SPEARHEAD
ASSAULT

Also by John Geddes

Highway to Hell

JOHN GEDDES

SPEARHEAD ASSAULT

Blood, Guts and Glory on the
Falklands Frontline

CENTURY

Published by Century 2007

2 4 6 8 10 9 7 5 3 1

First published in Great Britain in 2007 by
Century

Random House, 20 Vauxhall Bridge Road,
London SW1V 2SA

www.randomhouse.co.uk

Addresses for companies within The Random House Group Limited can be found at:
www.randomhouse.co.uk/offices.htm

The Random House Group Limited Reg. No. 954009

A CIP catalogue record for this book
is available from the British Library

ISBN 9781846052477

The Random House Group Limited makes every effort to ensure that the papers used
in its books are made from trees that have been legally sourced from well-managed
and credibly certified forests. Our paper procurement policy can be found at:
www.randomhouse.co.uk/paper.htm

Typeset in Bembo by Palimpsest Book Production Ltd, Grangemouth, Stirlingshire
Printed and bound in Great Britain by
Clays Ltd, St Ives plc

This book is dedicated to The Seventeen.

THE ROLL OF HONOUR

THE FOLLOWING MEN OF 2 PARA GAVE THEIR LIVES AT GOOSE GREEN:

Lieutenant-Colonel 'H' Jones OBE	Commanding Officer
Captain C. Dent	A Company
Captain D. Wood	Adjutant
Lieutenant J. A. Barry	D Company
Corporal D. Hardman	A Company
Corporal R. S. Prior	A Company
Corporal P. S. Sullivan	D Company
Lance Corporal G. D. Bingley	D Company
Lance Corporal A. Cork	D Company
Lance Corporal N. R. Smith	D Company
Private S. J. Dixon	D Company
Private M. W. Fletcher	D Company
Private M. H. Holman-Smith	C Company
Private S. Illingworth	B Company
Private T. Mechan	D Company

Two other men from attached arms died with 2 Para's fallen. We count them as our own.

Lieutenant R. J. Nunn	Royal Marines
Corporal D. Melia	Royal Engineers

One man's view of a battle can differ completely from the view fifty metres away and in every battle there are as many stories as there are participants.

This is my story of Goose Green told as faithfully as I can remember it and helped by the recollections of many comrades who were on other parts of the battlefield. I acknowledge their help.

I have not related every story of heroism, sacrifice and unflinching duty performed by the men of 2 Para at Goose Green. There were too many to tell.

John Geddes, April 2007

CONTENTS

LIST OF ABBREVIATIONS

AA – Anti-Aircraft

Casevac – Casualty evacuation. This term is usually used in connection with helicopters.

CO – Commanding Officer. This means the top dog. The commanders of platoons and sections under the CO are known as OCs – Officers Commanding. It's a military thing.

CTR – Close Target Reconnaissance. Getting up close to the enemy to observe their deployment. Hopefully without being seen.

DF – Defensive Fire. If a position has been DF'd it means its range and coordinates have already been recorded for an instant attack.

DZ – Drop Zone.

EEF – Effective Enemy Fire. Enemy fire can be noted but only when they start finding their range does it become EEF and scary.

FAC – Forward Air Controller. Usually an officer who calls in and directs air attacks on enemy positions.

FOO – Forward Observation Officer. Same as above but he works with artillery.

FAP – Final Assault Position. The spot where troops form up for the final rush of an attack.

FUP – Forming Up Position. Where troops gather together before moving in for an assault.

GPMG – General Purpose Machine Gun. Commonly called a gimpy by troops.

HALO – High Altitude Low Opening. A specialist parachuting technique used for covert entry.

HQ – Headquarters.

LAW – Light Anti-Armour Weapon. The one used in the Falklands was the US-made 'fire and throw away' .66mm LAW.

LCU – Landing Craft Utility. A large navy landing craft.

LMG – Light Machine Gun.

L2 – High explosive fragmentation grenade.

MFC – Mortar Fire Controller. Same role as the FOO but for mortars.

MoD – Ministry of Defence.

MO – Medical Officer.

MV – Motor Vessel.

ND – Negligent Discharge. The accidental firing of a weapon.

OC – Officer Commanding. See above.

O group – Orders group where the senior officer briefs his subordinates.

OP – Observation Post. Usually a well-camouflaged and hidden outpost.

PTSD – Post Traumatic Stress Disorder.

RAP – Regimental Aid Post. A position at the rear of the battle where the wounded are taken for initial treatment.

RV – Rendez-Vous. In military terms a set of coordinates on a map where units meet.

RTU – Returned to Unit. That's what happens when the SAS sacks you. Back to your original unit.

SAS – Special Air Service

SBS – Special Boat Section.

SF – Special Forces.

SLR – Self Loading Rifle.

TAB – Tactical Advance to Battle. The abbreviation was taken as their own and used as the word for a cross-country march by the Paras. Hence 'tabbing' to Goose Green.

Tac – short for Tactical, which is the offensive mode of a mili-

tary unit. Hence Tac HQ will be a slimmed down HQ for battle.
VTOL – Vertical Take Off and Landing. The hovering capability of
a Harrier strike aircraft. It's still a miracle to me.

WP – White Phosphorous. WP grenades, also known as 'Smoke
Instantaneous'. They were designed to lay down smoke but because
of the burning effect of the phosphorous they were used as anti-
personnel weapons in the Falklands.

LIST OF KEY PERSONNEL

H – Colonel Herbert Jones VC, Commanding Officer 2 Para.

Major Chris Keeble, 2ic, the second in command of the Battalion.

Major John Crosland, Officer Commanding B Company, 2 Para.

Major Chris Neame, Officer Commanding D Company, 2 Para.

Major Dair Farrar-Hockley, Officer Commanding A Company, 2 Para.

Major Roger Jenner, Officer Commanding C Company, 2 Para. My boss.

Captain Paul Farrar, Officer Commanding Patrols Platoon, C Company. My direct boss.

Captain David Cooper, the Pardre, a fantastic bloke beloved of the Toms because he was a crack shot and trained the sniper team.

Captain Peter Ketley, the FAC, who captured the Argies' intelligence officer and a Land Rover!

My patrol Charlie Two Four:

Kev – Kev Butterton, our redoubtable gunner and an expert with an LMG.

Steve Jones – head scout of the patrol. A handsome Welsh bastard with a will of iron.

Pete Myers – the Patrol 'crow' or rookie who was the toughest eighteen-year-old in 2 Para and a young man on a steep learning curve.

Characters from other elements of 2 Para include:

Sleapy – Mark Sleap, who fought with another C Company Patrol and 'shot' the Colonel on exercise in Kenya.
Corporal Taff Evans of Recce Platoon C Company, who did a fantastic reconnaissance of the enemy positions.

A Company

Scouse McVeay, their MFC who saved our lives by knocking out an enemy mortar targeting us as we ran into the Gorse Gully.

Corporal Dave 'Pig' Abols – the man who broke the enemy at the Gorse Gully with a fantastic piece of heroism. He's the soldier that the 2 Para Toms think should have got the VC.

Corporal Gerry Toole, anther hero of the Gorse Gully, who fought alongside Pig until the enemy were broken.

Corporal Monster Adams. Not even the wounds from an Argy machine gun could keep Monster down. He was shot by the same gunner who later killed the Colonel.

Steve Prior, my best mate, killed at the Gorse Gully giving his life to save a wounded mate. RIP

B Company

Marty Margerison, one of the many Liverpool lads in the Battalion (all confusingly called Scouse).

The Bishop brothers. Big Bish was in one of the C Company patrols but Little Bish was in B Company. They're both huge – but Little Bish is actually bigger than his brother.

D Company

Corporal Tom Harley got the Military Medal for his exploits across the battlefield from the flank of the Boca House attack through to the schoolhouse.

Gaz Bingley and Baz Grayling – two more D Company heroes who made a frontal attack on a machine gun nest. Gaz died.

I'd like to name them all but there were nearly 400 out on the battlefield. They were all heroes.

TIMELINE OF THE BATTLE OF GOOSE GREEN

★ 2 April 1982. A large Argentine invasion force, including armour and artillery with air support, landed on the Falkland Islands at Port Stanley in Operation Rosario. They took the islands into the possession of Argentina after a brief firefight with a detachment of Royal Marines stationed on the island.

★ 6 April. The British government responded by sending a task force in a large flotilla of Royal Navy ships escorting cruise liners and car ferries commandeered as troop carriers.

★ 21 May. The men of 2 Para – re-designated the Spearhead Battalion of the British Army – were part of that task force and together with other British units they landed by moonlight at Blue Beach Two in San Carlos Bay.

★ In a forced march or 'tab' through the night 2 Para scaled Sussex Mountain without enemy opposition and dug in as best they could to await orders.

★ 22 May. As daylight broke over their new positions on Sussex Mountain the Paras watched the start of four days of intense Argentine air attacks on the British ships anchored in San Carlos

Sound. After their bomb runs the fighters swept very low in strafing runs over the 2 Para positions up on Sussex Mountain. The paras responded with a curtain of small arms fire. They brought down at least four enemy aircraft in this way.

★ 23 May. It's on! After days of debate over the satellite phone with the Chiefs of Staff in London a raid on Goose Green by 2 Para is sanctioned but it's called off when the lead company, D Company, guided by Patrols Platoon, was already tabbing its way onto the battle 'start line'.

★ 26 May. It's on again. The entire battalion moved off Sussex Mountain after nearly six days in the open and crammed themselves into the Camilla Creek House and its outbuildings for the night.

★ 28 May. The Battle of Goose Green is joined with the first phase of the attack on the Argentine positions on Darwin Ridge.

~ 2.35 a.m. H hour. A Company take up position on their start line for the advance over a white bridge crossing a stream called the Ceritos Arroyo. They were thirty-five minutes late. Their mission was to attack and take the Burntside House settlement. The other companies would follow across the bridge and home in on their assigned targets.

~ 2.50 a.m. The battle went loud as two light field guns open up on Burntside House while A Company advances on it. It would stay loud for fourteen hours. The house is attacked and shot up like a cowboy saloon but only the British residents remain there as the Argentines leg it. Thankfully the Morrison family are unharmed.

~ 3.00 a.m. While D Company is held in reserve at Coronation Point B company with bayonets fixed finally begin their advance and the long fight down the west of the isthmus to take Argentine positions at Boca House. A naval bombardment by HMS *Arrow* should have softened up the target first but *Arrow* reported 'Gun out' and sailed into open water.

~ 5.00 a.m. Initially B Company swept through Argentine positions rolling up the enemy but now the Argentines have stiffened and fierce resistance has stopped B Company and D Company too in their tracks.

~ 5.30 a.m. The Argentines have bought themselves time and are reinforcing their main trench line straddling the centre of the isthmus on Darwin Ridge.

~ 6.00 a.m. Daybreak. 2 Para reach the halfway point to the settlement along the narrow isthmus. Now 2 Para must fight in the daylight.

~ 9.30 a.m. Deadlock! The two leading companies A and B had been stopped in their tracks by a furious riposte from the Argentine machine guns.

C Company has been pinned down but is moving forward across open ground under intense fire to support A Company.

D Company is held in reserve but is sneaking along the beach on the north of the isthmus to outflank the Argy positions.

~ 10.00 a.m. 'Sunray is Down!' Colonel H. Jones is killed by enemy machine-gun fire charging a bunker in the Gorse Gully battle. His controversial action wins him the VC posthumously.

~ 10.20 am. The tipping point! Corporal Dave 'Pig' Abols of A Company has worked his way onto the spur of the Gorse Gully and stands up in the midst of a storm of machine-gun fire and coolly fires a .66 rocket into the Argy command bunker killing the machine-gunner who took out the colonel.

~ 10.30 a.m. B Company breaks the deadlock at Boca House now with Milan rockets fired to break the interlocking arcs of fire of the machine-gun bunkers. D Company help pouring machine-gun fire in from the flank. The Argy main line of defence along the ridge falls.

~ 10.40 a.m. C Company takes the point role from A Company and make their second advance across open ground in broad daylight towards the airfield and schoolhouse on the edge of Goose Green. D Company is hooking around to their right to join them.

~ 11.00 a.m. The White Flag incident when Lieutenant Barry is killed by Argies under cover of a flag of truce at a position near the edge of the airfield.

~ 12.00 p.m. C Company and D Company come under fire from Argy positions in the schoolhouse and some of its outbuildings including bunkers in the playground. They mount a bold attack on the building which is destroyed with the highest Argentine casualty toll of the battle.

~ 5.00 p.m. The battle rages on until fading light and at 7.25 p.m British Harrier jets attack the Argy artillery at Goose Green but their bombs overshoot and hit the sea.

~ 7.50 p.m. As darkness falls two Argy PoWs are sent forward under a white flag to deliver a stark ultimatum from 2 Para's new commander Major Chris Keeble. They have to give their answer before 8.30 a.m on the following morning of the 29th May.

~ 8.00 a.m. The PoWs return with an answer from the Argy Commander Colonel Piaggi. He surrenders. It's a famous victory for the paras.

Map of Goose Green

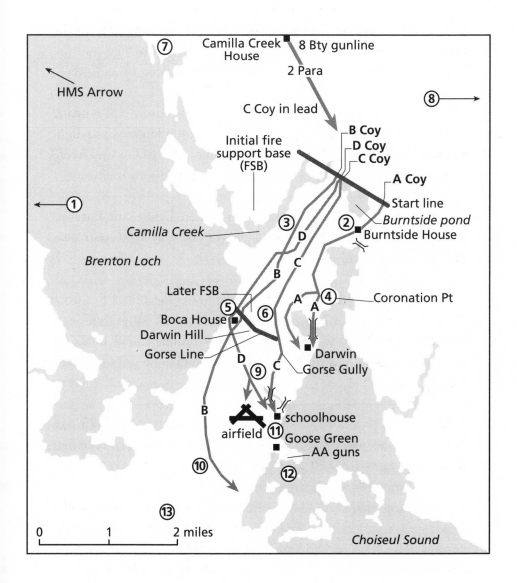

⑦ Camilla Creek ▪ 8 Bty gunline
House
2 Para

HMS Arrow

C Coy in lead

⑧ →

B Coy
D Coy
C Coy

Initial fire
support base
(FSB)

A Coy

← ①

Start line
Burntside pond
▪ Burntside House

Camilla Creek

③

D

② ❫

Brenton Loch

C

B

C

Later FSB

A ④ ⟶ Coronation Pt

Boca House ▪
Darwin Hill
Gorse Line

⑤ ⑥

A A
⬇

D C
▪ Darwin
Gorse Gully

D

⑨

❫

B

▲ ✕ ▪ schoolhouse
airfield ⑪ Goose Green
▪ AA guns

⑩

⑫

⑬

0   1   2 miles

Choiseul Sound

ONE

THE WAXWORKS

BLOOD POUNDED THROUGH MY head, almost drowning the sound of explosions and machine-gun fire all around me. My chest heaved and I greedily sucked in more air as I ran across the wet peat turf, trampling the tussocks of grass underfoot like babies' heads.

It might have been a bad dream but it was all too fucking real. The sky was washed grey and where it met the sea on the horizon you could barely see the difference between the two. We were on a narrow isthmus less than a mile wide; a chicken's neck of barren land that joined two halves of an island like a rain-pissed rock placenta.

Run. For fuck's sake just keep running. A seemingly endless stretch of freezing bog lay ahead of us and some South American fucker with a mortar was tracking us trying to drop high explosives on our heads.

In the midst of the battle, we'd barely registered that the black of night had given way to the watery light of dawn a couple of hours earlier, except that the vivid flashes from the tracer rounds no longer seared onto the backs of our eyes.

Move! Move! Move! Then another shrill whistle warning of an incoming mortar round. We hit the ground. All four of us. 'Boom!'

The bastard was getting closer. His first shot had been a hundred metres short. This was his third and it was gaining on us. Got to keep moving. We were up off the ground again and running hard;

we should have been trying to keep ourselves spread out to present less of a target.

Another whistle. We hit the ground. Another explosion. Forty metres. Too fucking close.

I knew what was happening. I'd served in a mortar platoon. You can set a mortar to lob bombs onto a target using a posh dial sight or you can have it on direct fire and quickly line it up on a moving target with fixed sights. That's what he was doing, that bastard; realigning the barrel and frantically chasing us with his bombs.

He'd caught us out in the open like bolting rabbits with nothing taller than the endless clumps of foot-high white bog grass to hide in. Not a rock or a ditch to bolt behind or dive into.

Dotted all around, the other patrols from our company were running their own race with the mortars and machine guns as they sprinted up the forward slope of the hill too. Explosions registered as small eruptions and bursts in the distance. They were muffled by the enveloping peat that sucked the bombs into the ground and smothered them. Their whistles and bass thumps played a discordant, jarring music on the battlefield.

We couldn't have been more exposed if we'd had our dicks out, and the lads in my patrol – Kev Mortimer, the gunner, Steve Jones, my second in command and lead scout and Pete Myers – were fanned out behind me as we desperately tabbed for a gully seven hundred metres away. To add insult to injury we hadn't even had breakfast. Breakfast? What am I talking about? We hadn't had hot food for thirty hours.

Me. I'm John Geddes and I was the corporal in charge of that patrol and I was running to stay alive. I shouted to urge the team on: 'Come on, lads! Move it! Run like fuck!'

And we did. Stumbling blindly, we sprinted across the soggy terrain, our hearts pumping frantically and muscles straining to keep up the frantic pace.

We were in light order. No bergen packs. Just 58 pattern webbing with pouches stuffed full of ammo and hastily grabbed combat rations. Tea and dried milk for a brew, garibaldi biscuits that were always damp, tubes of processed cheese and pâté, bars of chocolate. We had small gas stoves stowed in a pouch to make our brews. Light order? Believe me, nothing feels light when you're running for your life.

Behind me, Kev, a short battering ram of a man with a boxer's nose, was struggling to keep up. He was fit but Kev was carrying the light machine gun and he was festooned with a couple of dozen LMG mags that pulled him down into the soggy peat like lead boots.

'Come on, Kev, don't be a tart. You can do this!' Encourage, cajole, insult. It didn't matter. He was my mate and whatever it took to keep him going I'd do it.

Even Steve, a superfit Taff with the looks of a matinee idol, was feeling it after racing in what seemed like a continual-reel hundred-metre sprint with a triple jump to start and finish.

Pete, the tough little bastard from the Black Country, was panting hard but he was trying to give the impression he didn't give a shit, and he was only running because the rest of us were. He was eighteen and he didn't know a lot about fear. Not yet he didn't, but he soon would.

Steve just ran and ran and never complained. The only thing that weighed him down were his tattoos, the fucker thought he was Geronimo and every now and then he laughed uncontrollably and every time I looked at him he had a grin on his face. He wasn't hysterical. Far from it. The mad bastard was enjoying himself.

We sprinted on, struggling against the boot-clutching peat and then the next mortar round whistled and exploded. Forty metres behind us and closing. He knew what he was doing, that Argy on the mortar. I swear I could hear him in my head calling it out to his number two: 'Thirty metres left', or whatever the translation was in Spanish. Can't say they did Spanish in my Geordieland school.

We were dead men running. It was only a matter of time. That Argy was out there on the hill in front of us frantically resetting the sights again as he eyed us up for dismemberment. Pop! His number two dropped another round into the top of the tube and it fired again. We could hear it as it flew towards us like an executioner whistling a cheerful tune as he sharpens his axe.

The louder the whistle the closer the round will land. That's the rule of thumb when you gauge mortar fire, though a lot of people who've heard the loudest whistle never lived to talk about it.

We heard the crump of the explosion somewhere behind us, back along the trail we'd made across the boggy landscape sloping away towards a distant creek. We hit the soggy ground as it kicked sacks of peat into the air and shrapnel mixed with the peat to make a lethal potting compost. And we were the ones they were trying to plant. Thank fuck it missed.

Flat on the ground, my face full of soil, I put my head up and looked around at the others and wondered why we'd ended up so close together. We were trained to disperse and that was always the way we did it on exercise; we never squashed up like this. Why now?

I shouted at the lads: 'For fuck's sake, why aren't you spread out? What the fuck are we doing bunched up like this?'

One of them answered. I can't remember which of them it was but I'll never forget what he said.

'Because no fucker wants to die on their own, that's fucking why!' he shouted.

Whoever it was he was right. We'd instinctively drawn together in the face of death, seeking comfort in closeness.

'Come on. Let's go! And for fuck's sake spread out. I'd rather be lonely and stay alive,' I barked and we sprinted forward, willing ourselves not to collapse to the ground and wait to die liked frightened rats. We hadn't come to the Falklands for that; we'd come to fight, so we pushed ourselves on. I knew that next round was going to be close. To tell you the truth I thought we were as good as dead.

Pop! Here it comes. We all dived for the ground at the same time like rugby players on a training pitch, but it wasn't a coach who was blowing the whistle. This time it was loud, it was clear and it was jeering at us as it came in.

Whack! Something landed right in the centre of our pattern and I expected to die. I pushed my face into the ground and waited helplessly for the shock of pain and then oblivion.

Nothing.

I could still taste the earth in my mouth; still feel my heart pounding. Why wasn't I dead?

'Fucking hell,' said Kev, 'look at that!'

The rest of us lifted our heads off the ground at the same time, spitting grass and peat from our mouths. We looked around us. What the fuck was Kev on about?

Then we saw it and for a while we couldn't look at anything else. Nothing in the world seemed to exist and time stood still as we stared at the mortar bomb that had struck the boggy ground and failed to explode. It was stuck upright in the ground. A set of smoking tail fins marked the spot.

'Jesus,' said Pete, 'it didn't go off.'

'I can fucking see that, you dick,' said Steve.

'Move! Move! Move!' I yelled, urging them on and we began to sprint again. Fuck me, he's right on us that Argy, I thought. The next one won't miss. Three hundred metres to go. It may as well have been a lifetime away. I started to weave from side to side. How the hell I thought that would help I've no idea.

Not so quick now. That Argy fucker had been put off his stride by the misfire. Wouldn't be long though. Fuck! Here we go again. This time a rush of air flew about us and it wasn't the perpetual wind that etched the island. It was a mortar blast. Too fucking close. Then a rush of panic. I pushed it away but where the fuck was Kev. With the weight he was carrying he was always tail-end

Charlie and I couldn't see him through the wreath of smoke from the explosion.

I ran back towards him and then I saw him lying in the bracken. Oh no! Oh fucking hell no! Not Kev. Then he lifted his head off the ground and his body followed. Thank fuck for that! The blast had bowled him over but Kev had been a talented amateur boxer. Really gutsy; a London division finalist. He got to his feet but he didn't bother giving himself a standing count. He was dizzy and disorientated but he was game.

'All right, mate?' I called out to him. 'This way. Come on, this way.'

My voice was like the round bell and Kev came out of his corner running. I turned and ran too, fearing the fucker with the mortar might have zeroed us on his sights good and proper this time.

The Argies set it up well. To our right was a minefield. We'd watched one of the lads find it at the start of our race across no-man's-land when he stepped on one. Poor fucker. That meant we had to tab left – right into the arcs of fire of their guns. We'd walked into the killing ground they'd created and they were letting us have it.

Then a thump, thump, on the hill ahead of us and a lifting, billowing cloud of blue-grey smoke told me that A Company's MFC, their mortar-fire controller, had eyeballed the Argy position that had been persecuting us. Thank Christ for that!

He laid it on the line with white phosphorous smoke bombs to mark the spot, followed by two adjusting rounds of high explosive, followed by five rounds of 'Fire for effect' – the lethal mortar pattern the lads call dolly mixture.

Before he'd finished calling out the order, those five rounds were in the air and that short, merciless barrage spelt the end of the bastards who'd been chasing us with their mortar. Our luck was in. Theirs was out.

★   ★   ★

The firing had stopped and an eerie silence had fallen over the battlefield when we entered the Gorse Gully where A Company had fought their hearts out during the night. Here and there tracer rounds and WP grenades had set the gorse on fire and the peculiar acrid smoke of a heath fire blew over us, but it failed to fumigate the stench of battle.

The blokes from A Company who'd taken the brunt of the Argentine fusillade were standing in ones and twos; some were slumped on the ground drained of all feeling by the hours of fighting and fear. A few slept on rough beds in the furze.

Wounded men being tended by their mates were scattered around the position. Some of the lads who'd come out of it unscarred stared into the void and drew heavily on cigarettes; others busied themselves making a brew. Everywhere was the litter of war. Discarded weapons, spent cartridge-brass sown on the ground like seed, helmets thrown aside in surrender, empty magazines, blood-stained combat jackets and ration packs scattered like ugly confetti by mortar bombs. All around gorse smoke and cordite mingled like hellish incense.

My company, C Company, had arrived in the gully exhausted, but we weren't completely drained by the night of fighting. We were supposed to have come around on the left flank to link up with A Company and give them support by hitting the Argies on the hill alongside them about half a klick from the settlement of Darwin.

Like them we'd been pinned down by the immense firepower of the entrenched Argentine positions and their supporting artillery battery at the tiny Goose Green airstrip two klicks away. We hadn't been able to break free soon enough to come to their aid so what the hell could I say when I found one of my best mates, Gerry Toole, swaying like a tree in the tailwind of a storm almost too exhausted to move.

'All right, Gerry?' I asked. It was one of the thickest questions of my entire life but I didn't know what else to say.

Gerry shook his head. He was in shock.

'John, John, where the fuck were C Company?' he asked.

'Sorry, mate,' I replied, 'I'm really sorry. We got pinned down.'

How fucking lame did that sound? We got pinned down? Big deal, I thought. We should have done more. We should have unpinned ourselves. What use had we been to our mates in A Company?

I put my arm around him. Then he spoke again and his words were like knives stuck into my heart.

'They're all dead, mate. They're all dead.'

They weren't all dead of course, but a few of the special ones were, including two of our best mates and the colonel and Captain Wood.

'Who's dead, Gerry?' I asked as gently as I could in that harsh, uncompromising place.

He named two young NCOs in the battalion. Comrades-in-arms, mates; they were both men I would have died for. The trouble was they'd died for me – at least that's how I saw it then through eyes blurred by silent tears.

'Steve. Jock Hardman. They're dead.'

Two names, two body blows. He nodded towards a line of bodies covered by ponchos and told me, 'The boys are over there.'

Steve was Steve Prior, one of the best mates I'd ever had, and as I walked slowly across to the line of bodies laid out on an embankment in the gorse I felt as though my spine had been injected with ice. I had to see them and pay my last respects. I had to see Steve and say goodbye.

I pulled the ponchos away from their faces and paid silent tribute to both. For each of them I had a personal thought; memories of some shared danger or a great night out on the piss. When I pulled the makeshift shroud back off Steve's face I saw at once that he'd been shot in the head, but despite his violent death he looked at peace.

I made a pledge then that I would keep fighting for them.

Whatever else I did from that moment on I would fight for the men who'd died in the Gorse Gully. I'd sworn an oath to serve Queen and country and I meant it; but the Queen didn't live in Aldershot, her soldiers did and when it came to the balls of the matter it would be their memory I'd fight for. I've got a feeling Her Majesty would understand.

There was no time for long goodbyes, no time for indulging our mourning. We had work to finish. My platoon boss, Captain Paul Farrar, called us to order. 'Right, lads, let's move on. We've got a mopping-up job to do.'

That's a tactical situation, clearing enemy trenches, to make sure there's nobody left to fight. You don't just swagger through seemingly defeated positions playing the victor because that's the way to find the one bastard who still has a point left to make. If you aren't moving in support formation, covering each other and covering any enemy that are left in the positions, you might find yourself shot.

So we went into the enemy lines, rifles at the ready, to find and round up more prisoners and wounded and there we found some beaten, demoralised Argies still in shock. But it was mostly bewilderment that registered on their faces. When the battle had begun they'd been sitting on top of a hill holding all the aces. They outnumbered, outgunned and outpositioned the force attacking them, but they were completely undone by the ferocity of an enemy that had outfought them against all the odds.

The nightmare continued and as we moved into the Argentine positions in depth, we were entering a ghastly waxworks where the models were their dead. That's the only description I can put to what I saw, and I understood for the first time where the expression 'waxed faces' comes from.

Faces white and translucent in death stared out at us as we moved on through their trenches. Some of them were sitting up in their positions; a couple were still clutching their weapons, while others lay on their backs; a few of them were blown to fuck, but they were all as pale as ghosts and there was very little blood anywhere. I think when they died the cold was so intense that their blood quickly froze in their bodies.

It was a ghoulish and bizarre tour through the waiting room for hell, and most of those in the waxworks were Argentine conscripts and reservists taken from tropical towns and thrown onto a wind-scoured island far from their home.

They call those young soldiers *chicos* in the Argentine, but young as they were I didn't feel sorry for them. I didn't feel sorry for them at all because behind me were the dead and broken bodies of my own friends who'd been killed or wounded by those young invaders.

Some of them seemed to be looking at us, their dead eyes full of reproach. Few looked peaceful. Some had died trying to escape back into the foxholes they'd poured from. Many had fallen to the pinpoint shower of mortar shells that had dropped on them. None of them would see their homes again.

All around us were discarded weapons. Many of the rifles had brightly coloured images of the Madonna and Child on plastic cards taped to the butts. Some had rosaries tied around the neck of the weapon behind the trigger. Totems that were meant to protect them rendered useless in the fury of war.

'This is spooky as fuck,' said Jonesy. 'So this is what happens when you lose?'

'Looks like,' I said, then I nodded in the direction of our boys' bodies back down the hill and said, 'And it's not so fucking hot when you win either.'

'Stay down!' I heard a shout to my right. An Argy was crawling out of a foxhole with a gun in his hands.

We all moved into firing positions and then the silence of the waxworks was broken.

Crack!

One of the men in another patrol fired and killed the Argentine with a single shot and the guy paid the price for not coming out with his hands up. If he had kept them up then we'd have known he had no intention of fighting. The fact that he had a gun in his hand in a threatening position meant he was a potential danger. It was him or us. He ended up as a waxworks dummy. That's war.

We moved on, probing deeper into the layers of trenches and prepared positions that had already been fought over.

Pete spotted a movement and his gun was up in an instant. 'Over there!'

I moved up with Kev covering me and found another Argentine. He was in bits, half sitting up on the edge of a fire trench. A young bloke, he wore an officer's insignia and his helmet was discarded on the floor alongside him, leaving him wearing the black, woollen helmet liner. He was holding a .45 pistol but it was gripped loosely, not in any sort of threatening manner. He didn't have the strength to lift it.

I trained my rifle on him and registered just what a mess he was in and as soon I'd got that pistol off him I was going to try to help him. He looked like he'd been hit by mortar frag and then, as if that wasn't enough, he'd been unzipped by heavy machine-gun fire and he was on the way out.

We'd been told the Argentine officers are big on formality and honour. It's something they learn in their officer academies. Unfortunately, they also learn to be distant and disconnected from the troops they command. Anyway, he must have been a brave and honourable man and he offered me his pistol in formal surrender. I took the .45 automatic off him and tucked it into my belt.

Then he said something in Spanish and seemed to repeat it in poor English.

'We have fought the devil's battalion,' he sighed.

'We're 2 Para,' I answered and made a kind of mental salute.

I looked down at him more intently and I saw that he was about the same age as me. He was dark, Latin type and a handsome man. Maybe on a different kind of field he might have been a dashing Argentine polo player. I'll never know.

No more polo for this young officer. He didn't cut a dash any more. The man I was looking down at was smashed and broken before his time. It was a sobering sight and I wondered if the arsehole generals in the junta who'd sent him to such a pointless end would have been cured of their lust for war if they'd seen him in that state. I doubt it.

Then the faces of my dead mates came into my mind and any sympathy I had drained away. I thought, 'Why don't you just fucking die? What the hell were you doing here anyway?'

But the young officer lying there in front of me was beyond anger. He was about to pay the ultimate price for his trip to the Malvinas, so I just said what any decent para would say and told him, 'If you're ever in Aldershot, look me up and I'll buy you a pint.'

It was better than cursing the man but it couldn't have meant a thing to him. His eyes were empty then and he died a few moments later, sighing again as his life ebbed out of him. Still, that's one pint I'll never have to buy.

There's a mystery in all this that has haunted me ever since. When I looked inside the green canvas holster of his pistol, it had 'Capitan Bracco' written on the inside flap in indelible ink to identify the owner. But according to Argentine records the only officer to have died at Goose Green was Lieutenant Roberto Estevez.

Either the Argentines are lying about their officer casualties or perhaps more likely Lieutenant Estevez had been issued with a pistol that had once belonged to a Captain Bracco. It was probably Lieutenant Estevez that I took a surrender from, but whoever it was I'd met a ghost in the waxworks that day.

Captain Farrar called us together for a debriefing after we'd mopped up the Argentine positions.

We stood together in a semicircle around him, trying to get some heat from a smouldering gorse fire nearby. All we wanted to do was have a brew, get something to eat, have a kip and then go and find some Argies to fight. We'd been on the receiving end all night and unlike our mates in the rifle companies we hadn't had the chance to dish out any back or, in para jargon, 'get some in'.

I voiced all our thoughts when I said to Paul Farrar, 'Boss, when the fuck are we gonna get some in?'

The settlement of Goose Green was about two klicks away but the captain didn't think the Argies would put up a fight after the utter demolition of their positions on Darwin Ridge.

'Nah,' said the boss, 'don't think so, Geddes. They'll be surrendering soon, a walk-through talk-through. It's going to be pretty academic from now on.'

Some fucking understatement that. He couldn't have got it more wrong. The Battle of Goose Green wasn't over yet. Not by a long shot.

TWO

BABY SNATCHERS

DECEMBER 1981. BUENOS AIRES. It was a warm night in the capital of the Argentine but a cool wind was blowing across the mouth of the River Plate as a Fokker light cargo aircraft headed out over the wide estuary towards the sea.

On the northern shores of the river the lights of Montevideo, the capital of neighbouring Uruguay, twinkled in the night. To the south the lights of the much larger city of Buenos Aires lit up four times as much of the night sky.

The pilot, attached to a Special Forces unit called Battalón de Inteligencia 601, was relaxed. It was a fairly routine job and Christmas was only a couple of weeks away. He had some leave and maybe he'd take the children upcountry to visit his family on the ranch they worked in the pampas prairies of the Argentine interior.

In the cargo space behind the cockpit, an NCO and two soldiers from Battalón 601 sat on canvas bucket seats bolted to the side of the fuselage. They were resting their feet on a bundle lying in front of them. The bundle was breathing. Sucking in air through its nose. It was a young man.

His mouth was gagged so that he had to breathe through his nose. His eyes were wide. Terror? Probably. But they were glazed over and seemed more resigned than terrified; perhaps even a bit relieved that his ordeal was about to end. He was naked except for the engine chains wrapped around his body that bore the hallmarks of torture. Burns from electric probes, contusions from beatings, bloody gashes where boots had opened up his flesh with vicious kicks.

They'd picked him up from the torture centre at the Naval Mechanics School earlier that evening and driven him to the military airfield on the edge of the city. His crime had been to speak his mind. He was a student. A young firebrand, his left-wing ideals had marked him out for 'disappearance' in a country where a fascist military junta ruled with an iron fist.

In Britain he'd probably have been a member of the Labour Party and on the executive council of his students' union. In the Argentine he was a dead man.

Suddenly, the plane lost altitude and levelled off at about sixty metres over the water and cool air rushed into the cockpit as one of the soldiers pulled back the sliding door on the plane. It had been fitted for parachute jumps but there was no parachute that night.

The other soldier stood up, cut the tape, grabbed his victim's hair and pulled him towards the open door. He ripped the gag from the student's mouth and then his mate gave him a hand as they just toppled him through the door. One of them grinned as they momentarily heard his scream. Some of them screamed. Some didn't.

They knew from experience that at this point the currents would roll his weighted body along the river bottom straight out to sea while the fish and the crabs worked on it. The fish would eat his body within days. He'd disappear.

That had been an easy job. Just one consignment to deal with, but more often they had job lots to dispose of and they'd chain up three or four naked humans together, men and women, in obscene bundles and drop them out of the back of the plane.

Thousands of so-called dissidents disappeared that way in the

Argentine. A few nights earlier those same soldiers had guarded another bundle that was destined to vanish. It was small bundle this time. A baby. Boy or girl? It didn't matter to them, they were just guarding the female agent delivering it.

They'd collected it from the torture centre where its mother was having electrodes fitted to the breasts the baby should have been feeding on. Twenty minutes later they handed it to a nurse at a special government adoption centre.

The childless wives of senior military and police officers only need apply. The baby screamed for its mother all the way across town and they were glad to see the back of it. Anyway, it would be better off with a decent family and the socialist bitch who'd given birth to it wouldn't be fit to mother anything after the torturers had finished with her.

Hundreds of infants were snatched from their mothers in torture centres in the Argentine by the agents of the junta and given to couples loyal to the regime. Sometimes they arrested nursing mothers to order so they could supply a decent couple with the child they so longed for.

No one was safe. A couple of years earlier they'd even arrested a pregnant doctor called Silvia Quintela. She was no commie, far from it; she'd been a supporter of the right-wing Perónists.

But her crime had been to give medical treatment to the poor in the slums of Buenos Aires. Rumour has it that her infant son may have been handed over to a major in the Argentine army medical corps. Silvia was just twenty-eight years old when they took her in chains on a death flight; a *vuelo de la muerte*.

December 1981. Kenya. While the Argentine Special Forces were stealing babies and hurling students out of the back of aircraft, Patrols Company of 2 Para were lined out in the rocks on top of a sandstone bluff.

We were gazing out over an African plain that stretched away to the horizon in front of us. Out there in front of us was an endless sea of thorn scrub and elephant grass. Here and there the foliage of flat-crowned acacia trees looked like green smoke in the heat haze. The sky was vivid blue.

It was only an hour since dawn and already the heat was desiccating. Only an hour but it seemed much longer as we lay still as stone on the baking hot ground. To fight the boredom I started to count the drops of sweat that were falling off the end of my nose as the sun dried me out like a salted cod.

I settled down to concentrate on the view through the sight of my rifle as I looked for the enemy. Occasionally I blinked the tangy salt of my sweat out of my eyes as I struggled to concentrate. Flies? Plenty of them. But it was best to ignore them. Movement was not an option. One absent-minded swat at the cluster of the fuckers that had come to drink on my sweat and the game was up. We were all in the same boat. No one could move. We kept as still as stone and stayed flyblown.

We'd laid three long snakes of green parachute cord across the bush and they slithered invisibly through the landscape, defining the shape of the ambush we'd laid. The para cord would come to life when one of us spotted the enemy. We'd tug it to silently alert the others because everyone kept a hand on the cord. The platoon commander had a stick planted into the ground at his right hand as a junction for all three ropes.

It was simple really. We'd set a classic linear ambush. In the middle of it was a central killer group, flanked by the 'gun' teams on either side with their general-purpose machine guns. To the right and left there were others in cut-off positions to give a warning of the approach of the enemy and deal out withering crossfire to nail any survivors of the ambush. Twenty metres behind the killer group was a backstop of six of the lads to prevent our ambush being rolled up from the rear.

No one spoke, no one moved. Just wait and cover your arc of fire. We'd done it a hundred times before but nothing, not even experience, is an antidote for the mix of tension and tedium that is an ambush. Time in limbo numbs the brain. Fear of being caught in your own trap keeps pumping adrenalin you don't need to burn into your limbs. Ambushes are bad for the heart.

A predesignated code word passed on the radio meant the enemy hadn't come to dance and the ambush would stand down. A series of short tugs along the line meant they'd been spotted and it was time to tango. This time the wait was mercifully short before a rapid tattoo of tugs from the left and right cut-off points told everyone the advancing enemy was stepping onto the plate of our trap.

We watched them every step of the way. It was B Company and they were pepper-potting forward, knowing we were out there somewhere but not sure where. They also knew we'd be busting a gut to ambush them without being spotted first.

It was only an exercise. The yellow blank-firing attachments, or BFAs, on the muzzles of our rifles showed that. But the stakes were high. To the victor went the spoils and that meant the right to endlessly take the piss out of the losers over free beer. That was a prize not to be scoffed at.

Then I spotted him below. He was moving up through the scrub to the foot of the ridge we were lying on, right up the front with the point section. It was the colonel. It was H! What the fuck was he doing there? He should have been back with his tactical headquarters unit conducting operations, not up with the front platoons.

Mark Sleap saw him too. Sleepy by name but not sleepy by fucking nature. Mark was sharp as a tack and one of the top guys in C Company. We waited. No point revealing ourselves. We'd hidden well and so far they hadn't spotted us. They stopped to regroup and reorganise. H was handing out instructions to the point platoon commanders.

That's when Sleapy opened up. The ambush erupted as rifles and machine guns raked the enemy to our front. The fire was effective. Bang on the button. The colonel was dead. Mark had killed the 'enemy's' commanding officer. Direct hit. Sleapy had got the drop on H.

The colonel wasn't happy about it. No one likes to be killed. He grumped and humped about it and later told Mark, 'It wouldn't have happened. We'd have got you lot with our artillery when we softened up your area before moving in.'

Yeah, right!

'Maybe, sir,' said Sleapy diplomatically, before adding, 'But I did get you, sir.'

It was a prophetic moment, a glimpse into the future. Next time, though, we wouldn't be sweltering in Kenya; we'd be freezing our balls off in the Falklands and it would be A Company not B Company that H would be leading from the front.

And yes, he'd be up there again where he shouldn't be, and once again he'd be shot several times, but next time it wouldn't be an exercise; it would be live rounds and H really would be dead.

In December 1981 thousands of miles separated 2 Para in Kenya from those Argy Special Forces in Buenos Aires. It wasn't just miles that separated us either; we were light years away from them in the way we behaved, the way we thought.

We could fight. We were among the best in the world. But we kept the Queen's peace in the modern Britain of the Beatles and that didn't include torturing kids from colleges or stealing a doctor's newborn son.

In December 1981 the Argentine may as well have been on a different planet as far as 2 Para were concerned. But although we could never have known it then, events and the gulf in culture between a democracy and a military dictatorship had already set us on a collision course. We'd meet on the battlefield within six months and things began to look ominous to seasoned diplomats quite early on in 1982. Events were to unfold at an accelerating pace in the months that followed.

The Argentine had been in the grip of a military junta since

1974 when a general called Jorge Videla led a coup and toppled the Perón government.

Throughout those years Videla ran the so-called dirty war against those citizens who didn't hold extreme right-wing views, and as many as 30,000 of them, including students, trade unionists, aid workers, priests and even nuns, 'disappeared'. They call them *desaparecidos*.

In March 1981 Videla stood down and handed power to a rabid fascist called General Galtieri and he and his colleagues, including the heads of the navy and air force, ruled by main force. A measure of the man is that he and his mates had provided a safe haven for dozens of Nazi war criminals who fled to their country and found refuge at the end of the Second World War. And we're not talking about a few old SS men living out their days in peace reading Hitler's *Mein Kampf*. Real filth like Klaus Barbie, the SS butcher of Lyons in France, and Stefano Delle Chiaie, the Italian neofascist terrorist, were active in the Argentine. In 1980 those two bastards had joined up with a cocaine cartel and the arseholes from Battalón 601 to promote a coup in neighbouring Bolivia.

And a whole nest of other fugitive Nazis had helped reorganise the old, Spanish colonial-style Argy military on more modern lines. They advised them, too, on arms deals that saw the Argy forces using some formidable kit. They were undoubtedly an evil and malign influence on the officer corps of the Argentine.

However, by the time Galtieri took over in 1981, things weren't looking too rosy after a long period of military rule. Soldiers fight; very few of them can rule successfully. Hence the junta were faced with major financial problems. The Argy economy was in bits. The nation was in the grip of rampant double-figure inflation and a foreign debt that had increased fourfold in a year and was spiralling out of control.

Galtieri looked around for answers. The one he came up with was one that's been tried by countless dictators and despots around the globe and down the ages. If you can't sort out your own backyard, pick a fight with someone else. A patriotic dispute with a foreign power would unite the country and divert the attention of the population from the crap going on at home.

Once he'd made up his mind to start a war there were two options for Galtieri, because the Argies had two long-running international disputes going on. The first was with Chile and the second was with the UK over the Falklands, or the Malvinas as they call them, which they'd been claiming since we took the islands in 1833.

The dispute between the Argentine and Chile, over the possession of three islands in the Beagle Channel near Tierra del Fuego at the very tip of the continent of South America, had been going on for a decade.

There was a strategic pass through the end of the Andes mountain chain that would have been the obvious route for an Argy incursion to take back 'their' islands but the Chileans weren't daft. They knew the junta wanted to let off steam and that there were Argentine troop build-ups in the region, so they responded with a bit of sabre-rattling of their own. They had their own military ruler, a man called Augusto Pinochet, who didn't play by liberal democratic rules and wasn't going to be fucked around by anyone else's junta. Wind your necks in and piss off was the clear message from Pinochet.

That caused a bit of head-scratching in Galtieri's headquarters, and then the good old UK Foreign Office gave them an opening. They responded in a way that couldn't have contrasted more with the Chilean riposte to the junta.

Despite intelligence that the Argentine military was eyeing up the Falklands and some renewed diplomatic demands from the junta over ownership of the Malvinas, the FO decided to withdraw HMS *Endeavour*, the Royal Navy patrol ship based on the disputed islands.

We left a handful of Bootnecks (that's Royal Marines to the

uninitiated) on the island with a couple of blow-up boats and outboard motors. Fantastic, thought the junta. The Brits have given us a clear signal that the Malvinas are there for the taking. Back in Buenos Aires they immediately began planning the invasion.

We hadn't thought we were giving them a signal of course, but then the FO hadn't thought about much at all when they made that cock of a decision.

The truth is that we'd been caught out by the values of our own liberal democracy, together with a bit of Whitehall cost-cutting, and assumed that, like us, the Argentines would behave in a gentlemanly fashion.

You wouldn't credit it, would you? Diplomacy? Galtieri was a Nazi-trained thug who responded with violence as second nature. Those Oxbridge tossers in the FO knew full well they were dealing with a regime that snatched people off the streets, tortured them and then threw them into the River Plate while they were still alive!

Events moved quickly after the FO's cock-up, and by the end of March 1982 the junta had made their invasion plans to take the Falklands, code-named Operation Rosario.

Public unrest at home was building to a head, so the military moved the date of Operation Rosario and brought it forward from July to 2 April, when the Argentine Navy duly landed thousands of troops on the Falklands. There were some sixty or so Royal Marines in Stanley and they put up a short resistance, killing one Argentine commando in the course of a skirmish at the governor's house. The casualty was Lieutenant Gianchino.

The following day the Argies took the islands of South Georgia and South Sandwich after a short battle with a handful of Royal Marines.

Well, that did the trick for the junta. The streets of Buenos Aires were filled with joyful crowds. They'd got the Malvinas back. Hurrah! All was well with the world. Lieutenant Gianchino became a national hero and the military issued a poem written in his honour called 'The Malvinas Are Argentine'.

It was printed on a card, which their troops on the Falklands carried with them during the rest of the conflict. I've read it since and it's jingoistic bollocks. Poems? They must have been having a laugh. The only thing printed on a card that would have inspired the Toms in 2 Para would have been a ticket to a piss-up. Gianchino was the first Argentine to die on the Falklands but he wasn't going to be the last. We were the blokes coming to get them and we weren't poets.

Hot air followed the invasion, with the UN Security Council passing a resolution demanding the Argentines withdraw from the Falklands, which they duly ignored. Maggie Thatcher was the woman in charge in those days and while she went through the diplomatic motions she ordered her Chiefs of Staff to put together Operation Corporate – the retaking of the British islands of South Georgia and the Falklands.

By 5 April a Royal Navy vanguard set sail for the islands and we quickly followed in the task force. Meanwhile, the US and the EU condemned the Argentine and imposed sanctions against the junta. Interesting one that, because the French, part of the EU, kept selling them Exocet missiles throughout the war with devastating consequences for our navy. *Plus ça change*, or fuck all changes as they say in France.

Moves by Peru and others to get a peace treaty in place were sunk with the Argentine cruiser *Belgrano* on 3 May with the loss of four hundred of her crew. There was no going back. It was war.

That's why me and the lads were on the side of Darwin Ridge with the other patrols of C Company of the Second Battalion, Parachute Regiment – aka 2 Para – on 28 May 1982.

It was freezing cold and a lazy Falkland Islands wind, fresh from carving icebergs in the Southern Ocean, cut right through us. Even the sheep knew this was a bad place to be. They'd fucked off long ago.

I was a young corporal in 2 Para in those momentous days of the Falklands War, heading up a specialist four-man reconnaissance patrol, when we'd tabbed under mortar fire into the hellhole at the heart of the Battle of Goose Green. Our destination had been the Gorse Gully, which lay at the foot of Darwin Ridge, where the Argentine forces had been dug in with dozens of heavy machine guns and enough firepower to quarry the rocks from beneath our feet.

The destruction of the Argy mortar position that had been tracking my patrol seemed to coincide with the end of the battle at Darwin, but though we didn't know it at the time the Battle of Goose Green hadn't ended. When it did, several hours later, three hundred British paras, outnumbered by four to one, had taken on 1,300 well-dug-in Argentine troops with massive firepower and we'd defeated them against all the odds.

Goose Green was a moment of truth in my life and I've thought about that battle a great deal since, because I'm certain in my mind that it was a watershed battle in modern military history.

During the planning stage it was supposed to have been a raid, but what actually took place was a full-on battalion night attack, something the British Army hadn't done for thirty years. I reckon we were ordered to do a sharp right turn off the road to Stanley and take out Goose Green to give the politicians the early land victory they needed for the headlines back home.

Well, they got their victory and they got their headlines and the Argentines never recovered from the psychological blow it dealt their forces. But what 2 Para did we did more or less on our own. We did it without a tank in sight, with very little artillery support, no naval bombardment worth a mention and no air support when it was needed. We had no helicopters or Land Rovers to carry our ammo and supplies, so we carried every poxy bullet we fired into battle on our backs. I can still see men struggling under the weight of the machine guns, mortar barrels and bombs and Milan anti-tank missiles we used; we had to carry them all into battle too, in one of the most formidable forced marches in British military history.

Goose Green was a battle apart. It was the last no-tech battle of the twentieth century and we fought in pitch darkness without infrared sights to help our aim, facing murderous fire without a single piece of body armour. No bullet-stopping Kevlar plates for us.

There were no smart bombs to spank the enemy with pinpoint accuracy, no attack helicopters with Gatling guns and missiles to roll up them up before us. We rolled them up ourselves with aggression and guts, bullets and bayonets.

And modern warfare was never the same afterwards. The set-piece battles that followed across the world, particularly in Iraq and Afghanistan, marked a different era, with GPS navigation, JDam bombs, cruise missiles, aerial drone reconnaissance and computerised air cavalry. We'd have been happy with an armoured car at Goose Green but we had fuck all.

It was the hardest and longest battle of the campaign and probably the most controversial. We had no choice but to attack across open ground through the night and day, breaking all the rules of basic tactics. We assaulted uphill without heavy fire support, outnumbered and outgunned. Why? Because there was nowhere else to go. It was attack or die!

I lost seventeen para mates at Goose Green and in our turn we reckoned we'd killed 250 of the enemy, but the wounded on both sides were left to endure on their own for hours. I've read that at Waterloo many of the wounded were left to live or die for ten hours or more before they got any help. A hundred and fifty years later, GIs injured in the Vietnam War expected to be casevaced by helicopter to a modern field hospital and be under the surgeon's knife in an average time of thirty minutes.

It was back to the bad old days with a vengeance for my

wounded mates on the battlefield at Goose Green and there were some horrifying ten-hour waits before the casualties were taken off for treatment. One officer waited a staggering twenty hours before being carted away from the carnage. It was an element of the battle that sickened me and I lay the blame squarely where it belongs: with the pen pushers back home.

I saw plenty of courage at Goose Green too, and when the smoke drifted off the battlefield a total of one Victoria Cross, two Distinguished Service Orders, three Military Crosses, nine Military Medals, three Distinguished Conduct Medals and nineteen Mentioned in Dispatches had been awarded.

That didn't surprise me. The fact is that when we were ordered to the Falklands, 2 Para was not the spearhead battalion of the British Army. H bullied and badgered the high command until they gave us that role. We stole it from the Royal Anglians because we were honed sharp by endless training and were in a permanent state of readiness for action. We were looking for medals to win and eager to be unleashed like dogs of war when we hit the beach on the Falklands.

When I ran into the base of the Gully that morning I knew that our commanding officer, the formidable Colonel Herbert 'H' Jones had been killed in action. The Victoria Cross was given to him posthumously in what is without doubt the most debated award of the VC in British military history.

Generals talk about the fog of war. I think fog is too static, too muffled a word to describe the confusion of battle. I believe war is more like a ferocious blizzard. It stings your eyes and blinds you.

One man's battle can be very different to the one witnessed by men fighting fifty yards either side of him. But this is the story of my battle with the Argies, told from my viewpoint but from the perspective of some of my mates too. I'm going to tell the unvarnished truth about Goose Green and that controversial VC and I'm going to tell it in the plain-speaking way of a fighting

Para Reg soldier. We call ourselves Toms and this is a Tom's story.

So far, former officers and military historians have written the accounts of the battle. They're fine as far as they go, but they can't tell it the way a front-line para would tell it and they haven't told the whole story. But I can. I was there.

THREE

ABSENT WITHOUT LEAVE

I WAS A DAY late for the Falklands War, and I nearly missed it altogether.

We'd been given some leave and I'd driven with my wife and kids to the north-east to visit my folks in Newcastle upon Tyne. While we were there a telegram arrived for me at my mother's house. There was just one word on it . . . '*Normandy*'.

But it told me all I needed to know. The shit had hit the fan. *Normandy* was the code word we'd been given before we'd been allowed a couple of days' leave while the international turmoil over the invasion of the Falklands played out. *Normandy* told us that the hot air in the UN hadn't worked. The time for talking was over. It would be our turn soon.

We'd been told that when a telegram arrived with that cryptic word on it we were under starters orders to leg it back to the Para Reg depot in Aldershot on the double and then we'd be off to the Falklands.

The trouble was that the poxy telegram arrived a day late. If I'd stayed in Aldershot I'd have had to have been blind not to have noticed all the other lads coming out of their front doors with their kit and realised that something was going on. But I wasn't in Aldershot, I was in Newcastle, so I was in a right fucking spin when the telegram finally did arrive.

I can remember ringing the Para Reg depot to tell them

I was on my way and getting a beasting on the phone before piling into the car with my family and heading south with no time to spare, praying that I wouldn't miss the boat. Literally.

It was the longest drive of my life. I'd come within a whisper of being posted absent without leave, or AWOL as it's commonly known, and if I had missed the boat trip to the Falklands I know that I would have spent the rest of my days branded a coward who'd bottled out of the battle. The men I admired most, my mates, would have shunned me. I would have become a Para Reg leper and as far as I'm concerned that would have been the worst disease on the planet.

Anyway, I got there in the nick of time and as expected I spent my first ten minutes in the depot being reamed and roundly bollocked by Major Jenner who was wound up like a clockwork bomb like the rest of the battalion.

'Why the fuck are you a day late, Geddes?' he snarled.

'The telegram came a day late, sir.'

'The fucking telegram came a day late? Pull the other one, Geddes. What a load of fucking bullshit. You've been on the piss, man, that's where you've been. Don't you dare try to take me for a fool, Geddes, or I guarantee I'll have you spit-roasted for my fucking lunch.'

'Yes, sir.' No point arguing.

'You've cut it very close, Geddes. You've come within a fairy's fart of being posted AWOL. Now you and your men get your shit together and get on bloody parade while I compose a fucking telegram for you to deliver to General fucking Galtieri and I don't want it to get to him a day late.'

'Yes, sir!'

I was off with my tail between my legs like a badly booted terrier, but that's the army for you. I consoled myself that I'd provided some important de-stressing therapy for the ranting major whose blood pressure probably came down a notch or two after he'd had a good shout at me. Jenner was all right though. He couldn't help being a fucking Rupert. Not sure why, but in army jargon all officers are Ruperts.

There are all sorts of stories about that Normandy telegram. Kev Mortimer from my patrol was at his grandmother's hospital bedside when he got the brown envelope. His mum arrived at the hospital hot-foot from home with it in her hand.

Kev opened it and read it, then gently told his gran, 'I've got to go now, darling. I'll see you when I get back.'

Kev got back but sadly his gran wasn't there to greet him. She'd died just a day or so after he left her bedside. That's what happens when the Queen sends you a telegram and calls you to arms. All your loved ones get left behind.

We paraded, then I got stuck into the feverish preparations that were going on as the battalion swung into the well-rehearsed drill that leads to moving out in full battle order.

Kit was packed and repacked, checked and rechecked. Weapons were inspected and ammo counted and issued. It was not a frantic scramble because 2 Para was on round-the-clock call for a combat emergency. We were all but ready to go and the only atmosphere I can remember was one of professional industry and a buzz of anticipation. We were going to war! To most people that would have been a terrifying proposition but that's what we did for a living. Other people made cars. We made war.

I spent the night before we sailed in Aldershot with my wife, Laura, and our two young children, Kurt, who was four, and little Gracie, who was just two. Home was in army quarters provided by those bloodsuckers at the Ministry of Defence. Scores of paras and their families were stuffed into a block of flats called Willams Park which would have been OK had the dump not been condemned years earlier by the council as unfit for habitation. Presumably the officials who condemned it meant that it was not fit for civilian habitation, because Willams Park was still reckoned to be good enough for soldiers and their families.

That sort of 'squaddie' discrimination began in the days when Wellington treated his soldiers like animals and had them whipped for insubordination. It still goes on but it's been refined by the civil servants into a code of discrimination that basically says soldiers will put up with any shit at all because they've got an overinflated sense of duty.

Well, fuck the civil servants sitting on their backsides in Whitehall. Every soldier knows the permanent secretaries and their pen pushers are the first line of opposition that has to be overcome before we even begin to get to grips with the real enemy.

Anyway, my family and I spent our last night together before I went off to fight a war in a damp, cold dump of a flat with no mushrooms in the fridge but plenty on the wall next to the peeling wallpaper.

Worse still, some of the 2 Para heroes who were destined to die on the Falkland Islands spent the last night they would ever have with their loved ones in these communal shitholes, with draughty crumbling window frames, disintegrating plaster on the walls, leaking plumbing and toilets that didn't work properly. What a disgrace.

There was another downer in store on the night before we embarked. Normal procedure would have been for the lads to sign off duty then change into jeans, dessie boots and a maroon sweatshirt emblazoned with a Parachute Regiment badge. They'd be ready then for a few bevvies and a scrap with any soldiers from a lesser 'crap hat' regiment; in other words, anyone who wasn't a civilian but hadn't earned a red beret.

Well, it wasn't to be. Before we left the depot, Major Keeble called the whole battalion together and we all stood there thinking he was going to give us the old once-more-unto-the-breach routine. Well, he did, but it wasn't the Argentine breach he went on about, it was the one in the Aldershot boozers.

'Right, everybody,' he began, 'I've got a simple message for you lot. Anybody who gets into any trouble, anybody who gets seriously pissed or gets into a scrap, anybody who attracts a sideways glance from the police, in fact anyone who puts a foot wrong, will not be coming with us!'

There was a shocked silence on the parade ground. We couldn't have a beer or beat up a crap hat or two. How were the lads going to kill time before they sailed to war? These days we might have claimed it was a breach of our para's rights but Major Keeble was not a man to be fucked around and we knew he meant it. He was ordering a round for the whole fucking battalion. And it was half-shandies all round.

They still reckon it was the quietest night ever experienced in the pubs of the historic town where the army had been garrisoned since the days of Queen Victoria. No one, but no one, was going to miss out on a full-on war for the sake of a pissed-up skirmish in a pub.

Time to go to war. It's never easy and it's best done quickly. No point hanging about labouring the point. You're off to work and you might not come back. What's to say except goodbye?

'So long, kids. Be good. I love you. See you when I get back, love.'

I hugged and kissed my family as we were allowed some time to say goodbye on the dockside in Portsmouth but I couldn't wait to be off. The kids didn't know what was going on but I could see my wife was worried sick. All the wives were.

It's hard to say this, and it hurts the ones you love, but the plain truth is my eyes were firmly fixed on the Falkland Islands, not the family. I was itching to go and the pier-head farewells were not so much a chore as a bit of an embarrassment. I'm wiser now, I hope, but in those days the regiment and your mates were everything. We were paras – we didn't do the soppy stuff.

We boarded our vessel and lined the upper decks to wave goodbye to our tearful families who were seeing us off to war. I wondered how many times this scene had been played out with other families over the centuries as Britain's soldiers sailed off to conquer an empire.

The empire had long gone but we still felt that it was quite natural for British soldiers to be sailing to the other side of the world to help out some of our countrymen.

Most of us had never heard of the Falklands when the islands had hit the headlines a few weeks earlier after the Argentine invasion. When I first heard it mentioned on the news I assumed the Falklands were part of the Outer Hebrides, somewhere off the coast of fucking Scotland! And I don't think I was alone – half the country had never heard of the place.

That day, Portsmouth seafront was packed along its entire length as the ordinary people of Britain came in the thousands to wave their flags and cheer us off. That was a great send-off for an away match by the home team and we were all extremely chuffed and well proud of the folk onshore.

I remember watching my kids and waving until they became dots on the dockside. Later my wife told me that Kurt had stood alone waving at the ship while the rest of the crowd had broken up into groups of chatting people. He kept waving long after the boat had sailed out of sight. She said she could have sworn he would have been happy if he could have sailed with us. Looking back on it, young Kurt must have known something even then, because fifteen years later he became one of the brotherhood and joined the paras. But all I could think about then was making him proud of me and not letting him down when I went into battle.

The last thing on our minds as we waved goodbye to our families and friends was that exercise in Africa a year earlier, but within weeks the ominous prophecy made on the day H was 'killed' in Kenya would come to pass.

★   ★   ★

I was well established in the Parachute Regiment as a junior NCO when we got the call to war and I loved life in the battalion. But my route into the army and war had been a strange one. When I was a kid I'd wanted to be a movie star and do my fighting on the big screen, not in real life.

I didn't have a chance at getting any decent O levels at my Newcastle secondary school, but I'd been inspired by the screen heroics of my favourite stars, Lee Marvin and Steve McQueen. If they could do it so could I.

So I got a list of drama schools from the careers master and headed off to the Birmingham School of Speech and Drama for an interview. They didn't seem bothered by my lack of qualifications and gave me an audition. Then they gave me the verdict and told me exactly what they thought.

'You haven't got any talent,' said the chairman of the panel, 'but that doesn't matter because lots of film stars don't really have any acting talent. We'll give you a place and see how you get on.'

I went home to break the good news to my mother – Dad had died when I was young – and I was soon back in Birmingham sharing a room at the YMCA with a Jimi Hendrix lookalike.

They were right about the lack of talent and I could see I was going nowhere fast but I was still determined to be a screen idol and get my hands on a few tasty starlets. I decided I needed a new strategy and drew on the experiences of my heroes Steve and Lee who had both served in the US Marine Corps and seen action. I reasoned that if I left drama school and enlisted in the army I would get the battle experience that would turn me from a mere player into a convincing action hero. I'd just use the army as a rehearsal for my movie career. Simple.

That's when fate played a hand. Everything I'd done at the college had been absolute shite but the last project I did, while I was thinking about leaving, was right up my street. We had to take a piece of military history made famous in literature, study it and then give a recital based on it. Lots of people turned straight to Shakespeare and waded into Agincourt and the Battle of Bosworth as their pieces. All you could hear for days were the sounds of 'Once more unto the breach' and 'A horse! a horse! my kingdom for a horse!'

Me? I had my own ideas for a piece to recite for the military medley we had to put on in front of an audience of students and invited guests. I chose the Crimea and the awesome Charge of the Light Brigade as my subject and learned Lord Tennyson's poem by heart and put as much expression into it as I could.

Meanwhile, the tyrant of a principal, Mary Richards, had put the arm on one of her old acting mates to come along and we were told that the guest of honour would be the great Dirk Bogarde.

No sweat, I thought, I'll just give it my all. And I did, pouring heart and soul into my recitation, knowing that a real screen hero was out there beyond the footlights listening to me.

'*Half a league, half a league,/Half a league onward,/All in the valley of Death/Rode the six hundred . . .*' I strained to stop my voice erupting into a strangled shout as I rendered the best version I could of the epic.

My hands kept flailing around wildly like a cavalryman who'd lost the reins. I kept going, though, just like the Light Brigade, stormed at with shot and shell in my imagination. I ended the recitation sucking in a lungful of air as the words of the poem faded away. To be fair it was the best thing I'd ever done at the college and I got my first and last spontaneous round of applause.

Afterwards Dirk Bogarde came up and gave me an accolade that I'll never forget.

'Bloody good effort that, difficult to get that poem right.'

'Thanks,' I said, adding rather lamely. 'I just gave it my best shot.'

He laughed and told me he'd been a soldier himself during

World War II. 'I was in the Parachute Regiment, you know. Fought in Normandy at Plimsoll Bridge, unforgettable experiences, you know.'

That settled it. It was obvious that I'd been right and that the military was the place to learn acting and if the Parachute Regiment was good enough for Dirk it was good enough for me. A couple of days later I was back in Newcastle at the army recruiting office enlisting in the Parachute Regiment. A few weeks later I was in Aldershot at the para depot.

The dress rehearsal for the Parachute Regiment was about to begin; they call it P Company and what an unexpected fucking drama it turned out to be!

I've heard it said that 2 Para is a family, but that's a view that it suits officers to put forward. To me it's quite clear that we were a brotherhood and what bound us together in a solid fraternity was our initiation into the regiment. It's a horrible test of guts, stamina and determination called P Company and it's the only membership card there is to the Airborne Club.

P stands for Pegasus, the flying horse of Greek mythology which was taken for the insignia of the regiment. As a token of that, we always have a white pony called Pegasus as our mascot who parades with us and is looked after by the 'pony corporal'. Pegasus has the rank of a corporal but he's lost his stripes many times for crapping on the parade ground.

Pegasus Company is the toughest thing there is in the way of a military test, second only to the notorious SAS selection and only 40 per cent of entrants pass through it to get their red beret. It goes on for five days, with every exercise run against the clock. There are assault courses, stretcher races and a three-mile run with teams carrying telegraph poles on ropes competing against each other.

There's a melee with boxing gloves called milling, too. Everyone gets in a ring with their gloves on to square up to an opponent and then you punch the fuck out of each other until only one man is left standing. There are no points at all for presentation, but maximum points for battling aggression and a bloody-minded determination to batter everyone else to a pulp. The Marquess of Queensberry is not in the ring.

When it came to the milling I played it clever. Or so I thought. I'd been a talented ABA boxer from the age of fourteen and I just stood back, let my opponent come in, suckered him with a feint, then laid him out with a shot to the jaw. Knockout. Simple. Job done. Chuffed! Not for long though.

'What the fuck d'you think you're doing?' the training sergeant screamed. 'You were fucking boxing, weren't you?'

From the note in his voice when he bellowed the word 'boxing' I may as well have just raped the colonel's daughter.

'Yes, Sar'nt! I was, Sar'nt.'

'I clearly told you no fucking boxing, didn't I? You just stand there and trade blows, no clever stuff, I fucking said. Now that's not too hard to fucking grasp, is it?'

'No, Sar'nt.'

'I can't fucking hear you!'

'No, Sar'nt!'

'Right, mister fucking smart-arse boxer, we're going to have you on again. We'll see about boxing in my fucking milling ring!'

He looked around the parade hall, spotted the biggest bastard in the place, who stood head and shoulders above the rest of the room, and called him forward. He was bloody huge but I had no choice. There was no way I wasn't going to get a red beret. Nothing for it – I'd just have to scrap with him too.

We stood toe to toe as smack after smack landed around my head while I had a real problem getting a shot in above the giant's shoulders. But I just took the blows and kept banging away back at his belly and then I launched an uppercut with my left hand that felled him like a tree. No question of boxing that time. I'd milled him.

After the milling the P Company bollocks went on and on with endless runs and races and everything done at the double. There was a massive attrition rate too, as people dropped out left, right and centre, exhausted, injured or just plain pissed off with the process.

On and on it went until they decided that we were all knackered enough to have a go on a huge, forty-five-foot-high piece of scaffolding called the Trainasium. The Trainasium is an implement of torture dreamt up by some pervy training sergeant who enjoyed seeing grown men scared shitless. You have to shuffle along two parallel bars at the top and every couple of yards there are crossbars in the scaff which mean you have to lift your feet to go forward. Safety ropes are not an option. Then, on command, you have to stop and touch your toes.

After that, they offer you the once-in-a-lifetime opportunity to do a standing jump off a high tower across a six-foot gap, which by a trick of perspective looks impossible. Actually, it isn't that bad as there's a drop down to the landing ramp. Three refusals at the jump and you're fucked.

To be honest, I didn't find the Trainasium too bad. I'd been a bit of an alley cat back home in Newcastle and I'd spent my childhood developing a finely tuned sense of balance running along the tops of the back-alley walls. But the real key to it came from the training staff. I'd watched others going on the Trainasium rig and I'd noticed that those who trusted the staff and followed their orders and instructions seemed to succeed. I decided to put my trust in the instructors completely and I just followed the orders they bellowed up at me from below. It worked.

P Company ends with the log race, where teams of six carry a telegraph pole for mile after seemingly pointless mile. Sapped of all your strength, you just keep going, defying your body to give up. It only dawns on you what possible use that test of hauling stamina could be years later, when you have to drag a wounded comrade off a battlefield.

If you pass through P Company you get your red beret and that is a moment I'll savour for the rest of my life. I held it in my hands as though it were made of gold and encrusted with diamonds. To me it was the dog's bollocks and I couldn't wait to put it on. But that's not the end of the initiation, because then there's the small matter of earning another coveted military emblem: our parachute wings. We were driven off in a truck to Abingdon, near Oxford, where, in those days, the parachute course was run on an old airfield.

After we'd learnt all about the flimsy pocket of silk that's supposed to slow your descent when you jump into the void, they put us in the basket of a balloon that was tethered to the ground by a wire cable and then sent up into the sky for static jumps.

I stood there at the door in the side of the basket looking down onto the airfield and the very hard ground below thinking, 'Fuck! This is it. Do or die.'

All you can hear is the sound of the wind strumming on the balloon wires and your heart pounding inside your chest until the voice of the sergeant cuts in and his hand taps your shoulder. 'Go!'

I went and, believe me, it takes a lot more bottle to do a static jump than to hurl yourself with joyful abandon out of the back of a Hercules aircraft.

Same sketch as the Trainasium jump. Those who refuse three times are driven away in a Land Rover before they infect the other candidates with their fear and they are never seen again. Personally I don't believe the rumour that the sergeant takes them round the back of a hangar and shoots them. I think it's far worse than that. I think they're sent back to join units that wear crap-coloured hats.

So that's how you get into the paras. It's tough and by its very nature it attracts the toughest of men. When you've got your red beret the fun starts, with endless nights crawling through chalk slime on Salisbury Plain and weeks on the Brecon Beacons being turned into a shivering prune by gallons of wet Welsh drizzle.

It was autumn 1978 and we were in bandit country, South Armagh. Rain dripped from the moss-covered boughs of the oak trees clinging to the side of a steep Irish valley.

Boomph! The sandbag in front of our young lieutenant exploded as a machine-gun bullet smashed into it. An inch higher and it would have smashed the lieutenant's head into tomato purée.

'Go! Go!'

I leapt out of my dug-in position. There were no leaves on the trees and I'd eyeballed the spot in a copse on the other side of the valley where the machine gun had opened up on our positions. We were on the Northern Ireland side of the valley; they were more or less level with us in the Republic.

We'd already DF'd that spot – in other words marked it out as a potential ambush point, worked out the range and marked it on a map and a range card. It was about four hundred metres away.

I had an M79 grenade launcher and I dropped to one knee and fired across the valley, over a road and a stream and right down the throat of the ambush position. The explosion was right on the mark and it was followed by a ground-ripping burst of fire from my mates' M16 automatic rifles.

Then nothing. They didn't return fire. The exchange was over. The IRA terror merchants who'd attacked across the border then vanished.

We'd been dug in at that high position with a view over the winding road that followed the course of the stream below for three days. It was a road used by army resupply convoys and we'd been there to head off an ambush on one of the convoys. We'd succeeded. I think the Provos had come to set up for a hit on some trucks, but they must have spotted our positions and decided to let go a burst anyway.

Two weeks later we had an intelligence report telling us that two terrorists had been hit in that exchange. Special Forces had crossed the border to look at the scene and they found an M16 gun and an M1 Garand rifle from the Second World War. The shadowy blokes from MI5 also confirmed that both terrorists had been hit by frag from a grenade. One of them had died later from his wounds. It seems I'd made my first terrorist kill in the ugly war that blighted Ireland.

On 27 August 1979, the battalion was hit a hard blow when the IRA killed eighteen soldiers, mostly paras, in a bomb ambush at Warren Point. A Company were hardest hit but later it was D company who were to take the brunt of our losses in the Falklands, which both did with huge fortitude and courage. I lost good friends at Warren Point and, though it hurts me to say this, it was a well-laid trap and turned out to be the IRA's biggest single success against the British Army. But let's not forget that those so-called Republican heroes of the hidden bomb cravenly killed far more civilians in their 'spectaculars' before and after Warren Point.

I'd never have wished for Warren Point in a thousand years but it happened and we learnt from it. Those of us who were left to go on were harder edged and more effective troops because of those we left there on that bloody road. Northern Ireland's a long way from the Falklands but the point is that during four tours of the province 2 Para became used to real bullets, real bombs and exposure to a real enemy that will shoot back. We weren't exercise soldiers like those from some European countries.

'This is the track you take, *mes enfants*.' The Foreign Legion training sergeant pointed at a sweeping line on a classroom board. He was immaculate in his rigidly pressed uniform, his kepi hat welded to his number two haircut.

There was one more challenge I had to undertake, one more test I wanted to pass before I would be battle-ready. And this was it. I was on a special course with the French military and the sergeant was making an exception and instructing in English because he had a visitor from the UK on his course.

And yes, he really did call us 'mes enfants'. I was the 'rosbif' from England, Corporal Geddes, 2 Para, and I was learning how to HALO. To the uninitiated that's not a dance step and it's not a badge you get when you become an angel. It's the parachuting technique known as 'high altitude low opening'.

Basically you fling yourself out of an aircraft that's flying so high you need oxygen to survive the first phase of the jump. Then you freefall for a while, maybe as long as two minutes, 'flying' in the general direction of your DZ, or drop zone. Hopefully, that will take you below any enemy radar without your track being picked up. Then, at the last possible moment, you open your chute and drop in to enemy territory. Simple. Sometimes.

It's a technique used by Special Forces to effect covert entry behind enemy lines and it's a technique I had to learn to join the Patrols Platoon. I would be the first into battle to set up the drop zone and guide the rest of the battalion onto the right spot and into war. It requires specialist scouting, concealment and observation skills as well as the HALO advanced parachuting expertise.

I was at the French Army's parachuting school near the city of Po in the South of France and I was the first Parachute Regiment soldier to go on a HALO course. In fact, I also completed our own UK Special Forces HALO course a bit later and I think I'm right in saying I'm the only person to have done both.

Unlike many Brits I really love the French, so aside from revelling in the adrenalin rush of the new skills that I was learning, I loved the atmosphere, or maybe I should say the ambience of the French services.

I was attached to the famous Deuxieme Rep of the Foreign Legion who'd fought famous battles in Algeria and Vietnam (when it was still called Indochina). And while I was there, apart from free-falling, I acquired some new friends and a taste for decent red wine. The French serve it with their scoff in the canteen and they even give their troops minibar bottles of the stuff in their combat ration packs! Fantastic.

I'd volunteered for the HALO course because my big ambition was to go on to do the ultimate challenge of SAS selection. However, there was a problem with that because I had what are known as 'regimental entries' with the paras. Basically that's like having points on your licence and if you've got points you can't apply for the SAS. They don't want to consider knobs who make trouble. Fair one.

My 'points' on the regimental entries were for scrapping with other NCOs and insubordination. I had always been a spirited lad and in the discipline of service life it had got me into trouble. With a year to go before the points came off my licence, I decided to fill in my time with all the courses and skill-learning efforts I could find. Anything but fighting and insubordination!

With the HALO qualification on my army record I was soon back in Aldershot and playing an important role in redeveloping Patrols Platoon. I helped set up a Patrols selection process for Toms from the battalion who wanted to get on board. We were looking for men who were fit, determined and aggressive with the balls to work behind enemy lines. Well, the battalion was full of them – that wasn't the problem; but we also wanted patience and an aptitude for field craft as well as an ability to work alone for prolonged periods. It's a tall order.

In the months before the Falklands I came to be in charge of four other paras who had all those attributes in spades. I was proud to call them my patrol.

Kev Mortimer had come to Patrols Platoon from one of the rifle companies and he had all the skills plus an indomitable optimism born of his Kent pedigree. He was the sort of bloke who'd rename a rain-filled foxhole a spa bath then try and sell it to you. He was a tasty boxer and a fiend with a light machine gun, which was the weapon he loved.

Steve Jones was a 'crow' – that's a para term for a learner – when he joined the patrol, and I remember our first meeting in the NAAFI, the official army canteen, when I'd just got back from a long exercise on Salisbury Plain. I'd spent five days of it in one of those rain-filled foxholes on observations and I was caked in mud from head to toe.

The usual drill at end-ex – army jargon for the end of an exercise – was to finish the post-exercise briefing then head for the fry-up van stationed at the barracks where we'd scoff a couple of huge burgers. Then we'd head to the NAAFI to play Space Invaders – remember Space Invaders, the first of the addictive computer games? – and drink some beer. Usually a lot of beer.

Anyway, I pulled up a chair to a table in the NAAFI, a can in my hand, and there was Steve. He'd been waiting for us to get back. He was a handsome bloke but he was putting on a bit of a scowl. I reckon he was trying to look hard, which was a bit of a waste of time because he was hard. He didn't say much after one of the blokes introduced him. He just kept chewing away at his nails.

It was annoying me and I told him 'Stop biting your fucking nails.'

He glared at me and I stared straight back at him. It was a meeting full of menace as he gave me a look that said, 'Who the fuck do you think you're talking to? I'm as hard as you any day.'

There was silence around the table as the others watched the contest of wills. Then I just stared even harder and moved my face up closer to his and said it again with a menacing look that told him clearly I was the alpha male.

'I said, stop biting your nails,' I growled.

I'd won that time but his whole demeanour told me that if I'd had to take him on he'd be a real handful. He'd been a junior para, when we had such youngsters, and they tend to be very tough people indeed. Steve went on to prove himself and quickly went from crow to second in charge of the patrol and its lead scout.

The fourth member of the patrol was a young crow called Pete Myers who'd come straight to Patrols from the depot without first going through a rifle company. Pete and another crow called Chopsey had both sidestepped time in a rifle company because our platoon commander had been their platoon commander in the junior paras. Pete was another boxer. He was quiet and confident and he thrashed his way through the selection for Patrols while experienced Toms from the rifle companies struggled. He'd do. We'd all do. We had too. There was no one else to do it. Our call sign was Charlie Two-Four.

The truth is that the gruelling P Platoon selection process, those bleak and endless exercises in the Beacons and the fatal edge of Northern Ireland, equipped us for one thing and one thing only and it wasn't the diplomatic corps. It wasn't hearts and minds either; it was combat. You don't send the paras to deliver flowers. You send them to fight.

We were blooded, case-hardened like steel and ready to prove ourselves in an all-out battle. We were prepared for an enemy who wasn't a sneaking terrorist, an enemy who could be seen and who would stand his ground in classic battlefield dispositions. We didn't know it then but we were about to find one sooner than we thought on the other side of the world.

FOUR

BILGE

ONE LOOK AT THE rust-streaked blue hull and white superstructure of the MV *Norland* parked up on the quayside at Portsmouth had told me all my dreams of jumping into battle on the end of a parachute were fucked.

What was actually going to happen seemed totally bizarre to a young para. Rather than flying into battle, the bastard pen pushers were going to send us into our first full-scale war in a sea bucket that had been designed to ferry cars across the North Sea. I was pissed off. We all were. The truth is I'd seen canoes that looked more fierce and warlike than the *Norland*. It just didn't fit the Red Beret image.

But there was nothing for it but to make the best of a bad job, so after we'd said our goodbyes to our loved ones we went below decks and looked over the *Norland* suspiciously. We checked it out for leaks and realised that life jackets were a bloody poor substitute for parachutes. The eyeballing over, we settled in and made the *Norland* our home for the next couple of weeks or so and what a floating home from home it turned out to be.

A great no-bullshit bloke called Baz Greenhalgh was our company sergeant major at the time, and just in case we weren't already unhappy enough about being loaded onto a bloody car ferry he gave us the bad news about where we were to be billeted.

'Right, lads,' he said. 'The good news is that everyone's got a bunk. The bad news is that our cabins are at the bottom of the boat. We're in the bilges.'

'The bilges?' someone asked. 'What the fuck are they?'

'Don't worry, you'll be at home in the bilges,' said Baz. 'It's where the rats live. There's nothing between us and Davey Jones's locker but a couple of inches of steel plate.'

Usual rules, we thought, Patrols Platoon gets the shit end of the stick. But each four-man patrol soon set up home in a cabin with two sets of bunks and a washbasin and loo in it. The whole of C Company was down there except, of course, the officers who were billeted above the waterline with the rest of the Ruperts.

Fair enough, you might think. It doesn't really make much of a difference. It would have been nice to have a cabin with a view but we were going to war. True. Until, that is, you come to evacuation drills. We did quite a few of them and even though we were fit as fuck and could move a bit, not once did we make it to the bulkhead doors before they were slammed shut, trapping us below the waterline. It was clear that if the *Norland* was hit by enemy fire we were wet toast, so we decided to ignore the drills and relax.

It didn't take us long to organise the billet to suit ourselves. We had a gym set up within a couple of hours of setting sail and we were training hard and getting into a good routine, which would make sure we didn't hit the beach stiff and flabby. We were a specialist unit renowned for our fitness, so we took a full set of weights on board. We had medicine balls and boxing gloves too, so that we could punch the fuck out of each other and hurl the balls around.

Running was compulsory so we spent a good bit of time on deck pounding the promenades on dizzying runs around the ship. The other deck activity was rifle practice with a lot of time sorting out our SLRs. We'd throw 'gash' bags full of rubbish over the sight as targets then fire at them.

In the evenings we'd head for one of the two big saloon bars on board and drink beer. We were allowed a good drink every night until we got into the Falklands exclusion zone in the South Atlantic. The crew were OK but we didn't have much to do with them, apart from Wendy, the entertainments officer. Wendy was the gay piano player on the *Norland* and part of the ship's company. He was chubby with long unkempt hair but he played well and he had all the bunny of a gay entertainer. We had some great raucous sing-songs with Wendy and he was a great morale booster on the voyage down.

Over the decades the Merchant Navy has had a tradition of sending characters to war and Wendy was certainly one of them. What made him volunteer to sail into the jaws of a war I'll never know, but Wendy did his bit for the war effort. Tinkling on the ivories.

As we sailed out of home waters, the voyage south was marked out by what were for us paras some unusual events. Naturally enough it got hot as we approached the equator and one of the Toms from our company, Pete Myers's best mate, Dave 'Chopsey' Gray, decided to take in a few rays. We were all in the habit of clambering into the safety net slung around the helicopter landing pad built on the bow of the *Norland* for a bit of a sunbathe. You just lay there in the net with the sea foaming over the bows underneath you. Very relaxing.

One blazing hot day Chopsey decided to get on the shaded side of the netting for a kip. So he thought. Unfortunately Chopsey got his physics badly wrong. The reflection of the sun bounced off the sea underneath him and ended up seriously barbecuing his back and legs while he slept through the slow roasting.

By the time he was ready to be turned on the spit he looked like a lobster wearing fishnet stockings, but only from behind. His patrol commander was another corporal, a laser-brained mate of mine called Bish, who told me that the company boss wanted

Chopsey's arse in a different type of sling. And guess what? – it was me who had to put Chopsey on report. So I limped his sorry arse into the major's cabin and he was promptly charged with inflicting wounds on himself and fined £20 out of his pay.

The burns were bad and Chopsey was in the sick bay for the rest of the journey, but he recovered in time for the landing and the attack on Goose Green.

Sailing through the roaring forties, the stormy regions of the mid-Atlantic, was another weird one and a completely different experience for paras as the *Norland* threw us around like toys. We reassured ourselves that any vessel with the words 'North Sea Ferries' emblazoned on its side must be designed for heavy weather and I decided to enjoy the fairground ride.

A lot of the lads were sick as dogs but those of us who weren't decided that sympathy was no cure for seasickness. I'd wait until I saw one of the lads was going green then I'd produce a pie or an egg sandwich and munch it in front of him. It usually did the trick and saw them rushing off, puke drooling out of the sides of their mouths.

I loved watching the power of the sea and in the evenings I used to stand at the bar drinking beer with the lads from my patrol and every time the ship dropped into the trough of a wave we'd jump into the air. It was the closest thing to a parachute jump we were going to get in that war and no mistake.

The car decks of the *Norland*, where motorists usually park their cars up for the crossing, looked like a huge ferry boot sale of army surplus kit when we were on board. They were piled high with the green, brown and camo colours of army equipment, but there were no battalion vehicles loaded on the car deck – they were on another boat.

There were rows of brown metal ammo cases, with the type of munitions they contained stencilled on them in yellow, there were stacks of bergen rucksacks and pallets of rations. The heavy-duty weaponry, the mortars, the anti-tank rockets, they were all strapped down on the car decks too. All of this was sat on, clucked over and jealously guarded by the chief equipment hen, the battalion quartermaster and his team.

It all represented the paraphernalia of war needed by the military unit called 2 Para on the eve of battle and it's worth taking the time to explain what the battalion was and how we organised ourselves in 1982.

2 Para was one of the three battalions of parachute-trained troops in the regular British Army. In those days we also had a Territorial Army wing called 10 Para who were a credible unit of part-time airborne soldiers, but they have since been disbanded.

Fire and move! Fire and move! That's the mantra of the infantryman and when's all said and done, motivated and well trained as they are, paras are infantrymen. They're just specialist infantry who can be dropped in on a battle from the air. The idea is to close with the enemy and not to sit in some shell scrape exchanging fire with him like insults. The idea is to get up close and personal and then kill the bastard.

Firing without moving forward gets you nowhere. Moving without one of your mates supporting you with some fire is a recipe for disaster. So the British infantryman fires and then he moves while his mates support him with fire. Then his mates move while he supports them in turn. We call it fire and manoeuvre and British soldiers excel at it.

Every infantry battalion like 2 Para is a unique entity brought together for one purpose alone and that is to bring about the destruction or surrender of the enemy. It's the sum of all its individual parts and it only works if all the parts integrate and work well together.

In the case of 2 Para the fighting edge came in the shape of the soldiers who were organised into three rifle companies, A, B and D. Each of these had three platoons.

C Company, my company, were the eyes and ears of the unit.

We were split into Recce Platoon and Patrols Platoon. Recce were mostly guys who'd failed the selection for Patrols.

They used vehicles in the field to carry out long-range reconnaissance SAS style in short-wheel-base, lightly gunned-up Land Rovers. It was a role that was copied from the use of willys jeeps, called Pinkies used by the SAS from the El Alamein campaign against the Nazis in the North African desert right through to Afghanistan and Iraq. But Recces' Land Rovers were more Dinky than Pinky and they soon became a taxi service for lazy Ruperts on exercise.

Patrols Platoon, my platoon, went on foot and had to be HALO-trained because our job was to mark DZs for a battalion drop. We'd have to infiltrate ahead to set up OPs, ambushes or snatches of enemy personnel for interrogation. In short, we had to get close enough to the enemy to take their pulse.

We worked in four-man patrols but with the added refinement of being able to recombine into our two platoons and fight as a small, conventional company.

The battalion also had some heavy metal in the shape of Support Company, consisting of three platoons: Mortar, Machine Gun and Anti-Tank whose job it was to provide close fire support for attacks.

Regimental Headquarters provided the brains to identify the target and work out a strategy for bringing it down, with the colonel, the alpha of the outfit, supported by his staff officers and the intelligence guys.

Attached to HQ were the logistics guys, whose job is to deliver the backup like the ammo and the rations, but especially the ammo, to the rifle companies up front. In the case of Goose Green that came down to a bunch of drivers without vehicles, cooks, bottle washers, walking wounded and the regimental sergeant major on a commandeered motorbike.

There were also the medical teams and in the Falklands we had an interpreter, a naval officer to direct ship's fire, a forward air controller, a Royal Marine officer and two blokes from the media. They were all shepherded by a defence platoon whose job it was to protect the headquarters position. In all, the HQ panned out to about a hundred blokes.

I mustn't forget the battalion rumour control and that came in the form of the communications teams, also known as the signallers. Those poor fuckers live in a buzzing, crackling world of dodgy frequencies, nagging officers, poor reception and mule-heavy loads when they lump their radio sets on their backs and drag their sorry arses into battle. On top of all that, they are highly visible and make a tempting target for the enemy.

The driving force in any battalion is the colonel and famously in our case that was Colonel Herbert 'H' Jones. No prizes for guessing why he preferred to be called 'H'. I mean, who the fuck wants to be a Herbert?

The colonel moved about with his Headquarters Company, assessing, sifting the facts, weighing intelligence and incidents on the battlefield and then making his decision and committing the Toms to battle.

It's called command and control in the jargon and in 1982 the Yanks were partial to having their commanders flying over the battlefield in a chopper, directing the troops like chess pieces from above, but that wasn't the British way and it certainly wasn't H's way.

To give them their credit, our Ruperts preferred to be on the ground leading from the front, which irritated the life out of the section commanders. That way, they argued, they could appreciate the shock of combat and get more of a feel for the ground to outflank the enemy. In other words, they could feel the pain and know where to apply pressure and when and if it was working. As I said, the theory is that you have to get up close and personal to fuck the enemy and that's the way H liked it to do it: alongside his men.

When he'd committed his blokes and battle was joined, the

colonel would get out there in the thick of it with his men in a unit called Tac 1, which was essentially a light order headquarters component on the battlefield. 2 Para's Tac 1 was the colonel, his best mate and adjutant Captain Wood, and his mortar officer, a Captain Worsley-Tonks; he also had a Royal Artillery officer with him to call down fire from an artillery battery.

That was a bit of a moot point at Goose Green because we didn't actually have a battery in much of a fighting condition when it came to the crunch in the battle. One of the guns went tits up and the other one jacked not long afterwards. There were also half a dozen signallers with Tac 1; you needed that many to keep the sets manned round the clock.

Last but not least, two members of the Tac 1 team were the colonel's personal bodyguards, Sergeant Norman and Lance Corporal Beresford, who were to play key roles in the drama that was to unfold.

Just in case the head got blown off there was a spare head shed lined up to duplicate Tac 1 and that was called Tac 2. In the case of 2 Para, the Tac 2 team was led by an all-round good bloke called Major Chris Keeble.

The rifle companies each had their own small headquarters group too, called Company Tac, with the vital signals element, and beneath them three rifle platoons under the officer commanding, known as the OC. With the OC would be his own minder, two signallers and the bloke called the FOO, the forward observation officer, whose job it was to mark and record artillery through his own signaller back to the gun line. Company Tac was duplicated too, in case the OC and his team got wasted.

A Company's boss was Dair Farrar-Hockley whose old man was the first famous TV general, Sir Anthony Farrar-Hockley, giving talks on the world's great battles on the BBC. At the time the general, aka Farrar the Para, also had the honorary title of Colonel Commandant of the Parachute Regiment, a role since taken by Prince Charles. I think it's fair to say that the colonel commandant's son wasn't the most popular officer with the Toms. How he got on with his brother officers in the mess I really don't know.

B Company's OC was a different bloke altogether and that was Major John Crosland. He was an ex-SAS officer who was blunt, funny and didn't give a fuck. The colonel ordered helmets on in the Falklands, but Crosland continued to wear the black woollen hat that marked him apart so the boys could recognise him instantly on the battlefield. The lads in Patrols loved that. We wore black woollen hats too.

Crosland was a man apart in our eyes. We would have left our pints on the bar to follow him anywhere, anytime. We would have loved to have him as our boss in Patrols.

In fact, as far as I know, only two men in the battalion, both of them officers, had any experience of a full-on battle. One of them was John Crosland, and the other was Mike Ryan, the officer commanding Headquarters Company. He had a good name with the Toms too.

The third rifle company, D Company, was commanded by Major Phil Neame. He also came from a big-time, traditional military family, and with a father like his he had a lot to live up to. Sir Philip Neame fought at Neuve Chapelle in the First World War as a Royal Engineers' lieutenant and was awarded the Victoria Cross for his gallantry. Major Neame was tough, but he was quiet, thoughtful and fair. The Toms liked him a lot and he led by his actions, not by his mouth.

Each of the three platoons in the company had a lieutenant heading it up and each had his own miniature command structure with a sergeant as his number two. The lieutenant carried a small battlefield radio set to communicate with each of his three section commanders. He also had a radio operator with him to listen in and talk to the company and battalion headquarters. The lieutenant would also have the mortar man in his group carrying the 2-inch mortar which was used to lay down smoke and was a complete waste of space. The last of his group was a soldier carrying the 84mm Carl Gustav anti-tank weapon, also called the Charlie G.

The sections were made up of two fire teams with four men in each. The fire teams would normally have one general purpose machine gun, or 'gimpy', each, but that was changed for the Falklands where the sections were issued with two each and they were used with devastating effect.

When war broke out, the Anglian Regiment were the spearhead battalion of the British Army and they should have gone to the Falklands, but H was a determined bastard and he was having none of it. We'd been the spearhead the year before, so H abandoned a skiing holiday and rushed back to Whitehall where he browbeat the generals into giving us the Falklands War instead of the Anglians. We jumped the queue and went to the Falklands. The Anglians went to Belize on exercise. Shit happens.

H had stolen the spearhead back from the Anglians because that's what his battalion was, a spearhead. It was a spearhead and he'd forged it himself like a Damascus blade, layer beaten upon layer during months of training to create a durable weapon that won't buckle or yield on impact.

Mutiny was afoot on board the *Norland*, as the C Company crows decided they were fed up with making constant brews for the NCOs and making up their beds in the mornings. Pete Myers and his mate Chopsey, the self-grilled lobster, those two hard nuts from the junior paras, were the ringleaders and Pete was my crow.

The way it works is that the youngest member of a patrol is the crow and he does the chores for the corporal, but one morning Pete simply refused to fan me in my pit. I was shocked. It was steaming hot down in the bilges, especially around the equator, and there was no air con on board so we used to fan each other with towels after a workout in the gym.

'I've had enough of it. I'm going to fight a war, not work as a fucking chambermaid,' he snarled at me.

'Right, Pete. I'm giving you fair warning and one more chance.'

I lay there, sweating my tits off and waiting for Pete to come round and pick up the fan.

But he looked at me and uttered the awful word, 'No.'

'No? Are you sure.'

'I'm not doing it.'

'Oh really,' I said. 'We'll fucking see about that!'

I had to act swiftly and harshly. I picked up a piece of wood and battered him with it, then I grabbed him, hauled him to a handrail running through the corridor and handcuffed him to it. All around the bilges the shouts and cries of a mutiny being swiftly crushed could be heard and another crow was soon chained to the rail as well. We left them there for hours. Pete was snarling like a rabid dog and kicking at Toms as they went past him, possibly because they were all aiming blows and kicks at him as they walked down the corridor.

I went on the beer and forgot about him and then on my way back to my berth I noticed he was still there and put it to him. 'Right, Pete, the mutiny is over. You will make my brews and you will fan me. Agreed?'

He said nothing, but looked at the floor and nodded his head. Unlike Captain Bligh, I had decisively crushed the mutiny in the bilges.

OK, it definitely had a touch of the *Tom Brown's Schooldays* about it but I make no apology for defending the crow system. The next time the brews went on it would be me making it for the patrol as we came under fire for the umpteenth time on the outskirts of Goose Green. Shared hardships and rigours of battle proved to be more binding between us than a mutiny on the high seas.

Talking of crows, I was involved in another fracas as we sailed south, and it was one that could have led me into serious trouble when I dropped a senior Tom known as Wang Eye because he had cross eyes. He also had a brother in the battalion – called, naturally enough, Wing.

Wang was all right and a good mate, but when he was pissed he used to let his mouth run riot. We were in the bar and beered-up when he decided to have a go about the crow situation. Wang thought there were too many of them and the Patrols' crows were all wankers who'd get the old sweats into trouble and killed. He was vociferous in making his views known, despite the fact that the bar was full of crows.

'I'm telling you, John,' he said, 'we'll pay for it. The fucking battalion has got too many inexperienced youngsters. It's the experienced Toms like me and blokes like you with a stripe on who'll have to pull us out of the shit when it goes down.'

'Oh fuck off, Wang,' I said. 'I'm telling you, these crows will fight like fuck when it comes to it. They're fucking paras, man. They're here because they are paras and they'll do the biz.'

'Bollocks,' he replied. 'What the fuck do you know anyway?'

I said, 'I've trained some of those crows and most of them are better now than you've ever been.'

With that, I launched him down the stairs with the left hook from hell that I'd perfected as one-time 2 Para light heavyweight champion.

I shouldn't have done it but me and Wang had been Toms together once and we were always scrapping, although we always shook hands later. Luckily Wang, being a para, landed perfectly and wasn't injured. It's also the measure of the man that he never made any complaint about it at all so that I wasn't put on a report and busted quicker than a virgin in a NAAFI queue. No more points on my licence.

Work on board the *Norland* went on and significantly there were two skills that the head shed wanted us to hone to perfection. One was the operation of the new Clansman radio sets that we'd been issued with. They were reckoned to be superior to the old A 41 kit, but then again two bean cans and a piece of string were better than an A 41 set. When I say the new Clansman radios, I mean new to the paras as most of the 'hat' units in the army had already been issued with them.

The paras in those days were always at the back of the queue when it came to new kit and it seemed like a strange time to issue us with new signals kit, as obviously comms are absolutely vital to the conduct of a modern battle, but that's the way it was. Once again the hard-pressed ordinary soldier has to stretch himself to cover up the shortcomings of the MoD pen pushers in the procurement department.

Getting new radios was enough of a challenge, but the other skill we were being schooled in was really ominous. The top brass must have already realised that there were not going to be sufficient medical services available on the island to first evacuate and then treat any injured soldiers. We knew for sure that was going to be a problem because the Parachute Regiment Band wasn't coming with us. We didn't need them to accompany Wendy on the piano, though that would have been nice; it was their skills as trained battlefield stretcher-bearers and paramedics that would have been reassuring. As it was, they were back home in the Shot practising 'Colonel Bogey'. That was another case of MoD loony-tunes if you ask me. Not as bad as eight stretchers issued for every battalion at the Battle of the Somme but near enough.

OK, we had no stretcher-bearers and no real means of evacuation worked out for the wounded on the island, so what was the answer? It was simple. Para heal thyself was what the head shed came up with and we were put through an intensive course in what was really battlefield self-treatment and a bit of first aid to help our mates too.

The battalion medical officer, or MO, was an all right officer called Captain Steve Hughes. He decided to use the fancy medic's name of 'battlefield resuscitation' and issued us with double the normal helping of field dressings which he cheerfully called our 'puncture repair kits'.

'Slap one on the bullet entry wound and one on the exit wound then tie them both in place with one of these elasticated crêpe bandages. They'll keep it all nice and tight until help arrives,' he told us.

Four men from each platoon were also trained up as battle-field medics, but the MO hit a snag when a few of them proved they'd be useless as junkies because they couldn't find a vein to get a fluid line into.

As well as our field dressings and bandages, we all carried morphine phials and our drip, a half-litre of Hartmann's fluid, a standard battlefield solution, which we stashed close to the body in the Falklands to stop it from freezing.

What was going to happen if the pillock who came to treat you was too clumsy to find a vein? Captain Hughes must have had a vision because he came up with a solution – that's a solution to the problem – which involved chucking the needle and ignoring veins.

'Just stick the IV tube up your mate's backside and infuse him with fluid through the anus,' he told us.

Nice one, Captain. You can imagine the variations and interesting ideas the Toms came up with based on the MO's new, unproven battlefield colonic irrigation method. It earned the captain the name 'Arsey' Hughes among the Toms. I wonder where he is now.

Most of the Toms joked they'd rather bleed to death than drop their trousers and have a Stevens tube rammed up their arse in the freezing Falklands wind. But a few of the captain's medics, men like Gibbo, Hank and Bill Bentley, came up trumps later and performed major life-saving feats under heavy Argy fire.

So the routine went on, as hour by hour we got closer and closer to our enemy and the *Norland* slowly chewed up the nautical miles at a steady twenty knots.

The voyage to the Falklands took us about seven weeks. We steamed slowly while the politicians and the diplomats tried to find a way out of the mess. We made two stops: one off Sierra Leone where we had the chance to practise our landing-craft drill and get ashore for a bit of beach rest, and another off Ascension Island where we did a bit more landing-craft drill. They didn't inspire us with confidence.

Eight thousand miles out of Portsmouth and a few days from the Falklands and H joined the battalion. He'd been back in London gassing with the high command in Northwood and had then flown to Ascension Island before being helied out to the *Norland*.

The routine was already tight, but with the task force closing on its target and the colonel fresh on board it tightened up a notch or two again. For a start we'd been running on the decks in gym shoes to spare the woodwork and keep the noise levels down.

'Bollocks to that,' said the colonel. 'They'll run in boots.'

So we started pounding the decks of *Norland* in our boots and I must admit it was a martial sound that really started getting us into gear for the fight to come. We sounded like soldiers again.

Earlier on the voyage there'd been another great morale booster, which came when we discovered that the battalion was larger in number than we'd thought when we left Pompey. The reason for that was that eight guys had actually stowed away on the *Norland*, unable to bear the thought of languishing in the UK while the battalion was in a fight. They'd been men written off through minor injuries or assigned to other units or duties and not part of the battalion's muster. There was only one answer, only one way to protect their warrior's honour. They smuggled themselves on board the *Norland* by various means, often with the help of their mates. I was told that one Tom stole a P&O steward's uniform to disguise himself as one of the ship's company to get on board.

It was no more than we expected and though they were given bollockings by the officers they were told to take their places for the grand finale on the Falklands.

Another ace in the battalion's moral-boosting efforts came in the shape of the padre. He was a man called Captain David Cooper and he was close to the Toms, not least because he was an international rifle shot who had been blessed by the Lord with the ability of a top sniper. The padre helped train the battalion's snipers and he was a no-nonsense man who believed in a no-nonsense God. I'm not religious, never have been, but I admire the faith of men like David Cooper.

During the voyage he'd called for us all to join his daily prayers and services and, like any shop, he had his regulars. My patrol didn't bother going to the services; not, that is, until the evening before we were due to sight the Falklands.

When me and the lads walked in at the back of the service he looked up for a moment and said, 'Ah, the lads from Patrols are here. Welcome, Corporal Geddes, nice to see you. Come to collect some insurance, have you, boys?'

We all nodded. It was true.

The padre didn't manage to convert us; we just had some quiet moments of reflection with him on the eve of war that we'll always look back on with gratitude.

A couple of nights earlier, though, there'd been an exchange between two paras that I counted as a moment of inspiration, and it happened when we all got shedded on beer up in the saloon bar.

One of the two was a young Tom who was obviously fretting about the battle to come. To be honest, we were all anxious about our fate; it's just that most of us had learnt to cloak our feelings better. That crow was only eighteen and he was wearing his heart on his sleeve.

The other was Steve Prior. Steve was beered up too but he leant over and grasped the crow firmly by the shoulder with his right hand and spoke to him confidently, not a trace of a drunken slur in his voice. I remember that quite vividly. Something had sobered Steve up and his voice was firm and full of resolve.

'Listen, mate,' he said, 'don't worry. If it comes to it I'll die so that you can live.'

Those words summed up the deep feelings of loyalty that one comrade-in-arms can have for another. They demonstrated notions of comradeship that have echoed down the centuries and have been translated into actions of pure, unselfish heroism on the field of battle many times.

Steve's words had a powerful effect on me as we sat together in that group at the bar on board the *Norland*. Events on the battle-torn slopes of Darwin Hill were to etch those words on my memory forever.

FIVE

THE LANDING

SARDINES HAD NOTHING ON us. Packed shoulder to shoulder in the landing craft with 120 pounds of kit and ammo on our backs, we were more like tinned fucking turtles.

We were paras so we'd all suffered the terrible claustrophobia you experience inside a Hercules transport plane before a combat jump, but that had fuck all on the landing craft. On a C-130 the confining weight of your kit, adrenalin and apprehension leave you with a trembling urge to be sick. You begin to sweat, your hands get clammy and all you want to do is to get out of that fucking aircraft and be free. The jump comes as a total relief.

Well, the cloying, stifling cram of soldiers inside the landing craft magnified the tensions felt before a jumping a hundred times. The stench of a throbbing ship's diesel engine blended with the iodine smell of the seaweed on the beach. It was an overpowering mix, trying to claw vomit from the back of our throats. The boat swayed and dipped in the swell that surged with the tide into San Carlos Bay and that made us heave too.

But seasickness wasn't the real problem. There was something else in the air. Raw fear. It was the fear of being shot up or shelled while you were still stuffed inside that floating tin can unable to fight back. It was the fear of being sunk and drowned like rats. No soldier can swim with a bergen on his back. It was the fear of failure.

Crammed like that into the landing craft, not knowing if or when the enemy would open fire on us, we were assaulted by a whole jumble of senses and stimulations. Vulnerability competed with the terrible claustrophobia and overpowering stench and in the end some of the guys couldn't hold back any longer and puked up where they stood. That gave the rest of us the stench of their vomit to deal with and it was all I could do not to throw up onto my boots. When the fuck were we going to land? How the fuck had it come to this?

We'd mustered on board the *Norland* at ten the night before. It was on and off all night and then in the early hours, at about two, two thirty in the morning, we finally scrambled down cargo nets and through the side doors of the ferry onto the four big landing craft utilities, or LCUs as they were designated, needed to take the whole battalion ashore.

The battalion vehicles were staying on board one of the other vessels because of intelligence, reputedly from some old fart living on the islands, that Land Rovers would not be able to drive across the terrain on the Falklands. They took the word of some twat and it turned out to be a load of bollocks. What the fuck did they think the Falkland Islands' sheep farmers were using to get about? Magic carpets – or Land Rovers?

Anyway, that duff info meant that we had to carry everything, and I mean everything, that we'd need on the island for at least two days' fighting. We had our own weapons of course and everyone was supposed to carry a minimum of seven full mags of ammo, although I seem to remember I took a dozen. We carried four grenades each clipped onto our webbing and rations stuffed into the webbing pouches. Even though the islands were awash with rainwater much of it was filtered through sheep shit after falling to the ground, so we had to take two full water bottles. We took purifying tablets as well – and we'd need them.

Our bergens were stuffed with spare Arctic clothing, a sleeping bag, a green zip-up, quilted Chinese-style jacket and pants and lots of spare socks. I had about eight pairs with me but I knew that after a couple of days none of them would be dry, just that some of them would be drier than others. Strapped onto the bergen we each had a trenching tool for a spot of combat gardening, but it could also double as a useful weapon for hand-to-hand fighting if it came to it.

That was our personal kit sorted, but each of us had to carry a load of extra kit for the collective battalion effort. It was different for everyone but the humping list included bandoliers of GPMG ammo, spare batteries for the radios, 40mm grenades for the M79 launcher and 66mm rockets for the LAW.

As we got up onto the deck we were each handed a little gift to take – a tube containing a couple of mortar bombs each. The tube and shells weighed twenty-six pounds. A heavy present to be delivered to the company mortar team. By the time we'd packed our kit there wasn't enough room in the webbing to slip a credit card in the gap.

The lads in Support Company had weight problems of their own, as their mortars had to be dismantled into base plates, sights, barrels and bombs, and carried on their backs. They had to carry thousands of 7.62 link ammo for their sustained-fire machine guns and the Milan and LAW anti-tank rockets too, plus lots of ammo to feed their hungry personal weapons.

At a stroke the battalion had been turned into mutant turtles with shells on their backs or killer mules laden with kit for the landing on the Falklands. I swear one lad from A Company had a kitchen sink strapped onto his bergen. What a farce. Still, the top brass had promised us that helicopters would fly in and do the heavy lifting once we'd established a beachhead. Really? Helicopters? That was rocking horseshit.

Just to add to the chaos none of us had been given any night-time training in the drill for disembarking into a landing craft, so it took forever to board the fucking things. Slipping, cursing Toms teetered over open water as they climbed slowly down to the LCUs with their huge kitloads on their backs. We were ponderous and out of our element and we knew it. Our timetable was beginning to make British Rail look punctual.

According to the briefing we'd had before the landing, which was code-named Operation Sutton, C Company would be on the first LCU and lead the landing. It was assumed that an SBS patrol would signal green with a torch if the beach landing was unopposed. A red light would signal 'You're in the shit and fighting off the beach D-Day style'. When it came to it there wasn't a red or green light, not even fucking amber. They were late making it to the RV.

A Company was to be on the same LCU and they would follow us in a right-flanking assault if there was going to be a fight. Tac 1 would be with us to provide battlefield leadership and there would also be a small party of engineers. Their job would be to clear minefields and booby traps.

The second LCU was going to take B Company, who would provide the left hook for any assault, and a load of mortar guys and the Assault Pioneer Platoon as well as Support Company HQ and the bods from the main battalion HQ.

D Company was stuffed into the third LCU and they'd be the reserve company in any attack, together with medics, air defence troops, the Machine Gun Platoon and a mortar section. The fourth LCU would carry the Defence Platoon, which guarded the battalion HQ, more medics, mortar men, the snipers and Tac 2.

The whole thing was carefully arranged and planned by H so that if one of the LCUs were sunk by the enemy the battalion's fighting and its command and control capabilities wouldn't be sunk with it. It was a bit like royalty not all flying together so that one of them can carry on if there's a crash.

My lot, C Company, duly boarded what was supposed to be the first LCU with A Company, the engineers and Tac 1, which meant that the colonel was with us, though I never saw him. I wouldn't, would I? There were 180 of us stuffed onto the deck of that landing craft but H was probably up on the bridge with the chief Booties.

And he'd have been gnashing his teeth and snarling at them because we should have been on the LCU in line to land first, but the senior naval officer had taken command of that one and he'd picked up B Company to land them first instead. Colonel H's order of invasion was going down the pan. Delays were building up and so was his temper. There were about 620 of us loaded into those LCUs. Fuck knows where the Argies were.

Fools that we were, we assumed that we'd head straight for land and storm ashore to take the beachhead. Wrong. A couple of hours after boarding them we were still going round in endless circles on the landing craft like day trippers on a municipal boating lake.

And just in case the enemy might have any problem spotting us, the whole fucking performance took place in the silvery light of a near full moon that picked out the whole scene like a search-light. We cursed the navy and cursed the Booties driving the landing craft too. What the fuck was this all about? It was supposed to be an invasion and it felt like a badly organised exercise for Boy Scouts.

Meanwhile, the fighting ships that should have been supporting our splashdown had been delayed because they couldn't navigate their way into the bay. Apparently there was fog at the entrance while we were bathed in moonlight!

Round and round we went. We were supposed to be running silent but the sounds of naval goings-on echoed across San Carlos Bay. Boat engines throbbed, chains rattled and clanked, and friendly Booties flashed lights at each other and called out to one another across the water. I was not impressed. Neither was H and we heard him bellowing a few times as he verbally castrated a few gobby marines.

Any moment now a fusillade from the shore might cut us up literally into pieces. The whole of my being seemed focused on some central point in my guts. The sheer horror of being attacked while I was jammed like a passenger on a rush-hour Tube consumed me. We were all revved up and ready to go – trouble was, there was nowhere to fucking go. We were at the mercy of the Royal Marines and we didn't like it.

Nerves were strung out like piano strings when a shot rang out across the flotilla of landing craft and echoed around the bay. Oh fuck, here we go! Inside our heads the shot amplified until it sounded like an artillery shell, and we braced ourselves for the attack from established enemy positions on the shore that we'd been dreading.

It turned out to be someone from the Mortar Platoon who'd cocked his Sterling sub-machine gun when he shouldn't have. It's a blowback weapon that uses the gases given off from each round to reload and it has a fixed firing pin. He must have whacked the stock of the weapon against the side of the boat and that was enough to set the antiquated SMG off then bang! He fired an accidental shot known in the trade as an ND – or negligent discharge – into the floor of the LCU. We didn't know what the fuck it was at the time and we were just relieved to hear curses and shouts follow the shot but no bombardment from onshore.

Tension was now at cracking point and the weight of our bergens, the stench of vomit and the shoulder-to-shoulder crowding made me feel like screaming, 'Get me off this fucking boat!'

A funny fucker at the front of our LCU must have been feeling much the same when he called out the familiar cry heard on boating lakes back home on a Sunday afternoon: 'Come in, number two. Your time is up.'

It's about then that the engines of the LCUs gunned up and they turned as one to face the beach and rush in to shore. The slapping of the bow wake on the square front of the landing craft and the sudden breeze in our faces came as a relief. It was just like when the doors of a C-130 open up before a jump. Within minutes we'd closed on Blue Beach 2, our designated landing site, for D-Day on the Falklands. The navy had sorted their shit out and our LCU was the first to splash down on the beach. I hate to think what H would have done to them if he'd been left at the back of the queue.

It was around four in the morning. Hydraulics whined and shoved and the big front doors of the LCU opened at last to give us the freedom from the tin can that we yearned for and reveal the scene in front of us for the first time.

'Shit,' said Steve who was standing alongside me, 'they're going to make us swim.'

Sure enough, the beach was still twenty metres away and our assumption that they'd drop the ramp on nice dry sand for us had been wrong. Our fault, we should have known better. No one ever makes it easy for the paras.

The Toms in front of us piled out and as their weight came off the bow of the vessel the LCU obeyed the laws of physics and moved back into even deeper water. Nothing for it: we couldn't just stand there, so we piled in after them.

Fuck, it was cold! I went up to my midriff into the freezing South Atlantic and my admiration for penguins went off the scale. We stuck together, the patrol and me, so we began wading ashore in a group. That's when Kev, who was just behind me, tripped on a rock and vanished under the waves.

'Kev! Kev!' I called out urgently but he didn't surface. My hand went down under the waves at the spot where I'd last seen him and I felt his body. I managed to grip his webbing and haul him spluttering and choking back onto his feet. He was halfway through the process of freezing into a fucking lollipop and we knew that as soon as he was ashore we'd have to strip him off and sort him out before he got a cold injury or, in civilian speak, life-threatening hypothermia.

Through all of this we'd been praying that the enemy were not waiting for us on the beach. Wading ashore under fire is every soldier's nightmare, born out of our knowledge of the epic heroism shown in the Normandy landings. Our prayers were answered and the task force landings were unopposed. For now.

So we'd hit the beach like fish flapping out of water. It was cold chaos and a bitter wind moaned ceaselessly over the islands. On either side of us in the moonlight men sorted themselves out into their sections, then the sections combined into their platoons and the platoons formed up into companies.

As 2 Para organised itself and prepared to file off the beachhead, my patrol had a different priority – and it was an urgent one if Kev was to survive. A nice big driftwood bonfire to warm him up would have been just the ticket but the middle of a seaborne landing wasn't the place to be lighting fires. Not if you don't want to get shot by the RSM.

Instead, we took Kev's top kit off and replaced it with the jacket of the quilted combat sleeping suit we all carried. That gave him a dry layer close to his body core to keep his inner heat up. We also changed his socks, but he'd have to put up with his soaking wet trousers like the rest of us.

'Fucking hell, Kev,' I said. 'What did you go and do that for?'

I knew exactly what had happened. It wasn't his fault. He was our gunner carrying the LMG when he'd stumbled under the weight of the twenty-odd magazines stuffed into his 58 pattern webbing and his bergen rucksack. But I wasn't going to be nice to him, was I?

'Because I fancied a fucking dip,' he countered. 'Don't have a go at me just because you're too much of a bitch to put your head under the water.'

The Kent sparrow was chirping again. He was going to be fine. While Kev was warming up the rest of us took the opportunity to dry our feet out and change our socks too. The old maxim that an army marches on its stomach is bollocks. You march on your feet and you have to look after them because if you get trench foot, blisters or frostbite you can't even march to get to your rations and fill your stomach.

Apparently, Royal Marines are called Bootnecks because in the days when they were Redcoats with highly polished thigh-length boots they'd learnt to take their boots off and tie them around their necks to keep them dry when they waded ashore on raids. I wish I'd taken a leaf out of the Booties' book on Blue Beach 2 and kept my feet dry. If someone had told us we were going to have to wade ashore I think most of 2 Para would have tied their boots around their necks as well, however much we disdain the Booties.

Kev recovered quickly and that was great, but his dip in San Carlos Bay had left us with a problem. Our orders were clear. In the great plan of things we were supposed to be up at the point of the battalion with the rest of Patrols Platoon, fanned out and probing forward to bump the enemy if they were out there. We weren't and that meant only one thing. We were going to have to catch up with them and that meant tabbing even faster than the rest of the battalion to overtake them and rejoin our company. Out in front.

It turned out that the delay in the landing and our circular trip round the bay had been on account of the SBS, who should have checked that the beach was clear and given the task force a green light. They'd been too late to complete that task in time because they'd been tied up neutralising a small Argentine force at Fanning Head overlooking San Carlos, which could have posed problems for the ships in the bay.

Well, that's the way it pans out as a military campaign takes on a life of its own. Across the battalion, unforeseen and multiple fuck-ups were being repeated, adding to the sum total of chaos and creating that impenetrable battlefield weather called the fog of war.

A lot of men would have a cock-up story to tell as dawn broke and the battalion began to move off the beach at the start of a tab that would make P Company look like a picnic.

Our patrol's little drama had been Kev's baptism in the South

Atlantic, but as we changed Kev's socks on the beach, on the track ahead of us someone else was facing another unforeseen problem.

He was a Tom from the Mortar Platoon lugging a mortar tube on his shoulder and weighed down with ammo. Strange, he thought, one foot's wetter than the other. He stopped to check his foot out and found that his boot was full of blood. That's when he discovered where the round from the ND on the landing craft had gone. Through his heel. Adrenalin and tension in the LCU and during the landing had been so overwhelming that he hadn't noticed he'd been fucking shot!

What we didn't know of course is where the enemy were. Not exactly, at any rate. The SAS and the SBS had been on the island sneaking around for some time but their intelligence on the enemy's deployment turned out to be poor. Poor? It was shit! Anyway, we'd discovered for ourselves that the Argies weren't on the fucking beach, which was a relief to say the least of it.

The next stage of the landing was to move forward and consolidate the bridgehead and that meant climbing up onto the high ground of Sussex Mountain. It was eight hundred feet high and faced the series of hills on the road between us and Port Stanley.

If the Argies had moved onto the mountain, while we'd been playing boats, then the battalion would have been in real trouble. Taking that mountain by force from a standing start on the beach would be a hell of an uphill struggle. We didn't need a lecturer from the staff college to tell us that. What no one, including the SAS, had told us was if there was anyone up there on Sussex Mountain.

Who were they anyway, these enemies of ours? As boys, most of us in 2 Para had been brought up on tales of battles with the Germans and the Japs in World War II. As soldiers we'd been trained to fight the war against communism and, of course, the terrorism of the IRA. But the Argentines? Who the fuck were

(*Above*) A team picture. Patrols platoon in a formal pose on the bow deck of the *Norland*. That's me, second left, back row.

(*Left*) The Task Force in the roaring 40s.

(*Below*) Gash bag target practice off the deck of the MV *Norland*. That's Steve Jones, Kev Mortimer and me, wielding LMGs and SLRs.

(*Above*) Planning. Big Bish is in the background, while John Yourston, Dave Trick and Steve Jones look at the map prior to the landing.

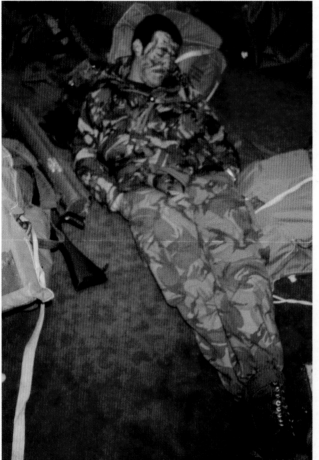

(*Left*) The calm before the storm. Me grabbing some sleep. The green tube is a 66mm LAW.

(*Above*) San Carlos Bay from Sussex Mountain.

(*Below*) Pete Myers, leader of the Crow Mutiny,
on patrol somewhere near Cantera Mountain.

(*Left*) Strung out on the ambush patrol east of Sussex Mountain.

(*Right*) Dave Trick with his LMG. I think this was in Camilla Creek House.

(*Left*) We're off! Leaving Camilla Creek House for the push into battle. We had incoming artillery fire over us!

(*Above*) Eddie Stokes after his probable hit on an Argy helo on Cantera Mountain.

(*Below*) Patrols platoon wearing our Red Berets for recognition!
Laid up near the Goose Green track.

(*Above*) Rick Tewson looking mean and magnificent at the forward OP on Sussex Mountain. Note the LMG set-up and the M79 'blooper' grenade launcher on the ground next to him.

(*Left*) Dennis Wheatley. There's always one. We caught him trying to cut the fingers off the Argy dead to steal their rings. I had to stick my gun in his face and threaten to shoot him. He's dead now. Hope he's got all his fingers.

(*Above*) Me in a basha listening to some Black Sabbath. Note the early Walkman the size of a brick. I've got it in a mess tin to keep it dry.

(*Below*) D Company. A classic view of the way we used tussocks as cover on the Falklands.

(*Right*) Kev Sisson, me, Bish and Bob McNally in the 'Waxworks' at the Gorse Gully. Hushed conversations.

(*Left*) Some of the Argy dead laid out at the Gorse Gully.

the Argentines? When the crisis started all I knew about Argentina is that corned beef came from there and they had cowboys called gauchos who used a thing called a bolas. That was something that looked like a pawnbroker's sign on rope, which they used to tangle up the feet of cattle when they wanted to catch them. Big deal.

We had been given a lot of briefings on the Argentine armed forces on board the *Norland* as the task force steamed south, and before we'd sailed out of Pompey I'd taken the trouble to read up a bit on the country.

What we were told in our briefings was that a large Argentine force had landed in the Falklands in what they called Operation Rosario on 2 May. The force had been made up of an amphibious commando company with some artillery in support and a platoon from C Company of the 25th Infantry Regiment. Mixed in with them were Special Forces and some US Ranger-style airborne soldiers.

That initial invasion force had taken Port Stanley after a short battle with a Royal Marines detachment in the island's capital and then the Argentine 9th Brigade followed them in to set up a garrison on the island. The leading unit was the remainder of the 25th Regiment and a battalion of Argentine marines with the 8th Regiment. The bulk of the force remained at Stanley on East Falkland while the 8th Regiment was stationed at Fox Bay on West Falkland, which is a completely different island.

West Falkland is connected to Lafonia, which would be an entirely seperate island but for an isthmus about ten klicks long by two klicks at its widest point; and lying more or less at right angles across it, blocking the way, is Darwin Ridge, crowned by Darwin Hill.

And it's on that precarious isthmus that the tiny sheep-farming settlement of Goose Green is situated. C Company of the 25th Regiment of the Argentine Army was deployed at Goose Green and they were only there because it had a short airstrip.

We learnt too that the Argentine Army wasn't a professional army of career soldiers but a conscript army of young men called up to do national service, and on top of that there was a huge social gulf between the ranks and the officers who were academy-trained professionals. Those Argy officers came from the upper classes of their country and made the snottiest of our Guards or Cavalry captains look like council-house curators. They never ate with their men, they talked to them like they're shit, and they had better rations too, with miniature bottles of brandy and wine in their rat packs.

Their regiments were about the same size as our battalions and also had three companies, although they had big US-style squads commanded by sergeants rather than small sections under a corporal.

The NCO cadre of the Argentine Army were also professional and full-time, and they too went to a training academy and then turned out with the rank of corporal, usually with a specialisation, like signals or mortars. They were the link between the conscripts and the officers and they glued the whole fucking thing together.

At the age of nineteen every man and his dog in Argentina is eligible for military service if they are fit and they do a year under the Colours, with a new intake starting to train in January every year. We were told it was all pretty Latin and relaxed, and as successive generations of the armed forces had never had to fight any war at all the army became a sort of right of passage for young blokes, who learnt a bit of weapons training and square-bashing then fucked off back home in time for Christmas the following year.

The intake in 1982 were only four months into their conscription cycle and weren't considered ready in any way to fight a war, so the military called up the reservists, men who'd done the full training regime in the previous year. The class of '82 turned out to be very lucky indeed.

When the task force left Britain the junta shat themselves and sent another brigade to bolster up their garrison on the Malvinas. It was largely a mechanised brigade, who left their tanks behind because there wasn't time to bring them, and an outfit called the

10th Armoured Car Squadron who apparently did have their French-built Panhard armoured cars with them.

This Argy invasion force was not as fit as the paras and marines sent to be pitted against them and nowhere near as professional, but they were extremely well armed, they could shoot and they would be fighting from prepared positions.

Our officers told us they would be dangerous because they had big fuck-off guns, but I can remember them impressing on us time after time during briefings, 'Hit them hard, lads, and they'll collapse. Just hit them hard.'

They told us there were elements of the Argentine Airborne in their ranks, and of course some of their Special Forces too, but we weren't worried about them. No fucking way. From what we'd been told they spent most of their time kicking the shit out of civilian opponents of the regime.

That's more or less who they were and roughly where they were. But there was only one way to find out for certain and there was no going back, so the battalion set off at a blistering pace to find out who was sitting on top of Sussex Mountain.

Fuck it! Me and the lads really had to motor to catch up with Patrols Platoon after wringing out Kev on the beach. By then they were well out in front of the main force advancing to contact as they looked for the enemy.

'Get your arses into gear, lads,' I ordered as we double-tabbed past the main column of the battalion that was already going flat out.

Every sinew strained as we leant forward to get the loads well over our backs and get a forward swing going with our arms to help the momentum in our legs. The idea is to get a rhythm going, but there on the slope rising off the beach it was almost impossible. We were on a narrow, rocky shepherds' track leading off the beach, but on either side of it there was just an expanse of grassy tussocks, frequently cut up by rills and fledgling streams which exposed the peat below. The whole sweep of the land-scape was booby-trapped by nature and we found ourselves stumbling into the soaking becks and constantly tripping over the tussocks, which the Toms soon began to call babies' heads with their usual macabre gallows sense of humour. But that's exactly what they were like as you tripped and fell over them in the dark, babies' heads.

Somehow we managed to rush on past A Company as they cursed their way up towards Sussex, then we came to the tail end of Tac 1, which we recognised from a gaggle of spare signallers bringing up the rear, stumbling through the dark under the weight of their radio sets. Luckily for us Tac 1 were holding back the superfit lads in A Company and we were grateful to haul along-side them, panting and sweating our way through to the head of the column.

I raced on with the lads behind me and that's when I tabbed past the colonel who as usual was leading from the front. Bad move. Poor etiquette. It's a bit like a member of the field racing past the master of a hunt in full cry after a fox. It's not the done thing for a follower to overtake the master and the colonel was out hunting. To make things worse I chose that precise moment to slip onto my arse.

'Who the fuck's that?' snarled H.

'Corporal Geddes, sir.'

'Where the fuck are you going, Geddes?'

'Patrols Platoon, sir.'

'Well, fucking well get on with it then.'

'Sir!'

I did get on with it too and his bollocking was still ringing in my ears as I tabbed on, desperate to get out of his sight. What with Kev falling into the sea and that bollocking from the colonel I wasn't having a very good invasion. Shame.

Later, stumbling up the side of that mountain, I looked at my map. It was covered in strange and unlikely names. Some of them, like Tranquilida and Ceritos, were obviously Spanish in origin;

others, like Brenton Loch and Ramsgate, definitely English.

But one name caught my eye. It was stuck out on the edge of my map area. Goose Green it was called. Why the fuck would you call a place Goose Green? I asked myself.

SIX

SUSSEX
BY THE SEA

STRADDLING ON THE CREST of Sussex Mountain the view to the west was of an expanse of pale, undernourished grass sucking a poor living from the peat. Here and there it was painted with wide bands of dark green gorse and there were splashes of brown where bracken had died back.

The whine of an aircraft cut through the landscape and out in front of us, maybe four miles away, we watched an enemy Pucara quartering the ground as it hunted for Brits.

There'd been two of them. They'd arrived over the three-mile-long harbour of San Carlos just half an hour after first light. One had taken a run at *Canberra* in the bay behind us but had thought better of it. He was too slow to fuck about with the flotilla. Then the second one had roared up the hill to strafe our positions on Sussex Mountain but he'd quickly ducked off too and circled away into the distance when we fired back. The whole battalion throwing a wall of lead into the air was far too close for comfort.

The junta had originally bought Pucaras as anti-insurgency aircraft. They had no real turn of speed but they had a low stalling point and they were manoeuvrable. That made Pucaras ideal for ground attacks, a bit like the far more sophisticated US A-10 tank-busters; it also made them a deadly threat to our meagre supply of helos. They were like dragonflies hawking for prey from the air.

The sight of it buzzing around was getting on my nerves but we didn't have to wait for long; it wasn't in the air for more than a minute after we spotted it again and that's when we had a glimpse into the future.

Suddenly, from a ridge that we could barely make out halfway to the horizon, a snake of smoke and vapour rose from the gorse. We heard nothing but just watched it cut loose and strike out towards the Pucara. I don't think the pilot saw a thing as the ribbon of smoke flew unerringly towards the banking plane then coiled itself around one of its engines before ripping it off with the sudden flash of an explosion.

Our eyes never left the aircraft as it began a wild uncontrolled dive towards the ground, the pilot grappling to maintain control until he gave up and ejected. The next thing we saw was the white canopy of a parachute floating lazily towards the ground. His aircraft hit the ground and was immediately engulfed in a fireball.

We knew that somewhere out there at the end of that trail of vapour was a Special Forces patrol and one of the troopers had simply lifted a missile onto his shoulder and let fly with a weapon that was destined to change the course of future wars around the globe. A Stinger ground-to-air missile.

Kev Mortimer, the patrol sage, summed up what we were all feeling at that point.

'Fuck me! That stung all right,' he said, adding a heartfelt and simple wish: 'I want one of them.'

We all grunted in agreement. It didn't need saying really. We all wanted a Stinger. We all wanted the ability to mount a deadly attack on the Argentine aircraft from the ground.

'That'll be the Regiment,' said Steve.

I nodded. It had to be them. The SAS were the only unit in the field forward of us and equipped with the lethal ground-to-air missiles. At that moment, exhausted, wet and footsore, our shoulders aching from the crushing weight of the bergens, we knew that it was going to be a fight to the finish.

Whoever he was, that pilot had been handed a calling card from the SAS in the shape of the one and only ground-to-air Stinger missile to be used in the Falklands campaign.

But even as his plane hit the ground in a spectacular fireball we knew that he would be the first of many Argentine flyers who'd swoop in to test our mettle and kill our mates. More were on their way and they were the real deal. Fast and furious supersonic fighters.

A hellish thump. Every cell in my body oscillated from the shock wave of another jet, as it broke the sound barrier ahead of its arrival announcing the attack that was to come. It was followed by a diabolical roar and another, louder thud as a bomb exploded.

The Super Etentard fighter lived up to its name and vanished almost as soon as I glimpsed it. Just the shadow of a delta wing and the bastard was gone, a deadly supersonic illusion as it streaked across San Carlos Bay in under twenty seconds and thundered over Sussex Mountain.

I may not have seen much of the aircraft but I did know what it sounded like and a Super Etendard it was. It was the sound of terror and they kept screaming in at sea level, five or six hundred feet below our position on the mountain, as our ships braced themselves for attack after attack.

We just had to turn and face in the opposite direction from the Pucara that had been downed by the Regiment to watch this new, more lethal enemy streaking in for the attack. We felt impotent and feeble in the presence of these multimillion-dollar, shrieking pieces of technology, but we knew we had to do something.

And as we watched from high on the mountain, the flotilla seemed to be scaled down to look like toy ships; Airfix kits that had been laid out on a superbly constructed modeller's display. The enemy fighters weaving in and out of the task force, almost slicing the tops off the waves as they looked for targets, completed the tableau.

Occasionally a beam of sunlight would run across the bay, bringing the waves to life and lighting up the ships one by one like a spotlight shining on a parade of stars. Now and then the MV *Canberra* was illuminated by the sun so that the old girl shone like an iridescent white whale breaching the lead grey waters of San Carlos water. That's what we called her: the Great White Whale. The stately cruise liner that had carried 3 Para to war was surrounded by the drabber outlines of her sister ships in the task force, and around her the frigates blended with the water like sinister sharks in battleship grey.

All was sound and fury in the bay, though, as anti-aircraft guns opened up on the incoming warplanes and the bombs that had missed their target erupted, spectacularly but harmlessly in the water all around the ships.

Then one got HMS *Ardent*. She was the first to go. The thunder of a jet echoing off the sides of the bay, then a delta-winged shadow picked out and brought to life for a microsecond by a sunbeam. A Mach 1 report that no one wanted to hear. Then the whole ship erupted from the centre turning itself inside out like a giant firework that had gone off in the box. Bright orange with streaks of vivid green and blue, showers of electric red at the edges as the fireball burnt onto the back of my eyes.

We stood there shocked, anger welling up. We knew that there wasn't much we could do to affect the air war, as the fighters came in to swat our ships at will, but we'd do what we could. British jacks in the crews on board the ships below us were being barbecued as we watched. We filed it under the heading revenge, then lay on our backs in the gorse and grass among the rocks to fire at them as they jinked over Sussex on their way home to reload.

And the jets kept pouring over us. Mirages, Super Etentards and Skyhawks. Dozens of them. They'd flown nearly four hundred miles across the sea from airbases in the southern Argentine state of Patagonia to wreak their mischief on the fleet. Fast as they were, we kept firing and thousands of rounds were put into the air as we tried to bring a fighter down.

On the voyage south we'd been given a talk by a Harrier pilot who'd told us, 'One of the scariest things for a pilot to face is small arms fire. It's random and there are no countermeasures for it. It's outside the pilot's normal experience. So if you get the chance, do fire at enemy jets. Don't try aiming; just lie on your back and swing your weapon in an arc and fire a burst as the plane comes over.'

We took him at his word and the whole fucking battalion lay on our backs and swung our arms in big arcs like a load of nutters all imitating windscreen wipers. But it fucking worked!

'Come on! Come on!' I shouted to myself willing one of those jets to come close enough for me to plug it. I was only firing an SLR. Hardly likely to bring a fighter down, but then if you don't try you won't fucking succeed.

The SLR was known as the widow-maker because it was a seriously accurate rifle. But it had one serious drawback, which once again had been organised by the desk dobbins at the MoD's procurement department. The SLR was basically a modified automatic FN rifle of a Belgian design, but the pen pushers in Whitehall had ordered a modified version which only fired single shots. We were single-shot soldiers fighting in a world firing on automatic; another triumph for the civil servants.

The ordinary British soldier is famed for his ingenuity though, and some of the lads had taken the problem of the SLR, turned it over in their minds, had a good look at the weapon and improved it beyond the specifications of the manufacturers and the clods at the MoD.

Their solution relied on an improvisation straight out of Heath Robinson, which had the advantage of using a component all the lads had in their kit: a matchstick snapped in half. Jammed into the sears of the mechanism it let you fire the SLR in short bursts. Hey presto, automatic fire, and 2 Para became matchstick warriors.

'Come on! Come on!' One lucky round. That's all I needed, one lucky round.

Even the colonel was on his back firing up at the fuckers. Every round counted and everyone wanted the glory of a kill. The machine-gunners did well and they claimed three hits. I witnessed the hits myself. All Skyhawks.

The steam of evaporating fuel streamed down the sides of their fuselages as it poured from the holes that gimpy rounds had made in their tanks. I watched our gunner Kev Mortimer pushing rounds into the air as one Skyhawk flew over us.

Several members of the patrol company reckoned they'd holed it, including me and Kev, as Avgas, aviation fuel, drenched us in our position and the Skyhawk banked and careered away in trouble towards Cantera Mountain and then dropped like a stone. The other one vanished over the crest of the loaf-shaped hill at Bodie Peak and I never saw it again. It had either limped off to Stanley under cover of the contours or hit the deck.

One of the lads from Support Platoon, a Tom called Scouse Worrall, became the first British soldier to fire a Milan anti-tank rocket in action. It wasn't a tank he was firing at though, it was a Skyhawk coming over the top of Sussex. We'd just been issued with the new Milans to replace the old heavy-duty Wombats, and Scouse, who was one of the fourteen sets of brothers in the battalion, reckoned that if one was coming low and fast straight at you a Milan could sort it.

So he tried. Fair play. His aim was true and he held his fly-by-wire missile right on the nose of the approaching Skyhawk, but at the very last moment the pilot woke up, spotted doom flying towards him and banked desperately out of its way. That was a ballsy attempt by Worrall. Keeping your nerve as a jet with big fuck-off cannons and a wing full of missiles heads straight for you takes a lot of bottle. If he'd hit the bastard, Scouse would have made his way into the military history books and he would have been given a big fat medal. More importantly, he'd have been on free beer in Aldershot for weeks when he got back home.

Later I watched another good hit when Colour Sergeant Cauldwell and his blokes had a Skyhawk right over them and let loose with everything they had. Aviation fuel was sprayed like aftershave from an atomiser all over the battalion as it flew on and then I watched it curl low and vanish out of sight into the next valley. It wasn't going anywhere far at all.

There was a moment during that first day of air attacks when everything stopped as we spotted a movement in the bay. *Norland* was turning around. We watched on tenterhooks as she upped anchor and steamed out of bomb alley towards open water. Would she make it? Every man in 2 Para was willing her to succeed. After all, she was the airborne's boat now and we prayed she would make it to open sea and out of range of the Argy flyers.

'I bet Wendy's sitting at the piano now bashing out "Land of Hope and Glory",' said Steve.

I could picture the scene myself and I said, 'I just hope the captain doesn't have to send down a request for "Abide With Me".'

I watched as great plumes of seawater thrown up by stray bombs erupted all around her. Eventually the *Norland* made it to safety but we couldn't watch her escape for long. More planes were coming over our positions and we were on our backs again weaving a curtain of lead for the Argies to fly through. Firing like fuck into the clouds.

As they came over, they'd be a couple of hundred feet above us; sometimes they'd be flying a lot lower, depending on the angle that they'd come off their bomb run over the water.

Often the pilots seemed too preoccupied with the results of their attack on the flotilla to be bothered with us. They were probably looking in their rear-view mirrors to see if they'd sunk a ship and got a medal. But equally often they'd strafe our positions on the mountains as they roared above us. Literally passing shots before they fucked off back to Patagonia to refuel and get ready for their next sortie. We'd watch the pale blue paintwork on the bellies of their fuselages, but we weren't plane-spotting, we were just lead-throwing, and for the next few days Sussex Mountain became a shooting moor with the Argentine aircraft the grouse.

All in all not a bad tally. Four Skyhawks wasted! Downed by small arms. One Skyhawk pilot rendered incontinent by an oncoming Milan, and a Pucara dispatched by the weapon that we all wanted to get our hands on – the new all-singing, all-dancing Stinger. After thinking there was fuck all we could do against their aircraft, we'd had a few.

As the attacks continued, a pattern emerged, and we worked out that if the Argentine pilots flew straight on after their bomb run on San Carlos they generally made it away safely. But if they veered left after they'd made their run, then they headed into some real trouble that made our small arms fire look like small beer. That's because a left turn took them straight into the sortie area of the Harrier fighters working off our aircraft carriers.

On the ground we'd be looking up at the Argentine fighters willing them to bank off to the left.

'Left! Left! Left!' we'd mutter under our breath. 'Please. Go left!'

Sometimes one of the lads would shout it out in frustration. 'Go on! Hang a left, you fucker! Go left!'

If they did, the Harrier pilots were waiting to give the Argies a lethal demonstration of a neat tactic they'd worked out using the amazing vertical take-off powers of their aircraft. They just angled their VTOL engines so that they did a bit of a handbrake stop in mid-air. That let the Argentine jets shoot straight past them and the Harriers fired their US-built Aim 9L missiles right up the exhaust pipes of the shocked enemy pilots. Couldn't be better. Fantastic!

Every now and then we'd see a huge red and orange smoke ball over the horizon, marking the place where the Argentine pilots had learnt that new trick from our lads, and the side of Sussex Mountain would erupt in a huge cheer. Result. One less bastard to come back and bother us.

To be fair, those Argentine pilots were courageous flyers who had plenty of balls, skill and commitment. They had families too, sure they did, but so did we. And they were the ones who'd started this bollocks, not us.

Ardent was the first vessel to be sunk in San Carlos, but it wasn't the only ship to be hit. In fact, bombs struck all the frigates moored in San Carlos, but amazingly a lot of the Argentine munitions just didn't explode. *Antrim, Brilliant, Broadsword, Glasgow, Sir Galahad* and *Sir Lancelot* were all hit fair and square by bombs that didn't go off.

Up on the mountainside there was talk of conspiracy theories among the Toms, with some reckoning the Argies had been sold dud bombs by the Yanks.

One thing was for certain: the French hadn't sold the Argentine any dud Exocet missiles but they just couldn't use them on the ships tucked up in San Carlos. Out in the Falklands Sound, where the jets armed with Exocets had a longer run-in to the target, it was a different story and the damage those French missiles inflicted is now part of the Falklands legend.

The more likely answer to the unexploded bombs is that the dashing Argy pilots simply weren't talking to their armourers when they got back to base. Their bomb fuses were being set for around two hundred metres of free flight when in fact they got so close to their targets the pilots were launching bombs away at fifty metres. Bomb fuses are basically propellers that screw in the firing pin as they travel, but if they don't fly long enough the pins don't wind in far enough. Job not done.

That's not the whole story though. Badly fused bombs saved the flotilla in San Carlos from a worse pounding than the one it got and that was bad enough. But the fact is that the Argentine high command got the plot completely wrong at San Carlos and missed the chance to completely obliterate the task force and Britain's retaking of the Falklands. Sat on their arses in Buenos Aires, the junta ordered their pilots to knock out the Royal Navy at all costs. Fair play to those Argy flyers, they did their best, but the whole point was that they were going after the wrong targets.

If they'd targeted the troop ships pressed into service by the navy instead, they'd have taken out hundreds of soldiers and tons of military supplies. When they turned San Carlos water into bomb alley, the *Canberra* and the assault ships *Fearless* and *Intrepid* were there full of vital military resources needed to prosecute the war on land. That war would have been over before it had begun if those ships had been sunk and Britain would have been humiliated internationally. It would have been another totally fucked-up invasion, reliving the scenes at the Battle of Gallipoli in 1915 when Turkish artillery raged down on the Allied battle fleet.

By the time the Argentines had woken up and smelt the Royal Navy rum ration it was too late. When they did, they sank the supply ship *Atlantic Conveyor* with its load of heavy-lift helicopters. In the harsh reality of war, that was a far heavier strategic blow to the British than the tragic loss of the warships.

Our pilots played a blinder of course, and shot down over a hundred Argentine aircraft in the frantic weeks of the war, but in those first heady days of the conflict it was the Argentine flyers who hit the headlines with their bold but useless strikes on our frigates.

I'm here to tell the story of one remarkable battle, the Battle of Goose Green, but I think it's worth pausing for a moment to reflect on the fact that there was another outstanding, watershed battle during the Falklands War. It was the battle in the air. It was the last time that two, more or less evenly matched air forces, both with highly skilled and supremely brave pilots, slogged it out in the sky. It was the last war of aerial dogfights and every major conflict since has been dominated by a single factor: the overwhelming supremacy of US air power.

Those strikes on our frigates turned out to be a false and hollow victory for the Argentine. The army that was going to defeat them wasn't sitting on the fucking frigates waiting to be popped off. We were on the Falklands and we were coming to get them!

The night of the landings, C Company had reached the forward slopes of Sussex Mountain to find that there was no need to mark out the start lines for a battle. There wasn't an Argy in sight and we got the foothold we needed on the Falklands without a serious land challenge.

The combined efforts of the other services – the Royal Navy, the Merchant Fleet and the Royal Air Force – had got an entire brigade onto the beach, with 3 Para and Royal Marines from 40 and 42 Commando deployed to the north of our position on the fingers of the inlet at San Carlos itself.

The Booties from 40 were dug in near San Carlos settlement where they were shooting at penguins. Seriously. A marine patrol was spooked when they glimpsed figures moving in the rocks behind the beach and they opened up on them. The 'figures' turned out to be penguins. Typical Booties. They must have thought they'd surprised a party of Argentine officers in full mess kit going to a regimental dinner. Worse than that, not a single fucking penguin was hit!

But while the war of sea and air continued unabated, the troops from the first British landing consolidated our positions on the beachhead. The fact that 2 Para was able to install itself on Sussex was a major plus because the nearest Argentine troops were about fourteen miles away at Goose Green and we were now between them and San Carlos. If they wanted to counter the landings they were going to have to go through us.

A guessing game was going on between us and the Argentines, who were well aware that we had another brigade nearing the Falklands sailing on the *QE2*. The riddle for them was whether the San Carlos landings were a diversion while the real invasion comprising the rest of the British forces was going to attempt to land a lot closer to Port Stanley.

While the Argies were trying to work out what was going on, the priority for the top brass was to deploy anti-aircraft kit to protect the brigade from aerial attacks and a huge effort went into deploying a dozen Rapier missile batteries around the beach-head.

They may as well not have bothered. The Rapier turned out to be pretty crap, because it was so delicate that the system didn't travel very well and it was thrown out of calibration when it was rocked around during the journey down south. That's just what you need, military kit that doesn't travel very well. Marvellous. Four-nil to the pen pushers so far and we'd hardly got going.

Meanwhile, our bosses on the ground had some other pressing problems. They needed helicopters, and were confronted by the grim fact that they'd lost three heavy-lift Chinooks and six Wessex choppers when the *Atlantic Conveyor* was sunk by a French Exocet.

For the moment, many of those tactical problems, like most of the Argentine air force, went over the heads of the Toms in 2 Para who had problems of their own. Only later would the logistics problems the bosses were fretting over hit home and it would be a hard blow to cope with. In the meantime, while the top brass were deciding our next move, 2 Para was in for a spell in the deep freeze.

Eight hundred foot up on the South Downs back home in late May is a pleasant place to be; you might even be able to have a picnic. But in the southern hemisphere May is the start of winter and eight hundred foot up on a mountain exposed to the blast of Antarctic winds is no fucking picnic at all.

Most of the battalion had to dig in on the forward sloping side of the mountain overlooking San Carlos Bay. That's because the Argentine jets might fly low over them as they came off their bomb runs, but they would have been able to completely fuck them if they'd all dug in on the other side away from any AA cover at all.

C Company, though, had to dig in on the Stanley side of the mountain, which faced south, and in the southern hemisphere south faces away from the sun. We were in shadow and it was freezing. We took over some observation posts that D Squadron SAS had dug earlier but we had to dig a lot more. We'd cut squares of turf to make our fire trenches and then pile them up to create a low berm or sangar in front of our positions. They were easy to dig but we soon discovered that when we got down a couple of feet we hit water. Basically there was no water table on Sussex Mountain – it was all fucking water and no table.

Result: the battalion had to spend days in shallow scrapes that offered little or no protection from the enemy or the wind and cold. The positions were so vulnerable that during the day you'd see Toms wandering around the mountainside scavenging for loose boulders to harden off their defensive banks of peat.

We had small bivouac tents that we could put over the top of our diggings to keep the worst of the rain and some of the wind off, but the pegs wouldn't stay in the peat so we had to tie them down with rocks too.

At night the temperatures plummeted and we just clung onto the side of the mountain, drinking brews as often as we could to keep the body core temperature warm and stagging each other on watch. Those that weren't on stag sought cold comfort in wet sleeping bags. It was debilitating stuff and the routine of standing-to for the air attacks followed by cold attacks took its toll.

I reckon about thirty of the battalion were taken off the mountain with various injuries. Some of them, like twisted knees and sprained ankles, were down to the terrain with the endless baby-head tussocks of grass and rock-strewn expanses of scree. But a dozen or so were taken off because of trench foot. It sounds funny, trench foot, and the expression has a touch of the Monty Pythons about it that attracts a lot of piss-taking when it's mentioned. But trench foot is actually pure torture for those who suffer with it. The blokes that get it swear it's like your feet are being squeezed until they feel like they're going to burst.

As I've said, an army marches on its feet, not its stomach, and the feet are particularly vulnerable to a combination of constant wet and cold. I never suffered trench foot myself but a dozen blokes out of action is a big deal in a fighting unit and the battalion went to great lengths to prevent cases of the condition.

The lads were encouraged to keep up a regime of regular foot care and there were regular foot inspections made by the medics, although because of the more independent nature of Patrols work we were expected to be grown up enough to make sure our feet were tended. The onset of trench foot made your feet turn as white as plaster and wrinkled like a bulldog's nose; they would be as cold as a block of ice to the touch. Every time it was possible you would whip your boots off, dry your feet, powder them and then put on dry or nearly dry socks to replace the ones that had inevitably got soaked.

Across the battalion lines you would see blokes wringing out their socks or holding them in front of their hexi stoves to dry them a bit while boiling up for a brew or cooking their scran. It was like a bizarre open-air sockfest. Spare pairs were put under the armpits or across the belly to dry them off with the heat of the body. I would even put socks in my underpants to dry off in my crotch. It was a bit of a risk but I can report that I never suffered from trench bollocks either!

The cold was another thing altogether. The Falklands are roughly the same distance from the South Pole as the British Isles are from the North Pole but what a difference. For a start, the Falklands don't have the sheltering mass of a nearby continent folding around them like Britain does. The Antarctic winds just rush in and scour the islands for much of the year. There's another crucial difference: they don't have the benefit of a warm current like the Gulf Stream bathing their shores and keeping the temperatures up like we do. The resulting weather is bleak. The winds, which are all cold, can notch up to storm force in minutes then die away again just as quickly; rain, sleet and snow can fall within the same hour, and when the wind drops off you get mist and drizzle, both of which are the chilled variety. The Falklands may be a penguin paradise but in winter it's hell for humans.

Those conditions would have also played havoc with our weapons had it not been an ingrained reflex to constantly check and clean them. But the damp affected ammo too, so we would spend a great deal of time emptying magazines and clips and cleaning off the rounds to prevent rust and verdigris, the green shit you get developing on brass. No use having a spotless gun if your rounds are covered in crap and jam up in the breach. No soldier worth his salt wants to deal with a hard extraction in the middle of a firefight.

Water caused huge problems too and not just because there was so much of the stuff. It was a case of water, water, everywhere, nor any drop to drink. Why? Because the whole island is covered in a layer of sheep shit and you couldn't risk drinking it fresh from the small streams pouring off the island towards the sea. Liver fluke from parasitic worms in the droppings would have followed.

Fresh supplies had to be helicoptered off the ships every day and when we went tactical we had to boil and sterilise the water for our brews and for our rations as well which were army issued freeze-dried Arctic packs. They needed a lot of hot water poured onto them to wake them up into the culinary feasts they were supposed to be.

Another very real danger came about if men from the different companies were sent on tasks to other units in the battalion. Moving up to headquarters for a briefing or to collect something became a risky business because the fat bastards in the Defence Platoon were very twitchy and had their fingers on their triggers.

Moving about in general was hairy and at one point our company's mortar nearly took out some lads from A Company who were foraging around in front of our lines. They weren't very happy and neither were the helicopter crew who'd nested up for the night nearby and nearly got shot up by some other A Company types who mistook them for the enemy.

In the end all these incidents were for the good, because it led to some rockets fired off by the colonel about tightening up procedures and communications so that blue on blues would be avoided. By the time 2 Para tabbed off Sussex they were good to go, and the only casualties up to that point were down to the cold and the terrain.

As the days on Sussex relentlessly mounted up and the lads were kept sitting there, watching the carnage being inflicted on our ships in the bay, the morale of 2 Para was certainly tested. But despite the appalling conditions and all the challenges I didn't sense that the battalion faltered at all.

In fact, it's my firm belief that we took whatever Sussex Mountain had to throw at us because if we faltered for a moment all we had to do was look down on San Carlos and remind ourselves that we had our mates in the Royal Navy to avenge.

Paras have never hidden from the realities of what they feel and what they do. We hadn't been that bothered on the voyage down but what we'd seen had made it personal. Revenge was what we wanted and we were up for a fight.

As it was, most of the battalion had six days on Sussex Mountain to think about it. That time waiting for the bosses to sort out their shit and decide what was going to happen was hardcore.

But Patrols didn't have to sit on our hands with the rest of them out there for long. We had work to do. Captain Farrar came to brief us. We were moving out.

SEVEN

DRINK YOUR DRIP!

I SWUNG THE BERGEN off my back and let it drop to the ground with a thud; as it fell from my shoulders my back snapped straight like an unstrung longbow. Soon I'd follow my bergen and collapse exhausted to the ground, but first I had to quench the thirst from hell.

Dawn was about to break and we'd just stumbled back into our positions on Sussex after a marathon tab through the night. All around me other men were standing like racehorses trembling after a steeplechase and wreathed in steam. They sucked in the freezing air and gasped with dehydration after the effort of a tactical advance to battle that had been a round trip to fucking nowhere.

Fifteen stumbling, mind-numbing, muscle-tearing miles. Fifteen miles of endlessly squelching babies' heads. Mile after foot-clamping mile of sucking peat and not a single stop for a brew. One of the guys in the company had actually collapsed with heat exhaustion after tabbing too far and too hard with too much Arctic clothing on. Heat exhaustion on cold-comfort island! But we may as well have been in the Sahara, after marching through the middle of a waterlogged desert where sheep shit had turned pure water into liver fluke cordial and we'd already drained the last drops out of our bottles hours earlier.

The moment the tab was over all I wanted was a drink. Nothing else was in my mind. There was drinkable water somewhere in the battalion lines but where the fuck was it? No time to ask. No time to stumble around looking for some. I had to have it. I felt like a piece of desiccated coconut standing on a soaking wet sponge. What could I drink? Got it!

I plunged my hand inside my combat jacket and pulled out the clear plastic pouch of saline drip that we all carry into combat along with our field dressings and morphine. I ripped the top off it with my teeth in my desperation to bolt it down. Fucking lovely! I squeezed the pouch to force the rush of fluid into my mouth and as I swallowed every cell in my body seemed to light up like a control panel with a surge of power. Christ, it was good.

The others were looking at me curiously. Wondering if I'd completely lost the fucking plot as I called out to a medic asking him to give me another pouch from his bag of tricks. He handed me another and I snapped the top off. Already the rush from the first plastic lifesaver full of minerals, electrolytes and isotonics had began to rehydrate me.

'Come on! Drink your drips, lads,' I urged them.

I didn't elaborate on the advice. I just glugged the next one and they got the idea. It was years before sports drinks had been invented but we'd found them on the Falklands.

The others did the same and then the word spread: 'Drink your drip.'

And we did. It tasted like stale, salty ham stock but we savoured every last drop of it. Cheers!

We had started that march the night before, on 23 May, when the brass had apparently got their act together and decided that Goose Green should be raided. D Company, under Major Neame, were to move up to Camilla Creek House, a sheep station a couple of miles on the Sussex Mountainside of the Goose Green isthmus. A and B Companies would follow and then the raid would go down on the night of the 24th and continue into the early hours of the following day.

That meant elements of Patrols Platoon would go ahead of the rest of the lads to recce Camilla and then lay out start lines for the attack. So my patrol was off on a furious tab to get ahead of the game as soon as dusk arrived.

The order to go had been given the day after the landings at San Carlos when the head shed, Brigadier Thompson, had visited H in a forward OP on the left side of the battalion lines and given him the good news. London had agreed to a raid on Goose Green.

H was on top form, according to all the reports filtering back from HQ Company. He had plans to formulate and there isn't an officer on the planet that doesn't love planning. That's what they're supposed to do.

The good news was that the four Sea King helicopters kitted with night vision would be able to lift a battery of three 105 field guns to Camilla in support of the raid. The bad news was there'd be no helicopters to airlift the men forward so they'd have to walk.

Why not attack from the sea in LCUs up Brenton Loch to land on Salinas Beach on the opposite side of the isthmus to the settlement? H's suggestion was sat on, because navigating the treacherous shallows of a loch full of hull-ripping rocks would be dodgy and would need sonar and radar which the enemy trackers would pick up instantly. Foot cavalry it was then.

There was another problem to sort first though, and that was a report from the SAS that a group of sixty enemy soldiers with a troop carrier were hanging around Cantera House to the west of Mount Usborne. That would put them about halfway between us and Camilla and make them the nearest known Argies, so they were well placed to raise the alarm or even fuck up the tactical advance to battle with an ambush.

Lieutenant Jim Barry and 12 Platoon of D Company were tasked to take the house and neutralise the enemy. They were dropped in by Sea King for a short walk to Cantera that turned into a four-hour-long tabbing nightmare. It only ended when Major Neame called artillery onto the house, then stormed it – only to find it was empty. The Argies must have legged it.

When the time came we set off down a track, utterly thankful to be leaving sub-zero Sussex to our rear, and the rest of D Company, minus 12 Platoon at Cantera, were tabbing somewhere behind us. We pressed on.

It was a cold, dark night and the clag of mist and rain soon soaked us. One of the unwritten laws of infantry fighting is that the weight of a bergen is twice the sum of the fucking rain falling on it. In other words, the wetter your kit gets the heavier it becomes and in your mind that can double the weight on your back.

On we went until we were not far at all from Camilla. Then a radio message. Turn back. The mission's off. Turn back? What the fuck were they on about? Later we found out that the weather had grounded the helos that had been tasked to move the artillery forward. No artillery, no raid. H kicked off like a firecracker when he heard and snarled, 'I've waited twenty years for this and now some fucking marine's cancelled it.'

Nothing for it but to do as we were told and we began the long, dehydrating slog back to Sussex where we learnt to drink our drip.

The way it panned out we weren't going to be there long, but it was during those last few hours on Sussex Mountain that I saw the colonel for the last time and once again it was going to be an odd encounter.

My patrol and another patrol were walking through the lines ready for the next 'on the truck, off the truck' mission, and as is my way I'd struck up a song. The lads all joined in. That's what Toms do. We like a song now and then and it's in the best traditions of the British Army. 'It's a Long Way to Tipperary' and all that.

Anyway, the song I'd chosen to brighten up the morning was a Beatles number, or more specifically a John Lennon song. It was the anthem he sang with Yoko Ono – 'All We Are Saying is Give Peace a Chance' – and we were singing it with a fair amount of piss-taking irony in the way of the paras. We were really belting it out when a head suddenly poked out of the command HQ tent flap. It was H. He didn't say anything. He just looked at us with an expression that said, 'Oh, it's those fucking nutters from Patrols.'

It has to be said H loved Patrols. He loved fit, aggressive soldiers, which is why I reckon he came to the paras from a crap-hat regiment in the first place. He'd actively promoted the Patrols concept. He was a Rupert who wasn't afraid of a fight and you can't say more about a CO than that.

He just looked at us like a patient father looking at some naughty kids and never said a word; then his head vanished back through the tent flap and we never saw him alive again.

We'd learnt all we needed to know about the terrain on the islands during that tab and it was fucking horrible. For example, Falkland Islanders are known as Kelpers, after the huge rafts of kelp seaweed that surround the place. And the islanders' name for the huge tract of open country that dominates the scenery all around is the 'camp'.

Basically, to visualise the camp you have to picture Dartmoor and imagine something very similar but the size of the whole of Wales. It's covered in gorse, bracken and tussocks of white moorland grass, and where it's dry enough the sheep crop the grass down until it's as short as a bowling green and covered in pellets of their droppings.

The coast is cut with deep inlets and fingers of bays very much like Scottish sea lochs and I'm told it's very beautiful. I assume that it must be beautiful if you're visiting in the summer and there isn't a war going on because I didn't think it was beautiful at all. I just thought it was a boggy shithole that I was going to have to fight on.

Most of the camp is made up of mile after mile of tussock grass floating on a bed of soaking peat that sheep graze on during the summer. There are quite a few peaks and mountains of around the same height and character as those found on Dartmoor or in the Brecon Beacons, with rocky tors eroded by wind and ice dramatically marking many of their summits.

I'm no expert but I reckon glaciers had sculpted most of that terrain during some previous ice age. You find long, wide ribbons of ankle-breaking rocks across the topography, probably the rubble that's been dropped out of a glacier. It's like a Stone Age mine-field and a bastard to traverse, especially in the dark and particularly if you don't want to be heard shouting in pain.

The gorse grows in long, wide bands too, with well-defined edges up against the tussock grass. Gorse likes well-drained soil and while I was crawling on all fours through the stuff, trying to not to get my arse shot off, I couldn't help noticing it was growing on a glassy, sandy soil. That was probably dropped in long strips by retreating glaciers too, and before you start thinking I'm some sort of rock anorak it's worth remembering that the way geology forms the terrain is important to soldiers. Why? Because we have to fight on it!

Another eye-numbing feature on the Falklands is the almost total lack of trees, which made the cloth-ripping, eye-jabbing gorse the best cover that was available. Remember, this is a place dominated by the wind; it's a place where any bees foolish enough to drop in for a visit are blown out to sea the moment they dare to stretch their wings again. So the chances of any trees surviving the rigours of the wind and the chomping of the bloody sheep are about zero. I think the lack of trees is another factor that makes the camp look so relentlessly big; there's not a copse or a hedge or a wood to break up the line on the eye. I seem to remember a few carefully tended excuses for trees, more like tall shrubs, near the settlements. But as far as trees go that was it. Give me England any day.

The only wood you do see out on the camp also tends to sprout up nearer the settlements and it comes in the shape of rather rickety sheep fences. They look like the decayed rib bones of half-buried whales sticking up at irregular angles and stretching into the distance. It's hard to work out why they're there at all, but they do at least break up the line of the endless tussocks of grass. Who knows where they got the timber for the fences; probably from their nearest neighbours in the Argentine.

That's what we tabbed through. An island the size of Wales without a tree to piss on where God scattered rocks around to trip you up and planted grass like babies' heads that made you think you were pulverising a kid's brain every time you put your foot down. Welcome to the camp.

'Right, guys. Listen up.'

Paul Farrar, our captain, was like a greyhound in the slips as he briefed us about the task we'd been given. The truth was that we were all straining at the leash. Despite the rigours of that abortive tab ahead of D Company, anything was better than clinging to the side of Sussex Mountain pissing into the wind. Our drip had revived us, we'd grabbed some kip and we'd had a scoff. We were ready for the off.

'Our objective is a track in a valley north of Bodie Peak, about five or six klicks from our positions here on the mountain,' he continued. 'There's some intel around suggesting that enemy patrols may be using this as a route to access OPs near the positions of 3 Para and the 40 and 42 Commando further north. Our job will be to tab out to this position and set an ambush on this route. Any questions so far?'

Silence. No one wanted to delay the move off Sussex for a moment longer than we had to. Anyone who'd opened his mouth at that point would have had a dig in the ribs. Anyway, what's to ask? A tab is a tab and an ambush is an ambush. Anything was better than sitting in a bath of freezing peat water waiting for another bone job from Tac HQ. We just wanted to get on with it!

'No? OK, orders are that we are to move off in light order. No helmets and definitely no sleeping bags. The idea is to get in there, hit any Argies who come down the track and get out again. You won't be doing much kipping. Any questions?'

Rumbles of complaint at having no bags but still no questions. Come on. Let's get on with it.

'OK. We move out in an hour. Synchronise your watches. Got that?'

'Yes, boss,' we replied as one, then fell out to get our kit ready. An hour later we mustered at the edge of our position, ready to move off down the eastern slopes of Sussex, when the boss turned up with the platoon sergeant, Eric Smith.

Shock and disgust registered on our faces at the sight of them both. The captain and the sergeant. We were standing there stripped down to our frames in belt order. No sleeping bags. No helmets. Just webbing with ammo and food and, of course, weapons. We were to travel light on the colonel's express orders. But those two fuckers had sleeping bags bungeed onto the back of their webbings. The cheeky bastards!

'Hang on, boss,' I said. 'Light order, you said. No sleeping bags, you said. So what the fuck's that hanging round your kidneys – a fucking cuddly missile?'

Free and frank exchanges of views with your immediate superior officers in the field are allowed, but he didn't like it because he'd been exposed as a man who needed a fucking sleeping bag when the rest of us could go without.

We didn't care about the sergeant much. But the captain? That was a different matter. You may think it petty but I can tell you things like this matter a great deal when you're up against it. When you're all supposed to be in the same boat that's where you expect everyone to be. You don't expect some of your number to be in another boat with a fucking cabin on it.

'That's a crap-hat trick, that is, boss,' Steve waded in with the ultimate condemnation.

'Look, you lot,' he snapped, 'I'm the one who has to do the thinking in this outfit. I need to get more sleep than the rest of you.'

Farrar was beginning to steam, but he didn't sound as though he'd convinced himself, let alone us.

'Oh, that's all right, boss,' I said. 'The rest of us think much better when we're fucking freezing. You just make sure you're tucked up nice and cosy. We'd hate to think you couldn't think cos you'd caught a fucking chill.'

'Don't take the piss, Geddes!' he snapped. 'Enough of this bollocks now. Let's move out, we've got a job to do.'

So we moved off in a snake with the lead scouts pushing out on point in front of us and we soon warmed up a bit, got into our swing and were going at the best pace that the babies' heads and boot-swallowing peat would permit.

We were about three klicks out and the wind had dropped. That meant an inevitable misty drizzle moved on to the island in its place, and there on the skyline was a figure. Sleepy was first to spot him and we all deployed into some old peat diggings.

As the whole platoon took cover, about fifteen men emerged onto the skyline in a snake heading straight towards us. The lads settled down and prepared for an ambush, laying a few spare mags to hand; a few 66mm LAW were also prepped for action.

We watched the suspect patrol approach until they were about two hundred metres from us and it was obvious they were UK troops travelling in light order. With the enemy lines behind them, they were wearing white mine tape bandannas to avoid blue-on-blue engagements.

Then suddenly their lead scout stopped, dropped to one knee and scanned the area to our front. They must have expected us to be in the area, so before they got too nervous we broke cover and then all met up for a chinwag.

They said they had been bounced from their OP by a Pucara aircraft. The bloke bringing up their rear was a big, bald-headed bloke who was wearing welly boots and was carrying a gimpy with the ammo belt trailing back into his bergen!

He just said, 'Give 'em plenty of firepower, lads. They don't like it!'

They were dishevelled, exhausted men, their faces harrowed and etched with tension and the pain of endless tabbing. But their eyes were sparkling and triumphant.

It was the patrol from D Squadron SAS; they were the guys who'd mounted a diversionary attack on Darwin when the task force flotilla had sailed into San Carlos Bay. As it happens they were the same nasty bastards we'd watched drop that Pucara with a Stinger, and they looked mighty pleased with themselves despite weeks behind enemy lines on covert operations.

We knew a few of them. They were ex 2 Para guys although ex is not really accurate. As far as the world was concerned they were still in 2 Para and if they ever put a foot wrong in the SAS they'd come back to the battalion, RTU'd – returned to Unit.

As they came through our line, there was a lot of backslapping and handshaking and I grabbed the big, bald-headed man. He was a mate of mine, Pete Peterson, ex 2 Para Patrols, who'd been a bit of a mentor of mine in the early days, a punchy fitness and health freak who got his crack at SAS selection before me – he had no points on his licence! Anyway, I bunked with him in South Armagh and he used to drag me out of bed, fighting tooth and nail, to go training over the Mourne Mountains at the weekends. It was good to see him.

We bear-hugged each other. 'Pete! When did you get here, mate?'

'Weeks back. We got a ride on a VC-10 to Ascension, then bounced over here for a covert insertion. What about you?'

'Jammy bastard! I had to get here on a fucking car ferry.' I turned three shades greener as I spoke.

He laughed and said, 'Time you did selection and travelled first class, Johnny boy.'

'Yeah, I intend to. I've got to get through this fucking lot first though.'

'Looks like you're off now, mate,' he said as our snake formed up again. 'Good luck. Stay low! Move fast! See you in Hereford.'

'Bet on it,' I said.

With that they disappeared into the mist on the mountain behind us. Later we came across the scene of their contact with the Pucara. There were some hexi stoves where they'd been brewing up still on the ground and the area was littered with cartridge cases. In the middle of it all was an unexploded Pucara missile stuck in the ground!

A few days later half of those blokes died when their Chinook ditched into the ocean in a tragic accident. Pete wasn't with them but a couple of my other mates went down that day. They were brilliant blokes. The country's finest.

We were out there beyond Sussex taking over the SAS OPs because A Company thought they'd spotted some Argy troops approaching their position on the northern flank of Sussex down the neck of this valley. They reckoned the enemy were trying to carry out a close-target reconnaissance on their positions; possibly trying to line up an attack and dislodge the battalion from the mountain.

That would have been bad news, so we were tasked to turn the valley into a death trap. We set off at last light.

There was the whole of the Patrols Platoon and tagging along was a group from 148 Forward Observation Party. It was a five-man patrol, with their para-trained Royal Navy radio operator, and their job was to call in the fire from the 4.5-inch naval guns.

The whole thing was obviously being taken very seriously. No one was going to take any chances on the Argy ground forces retaking Sussex, where they could join their air force in a turkey shoot on our ships.

We followed the ridge eastwards for about ten klicks, got to the ambush RV where we set a linear trap, and sat it out for the night in the rocks on top of Bodie. It was one of the coldest nights of my life.

We didn't have bags but we did have our Chinese fighting suits, the green, quilted pyjamas which we kept tied up tight on the back of our webbing. If we were on operations we'd slip out of wet clothes into the fighting suit under a poncho and at least we'd get a dry night. It was nowhere near as good as a kip in a sleeping bag but it was something.

I took to wearing my padded fighting suit jacket under my combat kit right through the Falklands campaign and I found that it kept me warm and worked well. I'd lost my gloves early on in an artillery barrage. One minute we were taking a vent stop, when you open up all your zips to let the steam out and cool your body during a tab. I put my gloves down on a rock in the sun and the next minute hell came to breakfast and the gloves and the rock were a smoking hole. Fuck knows how I survived. After that I spent the whole campaign with my hands exposed so I needed all the core heat I could keep. Resupply? New gloves? Forget it.

Meanwhile, Captain Farrar and Eric tucked up in their bags for a warm kip while the rest of us froze our bollocks off and shivered and rattled like old school radiators as we struggled against the bone-chilling cold.

The next morning we brewed up and ate cold rations for our breakfast with our tea among the rocks. Then we sat it out in the ambush spot waiting for a team of Argies who, as it turned out, would never appear.

Scouse McVeay was with us carrying an M79 grenade launcher, known as a blooper in the trade, which fires a huge fuck-off

40mm grenade, and the lads from 148 took a real shine to it.

They were about to call in HMS *Arrow*'s guns to register on the valley as a target that would close the jaws on the trap if the Argies did come strolling down that valley. We'd call in a volley from the navy big guns then pour our own nasty shit down on them from our ambush position.

The guys from 148 knew exactly where the shells would drop and asked Scouse to blast off his blooper a little bit up the valley. That way they could see it working under the cover of the bombardment and our position wouldn't be given away.

The battery commander gave a countdown to time on target for the naval shells. He was bang on and we heard the rounds scream in, arcing above our heads through the crystal-clear sky.

They landed with a massive flat crump and the valley lit up with a bright white light and a roll of explosions swept down its contours like the wall of a quarry being blown away.

With the 'bloop' that gave it its name, Scouse fired off his M79 which made quite an impressive bang in the valley, even along-side the 4.5-inch guns.

'Fucking brilliant that!' said one of the admiring 148 crew. We thought he was on about *Arrow*'s bombardment but it was the blooper they'd all been watching.

'Pound for pound that's a shit-hot weapon,' said their commander, nodding like a man who knows what's what. Well, if anyone ought to have known it was those big-bang navy gun fuckers, so we decided to be impressed with the blooper too.

After a while Captain Farrar was on the radio getting new instructions, and headquarters kept us in the area wandering along the top of the ridge at Bodie Peak, trying to get a look at a couple of the features that most interested the intelligence guys. They wanted us to look at Ceritos House and Camilla Creek House. They also wanted us to have a good look out towards Mount Kent and Stanley, but it was Camilla they were most inter-ested in. They had something on their minds, that was for sure.

The only excitement was when an Argy helo, a Vietnam War-style Huey, flew close to some of our OPs on Cantera Mountain and then hovered right in front of an OP to the west of the mountain.

Suddenly a long burst of fire rang out and the enemy aircraft took violent evasive action, peeling away from the mountainside, and smoke started billowing from the engine cowling.

It turned out to be Eddie Stokes, who was on stag at the OP when the helo came within about fifty feet of him. Eddie could hardly believe his luck and gave it a whole thirty-round mag from his LMG! We never found out whether the fucker made it back to Goose Green or not.

Then at about noon the following day the head shed called us off. That was it. Ambush over. Back to Sussex. Fuck it. No real action. Combat by the withdrawal method. Pull back before a climax.

'Any idea why?' I asked the boss.

''Fraid not, John,' he answered 'More briefings when we get back. I'll know more then. Meanwhile, let's get our backs into it.'

Personally I don't think an ambush was ever on. I think they were just sending us on a fishing expedition in case those sixty or so Argies from Cantera House were wandering around out there. But it was becoming pretty obvious to us that the Argentines weren't setting foot outside the settlements where they had their well-prepared positions unless it was absolutely necessary. Argentine troops out on the camp were like rocking-horse shit.

But we didn't care. We weren't turning into Sussex Mountain prunes like the rest of them.

About ten pay scales above me there were other concerns pressing on the colonels and brigadiers. It went like this. The entire campaign boiled down to one objective: the recapture of Port Stanley, putting a one-horse town on a giant sheep moor at the very heart of international events.

To do this, Brigadier Julian Thompson, the Bootneck in charge of our unit, 3 Commando Brigade, needed to consolidate his beachhead, wait for 5 Brigade, the Guards and the Gurkhas to arrive, and then move on to the objective, Port Stanley.

The trouble was that 5 Brigade were following us and weren't due for a week or two because they were sailing on the *QE2*. Rather than risk the pride of Britain's Merchant Fleet, the *QE2* was going to RV with the *Canberra*, *Galahad* and *Tristran* at South Georgia, and they would bring the troops into bomb alley. That was what was slowing down their arrival.

When they finally arrived Thompson would have eight battalions ready to take on the Argentines. By that time he also hoped to have a full muster of helicopters to move his pawns around the board; remember, Port Stanley and its defences were about ninety kilometres away from San Carlos across bleak countryside and it was the onset of winter. Thompson also hoped that by the time he had a full force under his command British air superiority would have been fully established.

So far, so good. It was all quite straightforward and made perfect military sense. There were problems and setbacks of course – there always are in war, and more would follow before it was over – but Thompson had a clear strategy in his mind and he was the man on the ground.

Now factor in the top brass back at the UK's strategic warfare centre in Northwood on the edge of London into the equation and then add the biggest X factor of all: Maggie Thatcher.

British warships had been sunk in the full glare of international publicity. Images of *Ardent* going up like a giant firework had been seen around the world. She didn't like it. Remember too that the Cold War was still very much in the freezer, and here we had the military power and prowess of one of NATO's leading members on display and up for detailed examination by our Soviet bloc enemies. You can imagine the generals in the Kremlin huddled around TV screens watching the images of the air-sea battle of

San Carlos. The fuckers were probably trying to get every Russian spy satellite in formation stacking over the Falklands to get their own view of events too.

Something had to happen. Troops were on the ground but they were just sitting there. Maggie wanted a result and she wanted it quickly.

Of course, the grunts in 2 Para and the other elements of 3 Commando Brigade didn't know exactly what was going on. We didn't know that satellite phone calls between Northwood and Thompson were sending the MoD's phone bill rocketing as they argued about what should happen.

One argument was to put a small force across the neck of the isthmus, isolate the Argentines at Goose Green and deal with them later. The other was hit them straight away with a raid and leave them so badly battered they wouldn't have the heart to cause trouble behind the advancing British force.

Things always filter down from above and we were aware that H was thunderous and tense, particularly since D Company's long march to Camilla and back after the aborted raid. But a raid on Goose Green was still on the cards and H was desperate to do some damage. Like any good commander he wanted action, and if there was any glory about he wanted it for 2 Para, not the fucking Bootneck Marines. The trouble was that Goose Green kept going onto the menu board only to be rubbed off again as the Northwood brass and Thompson slogged it out over strategy.

All that the Toms in the battalion could do was try to keep warm and wait for orders, but the military and the propaganda arguments for an attack on Goose Green were becoming more compelling.

We believe it was Maggie herself who tipped the scales in favour of an attack. She wanted a land victory to knock the Argy successes against the Royal Navy off the top of the worldwide news. Victory at Goose Green became a priority. It was down to us to provide her with one.

★   ★   ★

Captain Farrar had a brief vocal on the radio then told us the sketch: we weren't going back to Sussex where our kit was waiting for us; we were tabbing out again.

'Right, lads, we're going to slice across country and tie up with the rest of the battalion at Camilla,' he said. 'It looks like Goose Green is on. Our kit will catch up with us later.'

That meant we'd be going into battle without our helmets, which was OK because Patrols always wore our trademark black woollen hats anyway, and like the rest of the battalion we had our red berets stashed in a patch pocket on our trousers to wear when we marched into Port Stanley to liberate it.

'Not another false alarm, is it, boss?' I asked.

'I don't think so, John. Not this time,' he answered.

Well, that was something. It looked like we'd be getting to grips with them at last. I straightened up and put my best foot forward. And believe me, it was my best foot because I had cracked the secret for keeping trench foot at bay.

To be honest, my method attracted a massive amount of piss-taking from the battalion at the time. I hate to be anything but modest but I don't think I'm overstating the case when I say that my feet became part of the paras' legend of Goose Green.

Why? Because I was wearing jungle boots. You've got it. Jungle boots in the middle of the freezing fucking Falklands. And do you know what? They did the trick.

They were US issue green jungle boots that I'd managed to lay my hands on when we'd been on exercise in the tropics and the rationale behind wearing them in a cold climate was quite simple. The key lay in the fact that they were lightweight green canvas that had no waterproof qualities at all and although they let the water in they let it out again. You can get all sorts of nasty foot conditions in the jungle if you allow water to gather around your foot and putrefy, so it worked well in those steamy hot conditions. Fresh water kept moving over your feet.

You get a horrible foot condition in the cold too. So why

shouldn't the same principle work? OK, it wasn't jungle water, it was fucking freezing stuff, but it kept circulating through the boot, not wallowing around the foot and that seemed to help.

The boots themselves dried out quite quickly when they were given the chance. You could almost wring the jungle jobs out and once I'd done my foot routine and settled down I was reasonably comfortable.

The issue boots, on the other hand, were reconstituted cardboard posing as leather and appeared to have been specially designed as cold-water footbaths for the rapid culturing of trench foot. Some of us believed the civil servants who'd ordered them must have been in the pay of the Soviets.

The piss-taking about my jungle boots on the voyage down to the Falklands had been fucking relentless though.

'Did the foot fairy give you those boots, Johnny?' asked one wag.

'Oi, Tarzan, lend us your boots. I've got a date with Jane,' said another.

On and on it went. A few of the lads would sing that 'Awimbaway' song when I went by; the one that goes on about 'In the jungle, the mighty jungle . . .' but they'd add a line about Johnny's boots. I didn't sing along.

Now and then I'd manage to fist one of the cheeky fuckers in the face but by and large they had their escape routes planned before they launched their jungle-boot jokes. Was I worried? Was I fuck! If they thought I was mad that was their problem. If they really believed that I'd been ordered to wear jungle boots by voices in my head then they were the ones who were off their rockers.

No. The truth is that my jungle boots were a method I'd tried and tested and worked out for myself during the long, wet days of exercises on Salisbury Plain and the Brecon Beacons.

OK, I admit I have an unusually high tolerance for the cold.

As I said, I lost my gloves and went through most of the Falklands War with bare hands, which also raised a few eyebrows. Perhaps that tolerance to the cold is a Geordie thing. Maybe I've got Inuit blood coursing through my veins. One thing's for certain: I knew the old jungle boots would work for me and they did.

No one was laughing at my jungle boots after a couple of days on Sussex Mountain. There were no jungle-boot jokes on the abortive tab to Camilla and back either. By that time even the lads who'd taken care of their feet were beginning to suffer quite badly from the onset of trench foot. A few of them were so desperate they'd taken to stabbing their morphine phials into their thighs or directly into their feet so that they could kill the pain and keep going.

Kev was one of them. His feet gave him hell and he kept jabbing them with morphine. At one point he took his boots off and managed to warm his feet up a bit, but then he found that made his feet swell up. He wasn't going to miss the fighting, so one of the lads helped him out by putting snow on his feet to shrink them down enough to get his boots back on again. He wasn't the only one who did that. Hardcore or what?

In the end, though, I won the moral high ground in the trench-foot debate, but I didn't take the piss out of the blokes who'd tried to wire me with their barbed comments and their jokes. Not once did I turn round and say, 'I told you so.' That wouldn't have been fair when they were suffering so badly. But every now and then I'd do little tap dance in front of them. They got the bloody message then!

When the attack on Goose Green finally got the go-ahead it was billed as a raid and the military definition of a raid is quite clear. When you raid a place you go in hard and fast with the element of surprise. You put the boot in and kill as many of the enemy as you can and hit specific targets like radio masts, radar kit, ammo and fuel dumps. You then have a clear exit strategy lined up and

you fuck off as quickly as you can, hopefully with as few casualties as possible.

That's what the brass wanted us to do. They wanted a raid on
Goose Green but somewhere along the line that got transmogri-
fied into a full battalion attack. Quite how and when that happened
has taken up a lot of the hindsight thinking of a number of military historians and officer academy lecturers.

Personally, I think the reason is quite simple. I reckon H
persuaded all concerned that Goose Green should be lumped by
a full-on spearhead attack to open up the land campaign against
the Argentines. After all, he was a man of huge personal drive
and charisma and it was only thanks to him that 2 Para was in
the Falklands at all. He'd abandoned a skiing holiday, flown back
to London and almost battered down the doors of the Ministry
of Defence demanding that 2 Para should be part of the
Commando Brigade. He argued that it hadn't been long since
we'd been doing full battalion training with live ammo in Kenya.
H had asked what was the point of having a spearhead battalion on a high state of readiness if you didn't use them when
a war came along? Fair one. The result was we got onto the task
force.

I'd bet anything that he used that same force of personality to
press home the battalion's case for a full-on attack on the Goose
Green settlement with its airfield and Argentine garrison. On the
other hand, as I understand it, there's no record anywhere of the
brass in Northwood sanctioning a full battalion attack, although
the word 'raid' pops up here and there in their messages.

Maybe H was making it up as he went along. I wouldn't have
put it past him. One thing was for certain: the first time we'd
tabbed towards Camilla we'd had to do a Grand Old Duke of
York and we marched right back again. This time there was no
going back. We had a concrete feeling that we were going to see
some action and we were going to see it soon.

★   ★   ★

Thud! Thud! Thud! As we began to tab down the slope towards Camilla Creek House we heard the reports of an artillery salvo to the west. Not far away either. At first we thought the Argies must have worked out that a move was on towards Goose Green and opened up on our advancing battalion column.

Word soon came down the line that it was actually our own field guns that had fired a burst and that had been requested by D Company to clear the way into Camilla and help them find the place in the dark. An interesting way of map reading and not a very accurate one, especially as the fucking shells landed a good thousand metres behind D Company, not in front of them!

I remember the night well. It couldn't have been clearer. The southern sky was bright with stars and it was freezing cold with a light wind whipping our faces with ice. By the time we joined the lads from D company, we'd been out on the camp for a long time and we were starving and frozen. The house at Camilla beckoned.

When we got there we found it full of Argentine kit. The previous occupants had obviously fucked off in a hurry but they'd kindly left a load of their rations behind.

One of the officers cautioned us that the tins of Argy food might be poisoned. I looked at him as though he needed a session with a shrink. There was I, hungry enough to eat a goose with its feathers on, and he was trying to conjure up an image of Argentine soldiers with so little to do with their time that they could carefully inject poison into tins of grub. Maybe a hand grenade wired to the ration box, but poison? Bollocks.

'Don't think so, boss,' I said, stabbing my bayonet into the lid of a tin.

If that was poison I ate a hell of a lot of it and so did the rest of the lads. It was fucking lovely stuff. Not corned beef but beautiful tender cuts of beef in an exotic South American gravy. Fantastic. I can taste it now. There were moments then when I thought of defecting to the other side because their beef was so good, but beating the Argies would be better than eating all the beef in South America.

We'd been eating garibaldi biscuits that turned to ash in your mouth and cheese paste from a tube that you could use to grout wall tiles, so we filled our boots on those Argy rations. As we were tucking into yet more of the stuff I looked out of the window and saw the rest of the battalion winding into the settlement from the west.

They'd had a hell of a march in a long snake which, in the way of these things, had taken on a life of its own, like a drunken New Year conga dance, sometimes concertinaing and bumping into each other, sometimes spreading so thin that they had to tab hard to keep up.

At one point they lost the RAF guy attached to the battalion, a squadron leader called Jock Penman, who was supposed to coordinate any air strikes. He was aged fifty-something and a heavy smoker so how he'd got that fucking far is a testimony to his bottle. In the end, though, his fitness failed and he was found with an ankle injury wandering about nearly delirious with exhaustion on the edge of the column.

When they arrived at Camilla Creek House the bosses took a look around the collection of nine or ten out-buildings and sheep sheds that made up the settlement and decided the battalion would kip indoors to get at least one dry, warm night before the battle.

Bollocks! That left us no time to let our dinners go down. We had to find a decent place to kip before the rest of the fuckers swarmed all over the buildings. It was unbelievable. Nearly four hundred soaking wet, exhausted soldiers piled into the few buildings of the settlement for the night.

Wet clothing was steaming all over the place. I remember peat fires springing up in the grates in the house. A couple of blokes slept in the airing cupboard and a company headquarters guy kipped under the stairs. We got into the lounge with most of Patrols Platoon and slept with feet to faces. Some people slept sitting up, others got on top of the wardrobes and sideboards. A few cleared shelves and kipped on them.

The whole house became a pulsating, humid compost heap of sleeping soldiers but we loved it. After six days out in the harsh, uncompromising elements of the Falklands it was wonderful. It was dry and it was warm and the only wind in the house came from the soldiers who'd commandeered it.

EIGHT

RADIO GAGA!

WHAT A FUCKING RUDE awakening! The next morning, after a dry but cramped three or four hours in the house and the outbuildings, the battalion had stirred at dawn. Most of us were in groups around the Camilla settlement cooking our breakfast and having a brew. The men who'd taken the dawn stag on sentry watch, usually doubled in case of a classic surprise attack at first light, were just trying to grab a bit of sleep. We were all waiting for orders and wondering what was next.

Then suddenly there was a melee of officers and sergeants appearing among the various companies and platoons in a right fucking flap.

'Move out! Move out! Away from these building on the double! Grab your kit and fucking get out of here!' our sergeant major Baz Greenhalgh yelled at us.

All around us, the initial confusion was quickly replaced with action as the inbuilt conditioning to obey orders instantly cut in and paras moved out to throw a defensive cordon around the settlement.

In Patrols we were already in light order and we were first out into the terrain. That was our way of life; always first into the terrain. We were ready for battle and we sprinted out to a dimple of contours on the rising ground behind the house, fanned out and went tactical with our weapons at the ready. Ready for what we didn't know as no fucker had bothered to tell us what was going on, but we were ready anyway. Were the enemy about to steal our thunder, take the initiative and attack first? Was an air strike incoming on our position? We didn't have a clue.

Then someone, I think it was Mark Sleap, said, 'It's the BBC.'

The BBC? What the fuck did he mean? Why would the BBC attack us?

'What d'you mean, the BBC?' I said.

'I'm telling you. It's the BBC. They've fucked us up.'

Sleapy said their patrol radio operator had tuned into the World Service and they'd listened to a Beeb report telling the world that fifteen hundred paras were poised to attack Goose Green.

Captain Farrar confirmed it. 'It's true. We had to clear out of the buildings. The BBC have just run a report on the World Service news saying British paras are poised for an assault on Darwin and Goose Green. Not sure but I think Camilla Creek House was mentioned too.'

I can tell you I'd have been a lot happier if there had been fifteen hundred of us instead of six hundred. But we could hardly believe what they'd done. What the hell was their game? Signalling our moves to the enemy was taking the fucking piss.

Obviously the first thing we'd had to do was to clear out of the buildings in case Camilla had been revealed as our position to the enemy and the Argies were about to blast it to smithereens with air strikes and artillery.

We had a BBC correspondent attached to 2 Para, a bloke called Robert Fox, who was not responsible for the report. He had more sense than to file his position to the enemy and call doom down on his own head. I believe that some BBC bastard in London had been given a MoD briefing on an 'information only not for publi-cation or broadcast' basis. They just went ahead and broadcast it anyway.

In the event nothing happened. There was no artillery bombard-ment. No air strike. But it pissed us off to learn so starkly and at

grave personal risk that our country's national broadcasting insti-
tution had behaved like that. The foundations of a deep mistrust
of the BBC among British soldiers were laid that morning twenty-
five years ago. It's continued right up to the present day.

Did the BBC have an inquiry into who'd been responsible for
that broadcast? Obviously not, but I'd still be interested in meeting
whoever was responsible. I'd like him to explain what he was thinking
about at the time.

The irony of it is that, according to later reports from the defeated
Argy high command on the island, they had thought the World
Service bulletins were a double bluff, a load of black propaganda
meant to put them on the wrong foot. But at the time it was a
real jolt for the battalion, particularly for the colonel who had the
overall strategy to worry about and was left wondering how much
the Argies knew about his intentions. But there was no point in
steaming and frothing at the mouth over what had happened. We
just thought, bollocks to the BBC, and got on with the job in
hand.

Eight men moved slowly under the cover of darkness onto the edge
of a low hill overlooking Camilla Creek. They'd tabbed the four
or five klicks from Creek House to get to this point above the
narrow band of brackish water where the stream joined the sea
through the creek.

Armed to teeth with LMGs and 66mm rocket launchers, they
sized up the task in front of them, looked at the bank of gorse
stretching alongside the creek, shrugged and then plunged into the
thorny, skin-ripping vegetation. That's where they set up their OPs.
Then, like kids building dens, they busied themselves connecting
their OPs by tunnels through the damp gorse dust underneath the
shrubbery.

They'd chosen a spot that should give them a view straight across
the isthmus from the creek to the west side of the settlement of
Darwin, taking in much of the terrain between and on either side.

It was as good a view as they were likely to get without being spotted themselves.

They were in two patrols. Four of them were men from Recce Platoon, led by Lance Corporal Taff Evans, a jovial Welshman. The other patrol was the forward air controller's group, led by Lieutenant Colin Connor who was escorting Captain Peter Ketley, the officer who'd taken over as the FAC from the chain-smoking Squadron Leader Penman who'd fucked up his ankle earlier on the tab across to Camilla from Sussex Mountain.

They didn't know it at the time, but over the side of the creek on the Darwin isthmus were a load of Argies set up in layers of in-depth positions. Just as well there was a bank of gorse there or Taff and the lads would have stood out like ducks in a fairground shooting gallery.

The colonel was desperate for some good intelligence on the Argentine deployments out on the isthmus, because everything he'd been told up to that point had been general and non-specific. What the two patrols observed later was to expose the SAS and SBS estimates of the Argy strengths at Goose Green as wildly out and lower than a corpse's blood pressure.

Taff was carrying his bins and a Clansman VHF radio with a spare battery. He had his rifle, and a 66 LAW; crossed fingers too, because if he was spotted his weapons wouldn't be much use at all against a maul of machine guns four hundred metres away across the creek.

Dawn broke. At first they couldn't make out much through the pall of mist hanging over the creek, but as it cleared they had a bit of a breath-sucking moment as they spotted an entire Argy company dug in on the forward slope of a low hill stretching away to a small settlement called Burntside House. Seen through Taff's bins the Argies looked close enough to clout. He'd found his machine guns and there were lots of them.

Taff watched the enemy go through their routine as half of them stood down and went to collect their breakfast scoff from a field kitchen close to the house. Taff busily scribbled notes as he watched and he spotted a couple of big fuck-off .50-cal machine guns in the emplacements. He was staring straight down the barrel of one of them which had obviously been set up to protect the Argy positions from a flanking attack across the water.

All the time the lads were counting and taking notes. They spotted another half-dozen trenches near Boca House and a platoon position on a rise in the ground between Boca and the trenches opposite. That made about seventeen trenches in all reaching west towards them from Darwin Hill. And those were the ones they could see. A lot of the gun trenches were in 'dead ground', that's military speak for hidden behind hills and undulations in the terrain.

Taff was on the radio passing all the information back to the intelligence officer waiting at Camilla Creek House. The patrols couldn't see any Argy artillery but they'd realised at once that these positions were perfectly set up for an attack with our own artillery.

That option was ruled out because a bombardment at that point would have given away the position of our guns. They were best kept hidden until they were needed during our main advance. An air strike was on the cards, however, but a sanctioned Harrier strike was abandoned because of bad weather.

The lads even watched the Argies going through their trench-foot drill, washing and drying their feet outside their slit trenches. They watched the comings and goings in the Argy lines too, with a tractor and trailer arriving to unload recoilless rifles and ammo and an eight-man patrol leaving in the direction of the neck of the isthmus. That was slightly worrying because given an hour's tabbing they could have come round behind Taff's position in the gorse.

With the air strike off, the FAC was called back to attend the colonel's O (orders) group at eleven o' clock, where he was going to lay out his plans for the attack on Goose Green. O groups are vital because it's there that all the company and platoon commanders get together with people like the FAC and the gunnery officer and are told the whole picture. If they aren't told the whole sketch then horrible events can happen, like one company firing on another, or 'blue on blue'. They sometimes happen anyway even with the benefit of an O group briefing, but they're twice as likely to happen without one.

And when the boss of a battalion calls an O group he expects his top people to be there unless they're dead, they've lost a leg or no one's bothered to tell them about it.

Part of the problem was that everyone had scattered to all the points of the compass because of the BBC and letting those that needed to know had proved impossible. It was a fuck-up and H erupted.

Just before midday, after the FAC had left the gorse to head for the O group at Camilla, Lieutenant Connor's position was compromised by the Argies. Someone in his patrol must have shaken a gorse bush or stuck his arse up a little bit too high and the Argies had noticed.

They let fly with machine guns and rifle fire and Connor's patrol had to shoot their way out into dead ground before mortar fire toasted them in the gorse. Connor threw a white phosphorous smoke grenade onto the bank in front of his men to cloak their escape and then vanished into a billowing cloud of smoke like a pantomime genie behind his fleeing patrol.

After that the Argies started taking potshots along the entire length of the gorse bank, trying to flush out any more gringos who might be spying on them. But Taff Evans and his lads weren't going anywhere. They just sat there up to their eyes in gorse and bottled it out while bullets smacked around them and flew over their heads.

Meanwhile the FAC, who'd had to tab five klicks on the double to get to the O group, arrived at the colonel's side in time for fate to give him two fingers. Why? Because just as he arrived at the colonel's command tent, three Harriers roared over the newly discovered enemy positions back at the creek.

The Harrier wing took one tilt over the isthmus but they couldn't make out a thing and the FAC who should have been there painting the target with a laser target designator had been squashing babies' heads in the rush to get to the O group. The LTD was in his webbing. At the fucking O group!

The Harriers took a second run and screaming in fury they dropped their payloads, only to obliterate a load of peat with cluster bombs while the panicking Argies fired wildly after them and lived to fight another day. The very next day, in fact.

Taff Evans took the arrival of the Harriers as a timely moment to fuck off out of that position, because the Argies were certain to be looking for the OP that had called in the air strike. They'd have just strimmed the gorse on the bank opposite them with machine gun fire and then mortared the gorse to tease out enemy spotters.

As he was about to leg it, Taff watched as one of the Harriers make a third run over the Argy lines. Not a good idea. One sortie too many. By now the Argies were wide awake. Their Oerlikon anti-aircraft guns at the Goose Green airstrip were hot to trot, they were equipped with tracking radar and they probably couldn't believe their luck when they saw a Harrier coming back to make it third time lucky for them. They nailed the tail of the aircraft but the pilot managed to eject.

Seeing all this, Taff didn't hang about. He seized the moment when the Argies were all cheering the dropping of a Harrier and hurled a WP smoke grenade for covering smoke while his gunner Dave Theale emptied a magazine into the Argentines on the other side of the creek. In the confusion they both ran for dead ground and made it to safety.

Taff was immediately summoned back. The colonel wanted to have a chat with him about his sightseeing tour and he wanted it soon.

Meanwhile, the FAC made it back to the O group just as news of the fucked-up Harrier raid was reaching H. No way was it his fault, but apparently the air was blue as the colonel sent the poor FAC back to the OP with a massive flea in his ear.

It hadn't been the colonel's best morning and that's a fucking understatement. The BBC had revealed his intentions and his likely position. The Special Forces recces that he'd been relying on and their assessment of the readiness of the enemy were turning into fairy tales. Then a Harrier had been lost in a raid that had left the enemy totally unscathed and had only served to put them on the alert. On top of that, several of his key officers had failed to make it to his O group, which had to be postponed. On the eve of a battle that's something that would put any colonel into a spin. Nothing travels faster in a battalion than news that the boss is pissed off. The word was out. H was not a happy man.

But at least Taff and the lads had done their job supremely well, as you'd expect. When you've got your back to the wall you can always rely on the Toms!

Captain Peter Ketley was a jammy fucker though, because within half an hour of leaving Camilla Creek House with the colonel's blistering still hurting his ears he became the hero of the hour when he captured the battalion's first prisoners of war and got us our one and only vehicle into the bargain.

The captain was trudging forlornly down the track on his way back to join the patrols at the creek who in any case were just butting out of their position after the shoot-outs. With him was the colonel's driver, a lance corporal called Soapy Sloane, and a couple of Royal Navy signallers who'd been attached to the unit in the vain hope that at some stage they'd actually be able to call in some gunfire from HMS *Arrow*.

As they turned a corner on the track, they spotted the glinting from a windscreen coming towards them. It was a light blue Land Rover!

They dropped to their knees and took cover, weapons aimed, and then they waited until they could see inside the 4x4 properly. No point in shooting it up and then finding it was filled with a family of fleeing Kelpers. It stopped and someone got out of the passenger side just in time for a beam of sunlight to light up an Argy helmet.

The captain didn't need a formal invitation. He opened up with his SLR and the others gave it some with their SMGs while Argies abandoned the Land Rover like rats from a torch.

One of the Argies, a sergeant, returned fire as the FAC's team fired and moved up to the Land Rover. This same sergeant, who was evidently a man with a bit about him, then got inside the vehicle again and tried to get on the radio, but a couple of shots through the windscreen persuaded him that was not a good idea.

They gave in after that and the FAC found that as well as the sergeant he had captured two soldiers and there was an officer too. He'd been driving and he was none other than Lieutenant Morales, the commander of the Argentine recce platoon. Bingo! A full house for the FAC!

From the timings it's possible that Morales and his team had decided to go out and look for Taff Evans's and Connor's patrols as they moved away from their compromised OPs in the gorse overlooking the creek. The Land Rover, which the Argies had nicked off a Kelper farmer, may have been intended to act as a disguise but it was definitely the lazy option and it led to them being netted like fish in double-quick time. They may as well have sent a calling card. And perhaps they had, because the talk in the battalion was that, apart from that feisty sergeant, the other Argies seemed pretty much relieved to be captured. Maybe they were. We'll probably never know.

The prisoners were brought back to Camilla by a patrol from A Company, then given a grilling by the intelligence officer with the help of a Spanish-speaking Bootneck officer called Captain Rod Bell, who'd been attached to the battalion as interpreter.

H waited until the interrogation was complete before reconvening his O group for three that afternoon. It had been a busy and largely frustrating day for the colonel.

A Tom's view of events is usually quite different to an officer's. The boss would have been focusing on the intelligence harvested by Taff and Connor from the creek-side OP's. The Toms, on the other hand, were enjoying the chance to take the piss out of Connor's patrol for being spotted and they were big-timing Taff for having left the OP on his own terms, in his own time.

The boss would no doubt have been well pleased that the FAC had gone and captured himself an Argy recce patrol complete with an officer. His Toms, on the other hand, were chuffed that at last we had some transport to lug ammo around the vastness of the camp. And the arrival of a Land Rover led to renewed complaints about the wankers who'd said that vehicles couldn't move over the terrain on the Falklands. Especially as our own vehicles were still on board some fucking ship or other bobbing around on the South Atlantic.

And one thing was absolutely certain: unless they were completely loco, the fact that their Land Rover hadn't come home could only mean one thing to the Argies. They were going to be attacked. And it was going to be soon.

The job of every military commander is to formulate a plan of action and then try to execute it. The fact of the matter is that your enemy will try to thwart your action and most times the plan will change after the first shots are exchanged. Some you win, some you lose.

Whether it's a colonel mobilising a whole battalion into action on a complicated series of enemy positions or a lance corporal directing his fire team to take a single machine-gun emplacement, he has to come up with a plan, tell the lads what he wants to do and then get on with it. Lives depend on the plan. That is the stark fact. A lot of lives depended on the plan H came up with, so he spent every waking hour and most of the ones he should have been kipping through trying to get it right.

To understand the events that unfolded in the Battle of Goose

Green you have to understand how H's plan for 2 Para was supposed to work.

A battle plan has to take into account a lot of factors and they include the ground the battle is to be fought on, the forces you have available to prosecute your attack and the timing of your attacks as they unfold.

On the other side of the coin the commander must of course factor in the way the enemy have deployed themselves on the ground, and underpinning this is intelligence. You have to spy on your enemy to know where his forces are laid up, calculate the intelligence gained, make a plan and then execute the plan in the most effective way. It's a bloodstained game of chess.

All of these factors were going to be crucial the next day when H sent us into action in the spearhead attack of the Falklands ground war. But there are other factors in a battle and they include the fitness, fighting ability and will to win of the rival forces in the clash. These are elements that can tip the scales in a conflict and they are factors that can be planned for as well. To his credit H had done just that; he planned for the moment and he'd worked for a long time to tune up 2 Para into a hard-as-nails fighting machine.

I reckon that on the day before the battle the general morale and fighting fitness of the Toms under his command was the least of H's concerns. Of course he'd wonder how the lads were going to perform, but he'd seen us under pressure and under fire in Northern Ireland and it was probably the other factors in the equation that he would have been fretting over.

As I've already pointed out, the colonel had managed to translate the rules of engagement for the action at Goose Green from 'raid' into 'capture', and he was going to take the settlement lock, stock and smoking barrels from the Argies.

It wasn't going to be the original raid plan any more, with A and B Companies moving up swiftly to put the boot in while D Company hung back in support. H now planned a comprehensive smashing of at least two lines of entrenched Argentine positions before moving on to the settlement of Goose Green itself.

Everything I've heard since suggests that H was bang on, not only in putting forward Goose Green as a priority target because of the threat the garrison there posed to our rearguard, but in dismissing a raid as a potential propaganda blunder in itself.

If we'd run in, hit the Argies, then bugged out again, it wouldn't have taken the sly foxes in the junta long to portray it as a full-on assault by the Brits which their courageous forces on the Malvinas had roundly repelled.

No, H was right. If we were going to attack Goose Green at all, then it would be senseless not to destroy the Argy forces there. A comprehensive victory would leave Argentina with nothing to argue over.

H must have had his plans for a full-on battle OK'd that day because Support Company, who'd been left behind on Sussex to defend the high ground above the beachhead, were quickly relieved by a company of Booties and then tabbed up to join us.

With the objective given the thumbs up by the brass, H needed to know more about the enemy and that was a big problem for him in the hours before the battle.

The SAS and the SBS had been assigned deep penetration tasks of the Argy positions on the island, including of course the garrison at Goose Green, and they'd raided it on 21 May, the day of the landings at San Carlos, in a probing operation.

It wasn't their finest hour. Special Forces did some great work on the Falklands but frankly I've used shampoos that have penetrated deeper than they did at Goose Green. They banged off a few rounds from a klick away, got a few half-hard salvoes fired back at them and from that judged that Goose Green was defended by a company and that the troops at the settlement had no stomach for a fight. They were wrong on both counts.

More frustrating was the veto on patrolling because SF were supposed to be out in the sticks doing their CTR, or close target reconnaissance. The argument was that 2 Para might step on SF's toes or that we might instigate a blue on blue by shooting at each other in the mist. I know that H would have far preferred to use his own eyes and ears from Patrols and Recce Platoons but that was actively discouraged. At the same time, it has since become evident that what intelligence SF were coming up with wasn't being fed back to the battalion.

However, on the eve of battle we did know the Argentine 12th Regiment was holed up on the isthmus but we could have learnt a lot more if we'd been allowed to go and look for ourselves. Taff Evans's and Lieutenant Connor's forays into the gorse bushes helped rebalance things but a lot, lot more could have been done.

After Goose Green I vowed that if I ever got into Special Forces I would not conduct a recce on an enemy position from three klicks away. I did get into Special Forces and I always kept my self-made vow. No one was ever going to walk into a shit storm on my account just because I hadn't bothered to go and have a proper look at what the enemy was up to.

As things unfolded, H's knowledge of the enemy on the eve of battle went along the lines that there were a few Argies in Goose Green but not too many. Helicopters were roosting among civilian homes. The enemy were known to use the schoolhouse on the edge of the settlement as a shelter, perhaps a company headquarters; there were minefields along the beach and headlands but the roads and tracks were definitely not mined because the Argies were using them on a daily basis.

H also had Taff's sightings and maps of the trenches stretching across the width of the isthmus, from Burntside House to Darwin. He could reckon on three lines of defence across the isthmus, with another between Darwin and Goose Green itself on a line taking in the school and the airstrip. That would mean about three rifle companies with their supporting artillery dug in and waiting.

No one knew what was on top of Darwin Hill, the feature that commanded all the views around the isthmus, but we assumed there would be Argies up there and we'd have to fight them off it.

The ground they were holding was pretty much a defender's dream. The isthmus itself, at just under two kilometres wide, formed a natural bottleneck for attacking troops and the contours gave the Argies the initiative. Occupying the commanding set of hills, all they had to do was observe to their front and watch the enemy advancing up lovely rising slopes straight into their arcs of fire.

There was virtually no decent cover except for the lines of rank gorse and some dead ground here and there. There were a few dips and gullies etched in the terrain to hide your arse in as well, but once you opted to get into them you were going to have a hell of a job getting out of them, with all approaches covered by horrible overlapping, interlocking arcs of machine-gun fire and mortars.

H had already been told that an outflanking manoeuvre using the sea or helicopters wasn't on, so his options boiled down to an advance to contact onto a well-dug-in enemy who were waiting for us. It had the potential to turn into a turkey shoot on a pool table and we'd be the turkeys.

That's where timing came into the equation. If we were going to head straight through the enemy, timing was going to be of the essence because we didn't really want to be advancing to contact across those wide open spaces in broad daylight. If we were going to cross that ground we wanted to do it in the dark. Night would be our only friend in that terrain.

It's been estimated that the battalion had to cover fourteen kilo- metres to bring them up to the town sign at the edge of Goose Green. The first five or six klicks would bring them to the bridge at the head of Camilla Creek and across to Burntside House, where intelligence reports said the Argentines were waiting in company strength. That marked the point where the battalion would right wheel to attack down the neck of the isthmus. From there we'd lay a new start line and it would be another seven or eight kilo- metres to Goose Green through those well-defended positions. If we were going to do that under the cover of darkness we had from dusk at 4. 30 p.m. on the 27th until dawn at 6. 30 a.m. on the following morning. That's fourteen hours to march fourteen kilometres. More than enough time. Unless some bastard's shooting at you, that is!

The colonel opted for a really complicated sod of a plan involving six phases in a rolling operation that would start silently, without the usual softening-up bombardment. It would go loud when and where we had a contact with the enemy. It was timed to start in darkness and end just as light was beginning to dawn over the battlefield, giving us the cloak of night to make up for the lack of cover.

A rolling battalion action sees one company attacking, taking and securing a position, then a second company moving through its lines to go forward on to the next objective. While the second company is attacking, the first company regroups itself, takes stock, tends the wounded, then prepares to move on again if required. And so on. It's a relay race with a piece of hell passed on as the baton.

The regrouping phase is vital. Why not just charge on with the second company and overwhelm the enemy while your blood's up? Well, throughout the history of warfare fortune has favoured the brave who are also well organised and disciplined. The Romans were often faced with overwhelming numbers of extremely ferocious and courageous enemies from Gaul to the forests of the Rhine and in the rolling hills of Britain. But the Legions always took the time to re-form and regroup in the midst of battle, maintaining a ruthless discipline that conquered the world.

That's why we don't go whirling around like Viking beserkers. We have a head count, re-ammo, account for and process the dead and wounded, then await orders for the next move. It's fucking vital.

H's six-phase operation began with all four companies moving out of Camilla Creek House and advancing to a position just behind the start line. The start line was to be an RV point on the other side of a white-painted wooden bridge across the Ceritos Arroyo, the stream that emptied into the Camilla Creek itself.

The start line is just what it says it is, the place where the assaulting rifle company forms up before battle commences. It could be a bus shelter in Belfast or, in our case, a piece of flat peat near a wooden bridge over a stream. It's basically a grid reference on a map that makes tactical sense.

The start line for B Company was the responsibility of my company, C Company, and it was the job of the lads in Patrols and Recce to go forward and CTR the enemy positions, report their exact whereabouts, count bodies, weapons, assets and morale. Once that information had been passed back to the head shed, especially the section commanders, we would occupy the start line and wait for the rifle companies to arrive.

The other companies would follow over the bridge in strict order: Support Company, A Company Tac 1, B Company, Battalion Main HQ and then D Company.

After forming up on the start line, A Company would move off at 2 a.m. and attack Burntside House where the Argies were supposed to be nesting up, while B Company would attack any positions at Low Pass overlooking Camilla Creek.

At 3 a.m. A Company would roll through in phase 3 and attack Argy positions thought to be at Coronation Point, while D Company would move through B Company at Low Point and take on an another Argentine platoon to the south-west. By this time our artillery and the big 4.5-inch guns on HMS *Arrow* should be in play pounding the Argentines ahead of the rifle companies.

An hour later phase 4 would see B Company advance through D Company to attack the Boca House position, although this was complicated by an idea H had that it might be necessary for B Company to halt and let D Company through to finish that assault.

Phase 5 at around 5 a.m. and A Company would hopefully be moving forward to the outskirts of Darwin, C Company moving up as a small rifle company to clear the airfield along with D Company advancing behind us, while B Company remained in reserve.

Dawn at 6.30 a.m. would see the daylight that we would need

to identify civilians and keep their casualties to a minimum as we stormed into Goose Green, where we'd been told there weren't too many Argies anyway.

C Company were ready to lead the way for the rest of the battalion at the appointed hour, but the officers were still gassing their way through the plan at four thirty.

Later on, one of the big criticisms of H's plan was going to be that he hadn't allowed enough time for the battalion to move up closer to the start lines. In fact, the battle was destined to rage on for hours in broad daylight and critics reckon H would have been better off starting earlier and tabbing closer to the start line in daylight. He'd delayed the O group because of the fuck-up earlier when people hadn't turned out for it and then he'd decided to wait for the end of the interrogation of the Argy prisoners taken with the Land Rover. Better if he'd just set off towards the start line, then let whatever intelligence was going to come from those prisoners catch up with him, say the armchair commandos with hindsight.

Well, I think that this time they're right, but then they were probably sitting on their arses in a garden chair slurping on a glass of Pimm's at the tennis club while H was making life-or-death decisions in the field, the outcome of which he knew full well carried the pride of the entire British nation. At least he was out there doing it.

As they were rolling up the map after he'd given his orders, H told his officers, 'All the evidence suggests that if the enemy is hit hard he will crumble.'

Roll them up and hit them hard. That was H's plan.

I'd like to be able to tell you that we sat in the shelter of a low ridge of gorse quietly talking about the folks back home while we honed the edges of our bayonets ready for the hand-to-hand combat to come.

Well, we didn't sharpen our bayonets. We would have but you're not allowed to give bayonets an edge under the Geneva Convention. Apparently, a wicked needlepoint that will pierce through all an enemy's vital organs is considered fair while a sharpened edge to the same blade allowing a bit of evisceration isn't. I always thought that if you're unfortunate enough to find yourself at the business end of a bayonet then the Geneva Convention's too late to fucking help you anyway.

The fact is that we wouldn't have had any bayonets with us at all if H had had his way because he wanted them left behind on the boat. Sailing south on the *Norland*, he'd arrived at the conclusion that the coming battles on the Falklands would be won by sheer firepower. Hand-to-hand fighting wouldn't come into it, so bayonets would just be pieces of useless metal that would add to the already formidable load we'd be carrying.

D Company's OC, Major Phil Neame, then took some time persuading the boss that it was better to take the bayonets with us just in case. He knew that the battalion Toms would feel naked without their bayonets; he knew it would help them sleep better at night knowing they had a foot of steel to clamp on to the end of their weapons. It's an infantry thing. In the end H agreed they should be taken – when Neame pointed out that the lads' bayonets were also very useful as tin openers out in the field!

C Company knew that we'd be first off the blocks in our patrols and we'd already been briefed on what our different tasks were going to be. We were just waiting for night to fall before we moved off.

We cleaned our weapons, sorted out our webbing and stuffed them with ammo and two days' worth of fighting rations. More fucking toothpaste cheese and garibaldi biscuits. Shite! Then we checked everything; guns, ammo, rations, maps, radio. We checked it all, then checked it all again. Check and recheck. That's how you stay alive.

Time for a brew and a few people in the company were scribbling last letters to their loved ones with stubs of pencils. No one in my patrol was letter-writing though. Too wet. I'd written a few romantics to my missus on board *Norland* on the way down, but that was only when I was bored. I've never been much of a letter writer.

Then Kev said, 'Hey, lads, Pete's written a letter to his parents in case he doesn't come back.'

'Oh right,' I said.

'Yeah,' said Kev. 'He's told me where he's stashed it on the *Norland*. I've got to retrieve it and give it to his mum and dad if he doesn't make it back.'

Pete Myers was absolutely fucking furious. I would have been too, but I wasn't the one being baited so I sat back and watched.

'You're an arsehole, Kev! That's private. I thought we were mates.'

Kev laughed, the cruel laugh of a fully fledged Tom taking the piss. 'Well, if you do make it back, Pete, you'd better move fast because I bet you that I'll get to your fucking letter before you do. And when I do I'm going to copy it and show all the lads just what a fucking soppy crow you are.'

'That's it, you bastard!' Pete snarled. 'I'm not gonna die now. You're not getting your fucking mitts on my letter.'

And he meant it.

Scouse McVeay, A Company's mortar-fire controller, had jumped through a window when we all shell-burst out of the house at Camilla and he'd dug himself into a shell scrape with Captain Chris Dent of HQ Company.

As they lay there together, watching and waiting for the attack that never came, they chatted away. Scouse came from a classic family of Liverpool fighters. His brother was with him in 2 Para, making them one of the fourteen pairs of actual brothers in arms in the battalion, but his brother had a twin who'd arrived on the Falklands weeks earlier with D Squadron of the SAS.

Chris Dent was a fantastic bloke. He was telling Scouse about his family. I think he had a young baby boy and he was desperate to get home and see his son again; he was hoping to get a bit of

(*Above*) The School House. This is D-Company's fire-support angle on the assault of the Argy positions.

(*Right*) Don't look up! Rounds whistle overhead as a D-Company Tom takes cover near the School House.

(*Above and opposite page*) The surrender at Boca House on the fifty-foot contour.
Note the Argy bunker top left. In the centre an Argy is getting medical help.
We weren't sure the guy with the head wound would make it home.

(*Above*) Checking through Argy weapons in the first snow of the year. That's me, third left, in the bobble hat. In the background is the airfield and that large tin hut is where the Argy surrender was taken.

(*Below*) After Goose Green. The Union flag we liberated from Goose Green flies over our makeshift bunker.

leave when it was all over. As they chatted, Scouse shared his rations with the captain.

He was a great bloke but a typical officer – they're never organised – and he had no fucking scoff with him at all, so Scouse split his own in half and shared it with him. When they'd finished eating Scouse had just one packet of porridge left. That was it.

'We'll share that when the fighting's over, boss,' Scouse told him. 'I'll make it and then I'll come and find you and we'll share my porridge.'

'Thanks, mate,' said Dent. 'I'm going to get through this and so will you.'

That was my plan too. Just like Scouse and Captain Dent, I was going to get through it.

As we lay out in the open waiting for the Argy air strike that never came, I spotted Dave Woods who was a good captain and H's best mate; he threw his hand up to me and I acknowledged him. We liked Woods because he did illegal HALO jumps with us. He was such an adventurous fucker that he came along with us even though he didn't have the orders allowing him to do it. Because of that he pulled a lot of strings to make sure we got lots of flying time and got lots of jumps in. Perfect. He was a sound Rupert.

Normally I don't like officers much and all the dithering that was going on at the O group was getting on my tits. Patrols Platoon hadn't been utilised at all and relying on the SAS for information had provided us with a load of bollocks that put us all at a disadvantage.

Pulling out of Camilla Creek House should have been a positive, decisive experience but it wasn't; there was a sense of bluff and cuff, a lack of confidence in the decision makers, and just to prove it here we were again. C Company were about to lead-scout a battalion snake into the fucking void, like so many camouflaged mushrooms kept in the dark and fed on shit!

The colonel may have made his plans. But I had my own plan. I was planning to stay alive and I told the guys about it before we pulled out.

As we huddled together under a turf embankment with a crooked fence running along its top, my breath turning to steam in the freezing dusk air, I said, 'Right, lads. It's like this. We're in charge of our own destiny. We're mates so we stick together and we look after each other; we do our jobs and we don't volunteer for fuck all. We're going to get through this shit together. OK?'

'OK.'

Four voices answered as one.

NINE

WILD HORSES!

MY OWN BREATH SOUNDED like a storm in my ears. Surely they could hear it? They were only a dozen metres away. That's no distance at all. Fuck! You know that you're really scared when you think your own breathing is going to betray you.

I lay there trying to keep my breath shallow. I was listening intently and carefully scanning the scene around me. My senses felt like they were trying to crawl out of my skin as surges of adrenalin competed with the absolute need to remain calm and still.

But the adrenalin kept besieging me. My heart pounded and my brain was begging me to do something. Anything. I had to push those feelings away because the slightest sound, the least movement I made, could lead to catastrophe for the patrol. In the same way, sound or movement detected from the area in front of me could just as easily signal a violent explosive burst of action from the lads and me.

Every movement I made was carefully measured and weighed before I made it. I was soaked to the skin, and my knees and thighs were bruised from the rocks I'd crawled over. My hands were numb with cold, and the muscles on my neck and shoulders were clenched like a vice from the effort of crawling across the ground for fifty metres. But the discomfort and pain were nothing to the grief I'd feel if I were bubbled by the enemy. I had to concentrate!

One trench directly in front of me. No enemy visible. One

heavy machine gun in place. Couldn't miss that. I was staring straight down the barrel of the fucker. Still, I carefully made mental notes of it all.

Another trench twenty metres to the left. Five metres deeper than the first. Two enemy seen, talking and alert . . . Oh fuck, that stink! Unbearable!

I'd stuck my elbow into a piece of enemy excrement, a lump of Argy shit, as I'd crawled up to their position. The dirty bastards had not been digging latrines, they'd just been walking out of their slit trenches and shitting in front of their own positions. Bizarrely, there was pink toilet roll everywhere. We'd smelt their positions before we'd seen them.

But I was more concerned with that big fuck-off machine gun pointing more or less straight up my nose, although surprisingly no one seemed to be manning the gun. What was going on in that trench? If it was empty that would be great for B Company's attack. They couldn't be that suicidal though; no one would leave a forward trench empty with a fucking machine gun ready to be faced onto your own defences.

Better take a closer look. I lifted my arm, put my thumb down, then pointed in the direction of the closest trench, signing the enemy presence to the patrol fanned out behind me. Kev Mortimer was at the rear of the patrol and he'd watch me like a nighthawk. He was our gunner and he'd have to give me covering fire if it all turned to rat shit.

Behind me, in a rough V-shape with me at the apex, the lads were mapping out the enemy lines too and they would be mentally noting everything they saw. We'd exchange those notes later and put them together on a rough sketch to go back down the line to the boss.

Better get on with it. I slid my weapon into the crock of my arms. Softly. I inched forward on my elbows, pushing slowly, very slowly, with my feet. That's it, careful, steady. Not a murmur. Good. I was another half a metre closer.

I had a quick listening stop and let the sounds of my movement die away in my head. Then I listened to the sounds around me. Nothing. Well, not exactly nothing. Those Argies in the trench to my left were still chatting away in a low murmur.

What were they talking about? Girlfriends? Mothers? The state of their feet? The price of penguin meat? Who knows? All I knew is that their voices were quiet and relaxed, conversational. There was no edge of question or alarm; no hint that they'd heard anything at all. I didn't need Spanish to work that out. The tone of their voices told me we hadn't been rumbled.

OK. One more push. Same again. Ignore the biting cold. Ignore the stink of shit all around you. Weapon first. Elbows next. Push with the feet. Gently. Nice one.

If I'd reached out I'd have been a metre short of touching the ice-cold barrel of that heavy machine gun and if there were any Argies in that trench I'd got close enough to check their fillings. I paused and listened again. The same low murmur from the trench to my left. The mist was moving in fast. Thank fuck for that! Nothing else. All quiet.

Cloaked by the mist I lifted myself onto one knee, rifle at the ready, and peered head through the gloom down into the trench. Three of the fuckers.

The smell of their rations lingering from their last meal mingled with the stench of gun oil. They were sleeping like babes, tucked up nicely in their sleeping bags at the bottom of the fire trench, breathing in the metallic odour of guns and ammo. They were counting Falklands sheep in their sleep and I could have killed all three of them before they could say their Hail Marys.

What the fuck did they think they were doing? I should have been relieved that they were out of it and couldn't raise the alarm, but for some reason the soldier in me objected to their sloppy unmilitary routine. First the open latrines. Now this. They were a fucking disgrace.

Then I realised something. I could hear their breathing! Christ!

If I could hear them breathing then they would have been able to hear me too. If they'd been awake. Basically, they'd left the machine gun staring out into the darkness to do the stag on guard duty for them. At least the gun didn't feel the cold but it wouldn't start raising any alarms. With a bit of luck it would fucking jam if they tried to fire it; the ammo link was welded to the feed tray with rust and green oxidised scum.

I edged back away from that trench in reverse, with bulldog eyes staring hard to see until I was in dead ground. Then I signalled the patrol to pull back. It sounds simple but pulling back after sneaking close to enemy lines is an exercise in patience that would test a saint.

Everything has to be done in slow motion. Every moment has to be thought through. There's a voice screaming inside you saying, 'Come on! Get a move on! Just get out of here!' It's telling you it'll definitely be all right if you just get up and run like fuck. No one will notice. Just do it.

But you must never listen to that voice because it will ultimately get you killed. You have to move slowly and very deliberately if you want to live. We knew that. We'd trained for it.

As I crawled backwards I kept rubbing my elbow against wet babies' heads trying to get the Argy shit off my para smock. Eventually we were far enough away from their trenches to get off the ground and move low and fast, back towards the start line.

'Fucking hell, Johnny,' said Jonesy, when we stopped and regrouped, 'have you just crapped yourself?'

'You could say that,' I answered.

Earlier on, when we'd tabbed out of Camilla at last light to go on that recce, all we'd had was a set of coordinates chinagraphed on a map. They marked the sector of the Argy positions that B Company had been tasked to attack later on. We knew that the Argies were dug in around those grid references somewhere but what we didn't know is exactly how they'd deployed themselves.

It was our job in Patrols to go and look, and our orders were clear and simple: 'Find out exactly where the enemy are laid up; secure the start line!'

It was a CTR. Other five-man groups from Patrols were doing much the same job on other segments of the battlefront. And Recce Platoon were doing the same task for A Company over at Burntside House, which was to be their first target when it all kicked off. In fact, Burntside was to be the first blow of 2 Para's attack.

Once we'd had a good eyeball of the enemy we'd fall back, exchange notes, then draw a simple map of what we'd discovered, showing trenches, machine guns, estimated numbers and the general morale of the enemy.

The smell of those open latrines, for instance, told us that they had become slovenly and lazy. It told us that they didn't have a good sanitary routine. It told us that they'd been worn down by the wind and weather and couldn't be bothered to spend the time it takes to dig shit pits in the freezing cold. If they were similarly sloppy about their sentry duty and general alertness, then that was good for B Company. We'd learnt that much through our noses before we'd even seen them.

When we'd got closer and I'd found that unmanned machine gun in a trench, that was another symptom of a unit that was exhausted and couldn't give a fuck. Jonesy, my lead scout, had seen an unmanned machine gun in another trench too. Through his bins he'd looked at some of the trenches in depth and spotted Argies slumped over their machine guns asleep. That was all to the good for B Company.

As for the trenches, get the classic image of the First World War trench out of your head. In that war they dug huge earthworks with deep, wide trenches stretching for miles, complete with underground bunkhouses and command centres.

What we were coming up against is what are known as bunkers or fire trenches. They're usually about ten feet long and maybe three or four feet wide and they can accommodate three or four men with two machine guns. That's a helluva lot of firepower.

The longer you're there the more elaborate they become, and good soldiers will make sure they have a solid bank in front for protection and something above to keep rain, stray rounds and mortar shrapnel out. Usually that would be wiggly tin – that's corrugated iron to you – with earth piled on top. In the Falklands we also found a lot of the Argy trenches had wooden truck pallets for roofs with clods of peat banked up on top of them.

The secret of the fire-trench system is where you dig them. They should be positioned so that the arcs of fire from each trench overlap one another. That way there is no dead ground lying fallow from harvesting by rifle or machine gun; nowhere an enemy can seek refuge from withering fire. The arcs of fire are layered so that everything in front of the trenches is in a killing ground.

Either side of them a defender will usually lay minefields or take advantage of the terrain by using a river, small cliffs or the sea as cut-off points. A well-laid system of fire trenches can be lethal, but personally I'd rather be attacking a trench than defending one. Mobility is everything in war.

After our foray, we huddled together under the cover of some gorse back on the start line and worked out the enemy positions as precisely as we could in the light of a red torch beam. We'd done OK, but I wasn't entirely happy with our CTR. Not yet.

'I think we need to have a look at what's going on a bit further over to the east there,' I said nodding in the general direction. 'I've got a feeling there may be more of them over that way.'

I don't know why I had that feeling, but years of experience told me that there was no clear cut-off for their arcs of fire and that made the possibility of more fire trenches on the right-hand side of their positions a good bet.

'Me too,' said Jonesy. 'Best check it out.'

'All agreed?'

I was in charge, my word stood, but in a patrol like ours you lead by consent and I had to know what the other blokes were thinking. We were in it together.

Nods and grunts confirmed they all agreed that we needed to eyeball the ground further to our left just to see what we could see. There was no way we'd let our mates from B Company run into a lead storm that they hadn't been warned about. That wasn't our style. They were depending on us.

No clumsy bergens on our backs, just our webbing and our weapons; black bobble hats meant we could hear everything clearly without the muffling effect you get when your head's got a helmet screwed onto it.

'Right,' I said. 'Let's go take a look then.'

Jonesy led off with me behind, followed by Pete Myers, and Kev brought up the rear with the light machine gun. We were ready for anything.

What we weren't ready for was a herd of wild horses!

I think it was Pete who spotted them first in the middle distance swirling around each other like spirits in the mist. It must have taken him a second to work out what he was looking at but he still couldn't believe it.

'What's that over there?!' he growled.

'Get down!' I ordered.

We all hit the ground flat. I was still trying to make out what the fuck it was. We suspected the Argy lines were about seventy metres away and we were speaking in strangled half-whispers.

One thing was for sure: whatever it was out there they weren't spirits. These things were neighing and whinnying to each other, calling out as they rumbled on towards us.

'They're fucking horses,' said Jonesy.

Suddenly I could hear them. Thundering. That's the word you

hear used to describe a herd of galloping horses. And they were, they were fucking thundering towards us, and I can tell you it was as scary as hell.

What was going on? Had those fucking Argentine gaucho cowboys spotted us out there in front of their lines and decided to stampede a herd of wild mustangs onto us? Were they going to flush us out with those crazy horses, then waste us with machine guns?

We'd seen plenty of ponies on the Beacons but no one had ever tried to steamroller us with a herd of them! And these weren't small ponies, they were big bastards. Real mustangs.

'Fuck it. Let's drop the bastards!' I throttled my voice back to keep it low and to hide a twinge of panic as the horses loomed large, taking up the whole of the set.

'No, don't!'

It was Jonesy. What the fuck did he know about horses that I didn't? Had he been a hussar before he joined the airborne? I didn't think so.

'Just lie still and flat! They'll run over you! Horses hate stepping on living things!'

'You fucking sure?' I asked not convinced.

'Yeah. Positive!'

'Right! Do it, lads!'

With that, the herd was upon us. I'd never have believed it if I hadn't experienced it. I looked up at them for a moment before pressing my nose to the ground and squeezing my eyes shut. Heads and manes tossing, they snorted and called to each other as they charged on. Something must have spooked them as they galloped relentlessly on through the tussocks of grass.

A lot of them had patches of white on their coats which sprang out of the night like moving plasma. I felt the ground shaking and drumming all around me. Horses were literally pounding the ground in every direction, filling our senses. I could smell the dusty, stale ammonia and grass scent of the horses' coats and I could even feel the heat given off their bodies as they ran between us, round us and over us, but never on us.

Jesus! I opened one eye and looked up. A mustang leapt over me and I could see the blur of its shape above and the outline of its legs too for a split second. Then another. One of its big hooves slapping into the peat inches away from my head.

Then shots! One, two, three! The Argies had obviously stampeded the horses to pinpoint our position. We were done for. The Argies were going to mallet us. The fuckers were going to stomp us with machine guns and mortars and we were just laid out there in the middle of nowhere with only horseshit to take cover behind.

I braced myself. Another shot! Small arms. Maybe 9mm. It was definitely the Argies but there was nothing incoming. What was going on?

Silence. I got up onto one knee, my rifle aimed towards the Argy trenches, and I watched the pounding bunch of horses as they vanished into the darkness, the flashes of luminous white marking their course. Sixty, seventy perhaps, a hundred of them. They were pouring across the sloping plain in front of the Argentine positions.

A couple more shots. I couldn't make out any muzzle flashes but it was OK. The Argies were firing to scare the horses off, trying to turn them away from the trenches before one of them dropped hooves through the top of a trench position and onto one of their sleeping mates.

The sound of the horses faded away and there were no more shots. A few relieved shouts between the trenches and some nervous laughter from the Argies.

No doubt the sudden appearance of a herd of horses coming at them out of the dark had spooked them too. Panic over, they returned to the routine of eating and keeping warm while they waited for an enemy who was already a lot closer than they realised.

'Everyone all right?'

A quick head check confirmed that no one in the patrol had been hoof-minced.

'Christ, Steve. How did you know they wouldn't stamp the fuck out of us?' I said. 'Some Druid trick from the Valleys? I was sure I was going to hear about some piece of ancient Celtic folklore on horse handling.

'Nah,' he answered, 'Grand National. You know when those jockeys come off at Beechers Brook?'

'Yeah.'

'Well, they just roll into a ball and stay still as fuck, then the horses do anything they can not to put a hoof on 'em. I saw it on the telly.'

'Really?' I said. 'Fucking interesting, that.'

What I had to decide now was whether the Argies would be on a heightened state of alert just in case the horses had been spooked and stampeded by gringos, or whether they'd been taken by surprise but were quite relaxed about it.

I thought it was the second option. That was based on a gut feeling I had about the tone of their voices when they'd shouted between trenches after they'd fired the shots to scare the horses away. I just felt that these stampedes had happened before and they were more or less used to them. If that was the case we would be fine; if not, we could be in for a bit of a bad patch.

So there we were. We'd just had a herd of horses run over us in the dark about seventy metres from enemy positions and by some miracle none of the patrol had been injured and the Argies hadn't bubbled us. My heart was pounding, I'd just produced enough adrenalin to fuel a rocket and my second in command was telling me the reason we'd lived through it was all down to the Grand National.

And I still had to decide whether to sneak up to the Argy lines for another butcher's.

I put the dilemma to the patrol and said, 'My feeling is they would have called out the guard and mowed the grass out here with machine guns if they even suspected Brits had spooked those horses.'

'Yeah,' said Steve, 'I reckon you're right. It's happened before.'

'OK, lads, let's get on with it!'

Like or not we were going to drag ourselves up to the Argy lines again and have another sniff around their fire line.

While our hearts were in our throats watching a hundred tons of mustang bearing down on us, things weren't going entirely to plan with the rest of the battalion as they moved up towards their start lines either.

One officer thought the three field guns at Camilla Creek House were about to be attacked by an enemy section that turned out to be a flock of geese. Fair enough.

But the big problem was the clock; the fucking thing was ticking and H's timings for the battle were evaporating faster than a bottle of port in the officers' mess.

Recce Platoon, whose job it was to usher A Company into position, were having a really bad time of it, tabbing back and forth against impossible time schedules, and their legs were completely shagged out.

The problem was that the battalion RV was at a white-painted bridge across the Ceritos Arroyo, which was the second stream to flow into the northern end of Camilla Creek. The engineers had already checked the bridge for booby traps and mines, before a C Company patrol took charge of it and clocked the different companies over it on their way to their various start lines.

That wasn't so bad for those of us sheepdogging B Company to their start line because the Argy positions were only about six hundred metres from the RV at the white bridge. Pretty straightforward really and it gave us lots of time for our recce.

But the A Company start lines were a really complicated dogleg around two thousand metres of rough ground. They would have to tab between Burntside Pond and the enemy positions, which would take them to a fence line that had been chosen to mark their start line for a 2 a.m. attack. That start line was about four or five hundred metres from Burntside House where an Argy section was dug in, so all in all A Company's timings were tight as fuck.

But finding and marking the A Company start line took an age and it was a minor miracle that they were only half an hour late getting onto it. The timings were not going to get any better though.

Potentially worse than that was the fact that a patrol which should have been keeping observations on the white bridge had been sent off with poor orders and ended up watching the bridge across Camilla Creek Arroyo instead. That mistake left the real battalion RV unoccupied for hours but eventually the mistake was recognised and the right bridge was double-checked.

Confused? So were the poor fucking Toms. There's too much going on for the cock-ups and fatal errors that can happen in war to be caused by fog; it's a blizzard of events unfolding at such speed and so out of control that they sting your eyes and leave you dizzy.

My patrol's problem wasn't with the clock. It was right in front of us and it was more Argy trenches.

Keep low. Move fast. That's the mantra of Patrols Platoon and we were off again in a V-formation low to the ground, weapons at the ready, with lead scout Jonesy up front on point.

When he judged we were close enough it was down on our bellies again for the long crawl over the last fifty metres. Here we go again. Jonesy kept on point and then we saw it. His arm was in the air thumb down. Then he pointed.

More Argy trenches. A couple of soldiers in one of them. They were standing up with their shoulders outlined above the parapet of the trench. I heard the unmistakable click of metal on metal.

No, it wasn't a machine gun being cocked ready for action. It was a spoon clinking on a mess tin. One of them was eating. Wrong. When Jonesy got back he told us both of them were eating. That was more evidence of their sloppy routine. More evidence that the officers and NCOs in charge of this unit had lost their grip on the soldiers – if they'd ever had any real grip on them at all.

Careless soldiering costs lives. Those poor fuckers were going to discover the truth of that within the next three hours when the lads from B Company got stuck into them.

TEN

HELL BREAKS LOOSE

Click. Click.

Click. Click. Click.

It sounded as though somewhere out there in the darkness sinister insects were calling out to each other and the hairs on the back of my neck stood on end. One thing was for sure; there were no insects calling out in the Falklands winter.

It was B Company making the insect clicks as they slipped off the rough farm track that snaked along the isthmus from the RV at the white bridge, then strung themselves out along the length of the start line in their platoons and sections.

The insect clicks were the sound of their bayonets being fixed.

I was thrilled and I'm not ashamed to say it. I was electrified by that sound because I'm a soldier, and the thought of the fight to come and the idea of my mates out there preparing to do battle gave me a warrior's rush.

I knew them all, most of them by name, but they may as well have been strangers. They were unrecognisable in the dark; what features of theirs that could be made out were distorted by the camo paint smeared over their faces. Still, I didn't need to see their faces to know the comradeship I felt with them. They were my brothers in arms.

It's a deep feeling that's hard to describe and it's etched into the DNA of many men by the warrior gene. I had utter belief in those

Toms from B Company, and every cell in my body was willing then to win.

It was 3 a.m. on the morning of 28 May. One or two hands reached out and briefly clasped mine as they slipped by me into the darkness towards the battle. Mates made anonymous by the night in the midst of war.

Then a voice behind an unrecognisable face spoke in a gruff whisper: 'See you later, Johnny boy.'

I couldn't make out his voice either, but I caught the sugary tea scent of the last strong brew he'd snatched before battle on the cloud of his breath.

'You too, mate.'

I still don't know who it was but I hoped that I would see him later. I didn't want to acknowledge it in my heart but I knew in my head that some of them weren't going to make it.

I recognised one man, a good mate of mine, a heroic Scouser called Marty Margerison, who was breathing steam into the cold sleet that was already making streaks in his face camo.

I tapped his shoulder and whispered, 'Give 'em shit, Marty.'

He grinned at me and said, 'Too fucking right I will.'

Somewhere in the darkness a young crow puked up with the tension. He got that off his chest and went on to fight like a demon.

And out there in the drizzle Little Bish was leading his section up to the start line, still stinking of his sheep-carcass bedspread. Use the ground well. Personal skills will keep me alive. Fire and manoeuvre. Please don't let the fucking Argies have DF'd the routes or the dead ground! What about Mum and Dad and the girlfriend back in Stoke. I don't want to die at twenty-one! His mind was whizzing at a couple of hundred miles an hour.

But there and then on the start line he was hoping for one last glimpse of his brother before the battle began, but hard as he looked he couldn't see him.

That's because Big Bish was to my left looking as wary as fuck draped in the shining chain mail of machine-gun links and festooned in grenades and white phos like a peddler of death. Big Bish was anxiously peering into the gloom as well. Fierce and scary as he looked he wanted to see his brother too.

As B Company took possession of the start line we'd been holding for them so we began to move back a few metres through their ranks to wait and to watch events unfold.

Shapes brushed past us. Shadows moved to our left and right. There was no rushing, no stumbling, but there was no one hanging back either. I could feel their resolve. It was electric in the air around them, almost tangible. These were men who were going to take on the ultimate challenge. They were going to put their lives on their line for duty and country.

They were also men who were being led by Major John Crosland, their OC, and he was a man they were willing to follow to Buenos Aires if they had to. I glimpsed Crosland among them as he passed through their lines whispering words of encouragement to a group of Toms.

'Hit 'em hard, boys!' he said. 'You can do it!'

Crosland had his signature black bobble hat clamped onto his head. It had been turned into felt by constant use and had assumed the shape of the comedian Tommy Cooper's famous fez. The major was a bit of a comedian himself and loved a good joke, but no one was laughing when the fighting began; Crosland was formidable and seemingly fearless. As long as he was leading them, the word defeat wasn't even in B Company's dictionary.

I watched him come up to join his forward sections. He arrived just in time to overhear one of his junior officers winding Marty up with a succession of conflicting orders which would have been less confusing if he'd given them in Spanish with an Argy accent.

'You!' Crosland muted his bark to keep the noise down, but his voice still sounded vicious and he was holding the young officer's full attention. 'Fuck off back there and let the blokes get on with their job. They know what they're doing without your fucking suggestions!'

The platoon commander did as he was told and Marty and the boys gave thanks for the arrival of the OC, who, as usual, was right on time.

But that clipped, no-nonsense speech had a transforming effect on the young officer too. The major's words settled his nerves and he went on to give a bravura performance on the battlefield. That was the Crosland effect. Military magic! Bottle it and you'd make a fortune.

As my patrol stood there in the endless tussocks of grass, sleet dripping off our faces, peering into the gloom after them, we knew exactly how far the lads had to go to make contact with the enemy. After all, we'd crawled to their fire trenches and back on our bellies. It was nearly three on a freezing Falklands morning and we wouldn't have to wait long.

Officially, the Battle of Goose Green had gone loud an hour earlier with A Company's attack on Burntside House, which was maybe a long rifle shot away from B Company's start line. That's not so far off, but there was a hill between Burntside and us and that put their scene out of sight. They were in dead ground as far as we were concerned and we never heard or saw any of the action over at Burntside. At least we never registered it.

Logically you'd have thought that we must have heard the sounds of artillery and rockets and the glow of the looms, the illuminating shells bursting over Burntside. But I swear I wasn't aware of A Company kicking off the action and neither were any of my mates on B Company's start line. Maybe we were so absorbed, so totally taken up by our own situation and the storm that we knew was surely going to break in front of us, that our minds shut everything else out. I don't know.

What I do remember very clearly is that from where I was standing the Battle of Goose Green began at about three in the morning on the approach to Boca House. That's when all hell broke loose.

I'll never forget the scene. It's engraved on my memory. A fucking huge star shell from the 4.5-inch guns of HMS *Arrow* exploded somewhere to the right over Camilla Creek, lighting up the water and illuminating the battlefield. It was as if a potholer had lit a flare in a giant underground cave and the night sky was turned into the roof of an enormous infernal cavern.

The star shell should have been followed by a succession of high-explosive rounds from *Arrow*, which could launch them at the awesome rate of thirty huge shells a minute. But there was nothing but silence. No hammering for the Argies from the Royal Navy. This was because HMS *Arrow* was already making knots out to open water away from the islands.

Arrow had left a simple message in a quick radio call to the FOO: 'Gun out!'

Their fucking gun had jammed! Now B Company had to do the job on their own and the battalion would be left without any Royal Navy gunfire support for the rest of the battle. Thirty rounds of 4.5-inch shells a minute dropping on chosen targets would have been more than useful and would have shortened the engagement by hours.

B Company were among the enemy with bayonets fixed minutes before the one and only star shell burst over the battlefield, and they also used them in one of the Argy trenches before it went loud. The feedback was that they'd bayoneted a brace of them still in their sleeping bags when they'd tried to go for their weapons. Were they two of the sloppy fuckers I'd eyeballed? I wondered. If that was so they'd paid a terrible price for their incompetence.

Then it all kicked off a couple of minutes later when one of the lads from 6 Platoon, who were on the left-hand side of the company advance, the side nearest the track, spotted a silhouette standing in the middle of a field.

At H's O group there'd been some bullshit about the area on that side of the isthmus being the best arable land in the Falklands, so the young Rupert leading the section whispered, 'It must be a scarecrow.'

Uh? Arable land? Scarecrows? You can have too much fucking education. They were on the Falklands, the place was crawling with Argies and now they were seeing fucking scarecrows!

My mate Marty Margerison wasn't so sure about sodding scarecrows. A Scouse bruiser, his instincts told him this was no penguin scenario. Marty decided to believe what his eyes were telling him and he wasn't going to take any chances, so he called out a challenge. With that the scarecrow came to life and spoke.

'*Por favor?*' it said.

The scarecrow had suddenly come alive in the guise of an Argy soldier wearing a helmet and poncho.

Marty challenged him again.

'Hands up!'

'*Por favor?*'

At that point the Argy must have woken up and realised he was looking at gringos. Reaching under his poncho, it looked like he was trying to unsling his weapon. He shouldn't have done that, because at that moment two rifles and two gimpys opened up on him without a moment's hesitation. Bullets tore through him and tracer rounds from the machine guns ignited his clothing and lit him up like a Halloween pumpkin as they went through his body.

The 'scarecrow' was thrown into the air with the force of the machine-gun bursts, and later, when they looked over the body, they discovered several rounds had gone through a Bible he was carrying with him.

With a bit of Scouse understatement, Marty later told Crosland, 'He just fell over, boss.'

At that moment the star shell burst and the battle went loud. And when it did kick off it was unbelievable. They say nothing prepares a man for battle. But I suppose that what I'd seen and heard so many times on exercise did prepare me for the reality of a full-on battle. But only just.

The air was alive with vivid tracer rounds tracking across the sky against the darkness. The Argy tracers were green and white. Some were cobalt blue. Ours were red and orange. But if you looked at them for too long or too hard they merged into a terrifying, blistering lead migraine at the back of your eyes.

Sometimes opposing tracer rounds randomly hit each other like colliding comets, filling the sky with a storm of lead. There was so much tracer in the sky that you just knew lead was being fired at storm force. I was glad that my mates who were advancing into it didn't have the time that I had to stand and contemplate the sheer volume of fire. It was utterly awesome and terrifying.

Hand-held Schermuly illumes, a bit like emergency lifeboat flares, and illuminating rounds of bursting white phosphorous fired by mortar crews lit up various locations on the set of the battlefield at different times – it looked like a mad throwback to a medieval siege.

As C Company quit the area, we left behind us the flashes and explosive glows of WP grenades lobbed into trenches. Screams and cries of anguish competed with the relentless, harsh chatter of the opposing machine guns as they argued to be heard.

Machine guns, grenades and bayonets were being employed ruthlessly to clear the enemy trenches. Every section in B Company had two gimpys and an M79 grenade launcher, so they were packing a lot of hardware – and they were using it too as they tore down the west side of the isthmus, blowing trenches with the bloopers and 66 LAW anti-tank missiles, then tearing them apart with gimpys before burning them out with WP grenades.

Marty 'Scouse' Margerison charged off to attack a trench to the left, cleared it and then came charging back. His blood was up and he was screaming 'Hands up' in Spanish.

'*Manos arriba! Manos arriba!*'

'Scouse! Don't shoot! It's me, Bish!'

Little Bish wished he hadn't occupied an Argy trench as a firing position. It nearly got him a burst from Scouse.

During the CTR on my sector I'd counted five slit trenches, but B Company took out nearly twenty in a devastating attack on those

Argy trenches before clearing their company headquarters out as well. It was a good start to their battle.

As we watched I had to fight off the urge to go and join in. This was what it was all about. B Company was doing the biz. Fuck, they looked cool and professional, moving with assurance through the absolute mayhem all around them like well-trained tour guides in the mouth of an erupting volcano.

But we had to move off. C Company's business was on another part of the battlefield and we tabbed away to come round behind A Company in support of their own rapid advance up the left-hand, east side of the isthmus. That was the plan. Meanwhile B Company moved on relentlessly. Nothing was going to stand in their way. Not yet at least.

Battle had been joined. There were no bugles, there were no drums. Machine guns sounded the charge.

ELEVEN

BURNTSIDE!

IT WAS AROUND 2.30 A.M. on the morning of 28 May. A Company were on their start line to the south-east of Burntside Pond.

'Fire mission! One mortar! Illume!' The voice was urgent and demanding.

Scouse McVeay, A Company's mortar-fire controller, was on his radio set, feeding his mortar teams the fire missions as he asked them to light up Burntside House with their small 82mm.

Scouse's job may have been the MFC but for a few moments he was the MC, the master of ceremonies at Goose Green, lighting up the stage as the battle officially kicked off.

It was H-Hour and already a salvo of artillery high-explosive shells from the gun line on the other side of Camilla Creek had dropped on the tiny settlement.

A Company crossed their start line five hundred metres from the target under the eerie blue-white light of Scouse's illumes, which were soon beefed up with artillery star shells. Then the scene around the white-painted wooden house and barns at Burntside lit up like New Year's Eve in Trafalgar Square. It was unbelievable.

Scouse and the A Company lads had been waiting for the advance for a good while and that was a bit of a weird one. Those blokes who were still carrying their bergens were sitting on them, even though they were only a few hundred metres away from – and well within range of – the enemy, but there they were, silhouetted against the skyline in the dark.

When the word came, Scouse called in the first para-illumes and they were off towards the house. Intel reports had placed a platoon of Argies in the house and the surrounding area but there was no one returning fire.

Even so, Lieutenant Guy Wallis with 3 Platoon brought his 84mm Carl Gustav, his Charlie G, into play and his team let fly with a high-explosive anti-tank round, which completely missed the target.

The next two attempts with the Charlie G ended in misfires too, causing a lot of piss-taking among the lads, and at one point the boys on Charlie G had to prise out the round from the chamber and weren't very happy with the thirty-five pounds of dead weight they were lumbered with.

The large Swedish-made anti-tank sledgehammer had failed to crack the nut, so the sections moved in on the house and the outbuildings. They raked the house with machine-gun fire, and someone lobbed a grenade through a bedroom window – it was only a wooden structure so the grenade lifted the roof in one corner and set the room on fire.

All this came very close to a massive fuck-up, because when the lads burst into the building all they could hear were shouts of 'Don't shoot!' in very English accents. The shouts came from a family of Kelpers called the Morrisons and despite their near-death experience they seemed quite chuffed to see 2 Para.

'Oh, you're here,' said Gerald Morrison while his missus continued counting machine-gun holes until she reached 130. 'We've been expecting you. The World Service said the paras were coming.'

They were very lucky people, those Morrisons. They'd narrowly missed being obliterated by artillery, anti-tank rockets, grenades and hundreds of machine-gun rounds.

They were the only ones in the building, but they told the lads that the Argies had been in the shearing shed and must have bottled it and buggered off as soon as the artillery began to drop around them. But later on A Company found the bodies of two of their soldiers who'd been killed as they were legging it across open ground between the house and Burntside Pond.

The action had been short and sharp and conclusive, with two Argies dead and the Morrisons' dog wounded, but the minutes were now beginning to slip like sand in an egg timer.

H had been on the radio asking for a sit-rep, a situation report. The trouble was there'd been no officer nearby who could give him one, so the poor fucking signaller had to keep stonewalling the boss with the standard reply: 'Wait out.' H didn't like this. When he asked to speak to someone he expected to speak to them, battle or no fucking battle. He was getting increasingly impatient and demanded that the operator got an officer on the radio.

Chris Dent, second in command of A Company, should have been on the net, and when the dust had settled he was able to give the boss the news that Burntside had been taken with very little opposition. H then ordered Dent to carry the radio himself and stay on the net for the rest of the battle. He wanted to be able to contact an officer at all times.

The gorse had been set alight by the remains of the para-illumes and tracer, so Scouse and the lads stood in front of it trying to dry their kit off and get some heat into their bodies. No one said anything much but there was a general feeling that they'd seen at first hand how the Argies were going to perform.

The lads weren't left on the dryer for too long because H loomed up out of the dark and shouted at Dair Farrar-Hockley saying, 'Get a move on or I'll let C company run through you and take your next objective.'

No time for a chat over a cuppa with the Morrisons then. It was 4.30 a.m. and A Company had taken two hours to storm Burntside and make sure the Argy platoon that was based there was evicted. It hadn't taken much to shift the bastards and that fitted the sketch the whole battalion had been given. Pound into them and they broke.

The company's next objective was Coronation Point, which was a small piece of land jutting out of the isthmus with a bite of water between it and Darwin Settlement. They swept through Coronation Point as there wasn't a single Argy in sight and it was in their possession by 0520 hours.

A company were now ahead of the game and could have pressed on but when H was told this over the battalion net he held them up and refused Dair permission to move on. No, he told him, wait there I'm coming to look for myself. And like a bus inspector he crossed the back of the line to check A Company's ticket before he'd let them travel. The trouble was that it took him an hour to do that and by the time he'd let them go they were destined to reach the Gorse Gully in daylight.

A single platoon was left behind at Coronation Point, where they set up positions to provide supporting fire. They were overlooking the bay with a view across the water to Darwin Settlement, which was A Company's next objective.

As the rest of A Company set off to tab around the bay to come back towards Darwin, H was now following with his Tac 1 group. 0600 hours was approaching. The first strands of daylight were creeping like a sepia wash behind the mountains on the eastern horizon.

The whole shooting match was well behind schedule and H was whirling like a dervish behind his troops. A Company's battle had been easy so far, but that was about to change dramatically with the new dawn.

TWELVE

TACTICAL FAGS

ONE OF THE MYSTERIES of Goose Green is how the hell D Company got to their start line without getting their feet wet. The fact is that they never checked over the white bridge with the rest of the battalion. They admit they got 'a bit lost', but then they emerged through the darkness to take their positions with their feet dry, apparently without having crossed the Ceritos Arroyo stream.

No one in the rest of the battalion believes them but, as you'd expect, no fucker in D Company, from their OC Major Neame to the most junior Tom, has broken ranks to explain that particular trick. They must have it done with the use of bloody mirrors, because in the end they managed to get themselves in front of Tac 1 and the colonel and that's the one position they were definitely not supposed to be in.

That left Neame with a problem, because whatever happened he didn't want to lead his company out in front of either A Company or B Company. That way would lead to confusion, possible blue-on-blue shootings – and the wrath of the colonel.

In the end, they managed to track back into the wind and come up more or less behind the two lead companies, where they settled down looking out into the void waiting for the kick-off.

Tom Harley, one of D Company's superb soldiers, flopped down onto his belly looking into the blackness that he'd be entering, when an awful feeling of loneliness came over him. Then after about five minutes somebody lit the first 'tactical cigarette'.

The fact is that no amount of training can prepare anyone for the possibility that in the not too distant future they could be meeting their Maker. Tom noticed also that at those times the lads would sit very close to one another. Even when they were advancing it was a constant battle to get the men to space themselves out. No one wanted to die alone.

D Company must have lain there flat on the freezing ground for a good hour when Glen Grace, the company sergeant major of HQ Company, came marching up to the rear with a long line of stretcher-bearers.

'Is this D Company?' he asked.

'Yeah it is,' came the answer, 'and you're directly behind the point section of 11 Platoon.'

'OK, we're here,' Glen told his men and they settled in behind D Company with their stretchers, and however good their intentions, they had the air of expectant vultures waiting to feast on the carnage.

As soon as word got passed along to the rest of the company that a load of fucking undertakers had arrived at the scene, more and more tactical fags were seen being lit up along the line.

Neame was among the smokers. He never had fags on him and he didn't smoke very often but when he did he just bummed them off the lads. It was probably his way of keeping in touch with the Toms. He'd just sidle up and ask, 'Anyone got a spare ciggy?'

Towards the end of that stomach-churning hour, H came tabbing along and bumped into the back of D Company. To say the least, he was none too pleased to find his reserve company in front of his own position on the battlefield. The pawns had jumped ahead of the knight on H's chessboard.

'What the hell are you people doing here?' he asked Neame.

'Waiting for the battle to start, sir,' was the major's typically laconic reply.

'Well, you lot shouldn't be in front of me. My orders were quite fucking clear.'

It was a bit of a cock-up, though to be fair the wheels hadn't totally come off the pram, but then D Company reckon that was typical of the exchanges they heard between H and Neame. It seemed to me that the colonel was barely civil to him most of the time. Neame was their boss; they liked him and he led them like a lion.

The company just sat there on the ground smoking while H strode forward with his Tac 1 group; however, it wasn't long before the colonel and his team came under enemy fire and he was reluctantly forced to make his way back to D Company's position. He wanted the enemy ahead cleared off the track and told Neame he wanted them sorted out by his lads.

No fucker knew quite where the enemy troops H had encountered were situated exactly. Not Neame or the colonel or anyone else and it didn't matter which way up they looked at their maps.

This situation turned the plan outlined at the O group on its head. The battle was beginning to defy the maps and strategies to take on a life of its own. Fate would take lives or spare them and decide who would get the victor's spoils. And there was fuck all that H could do about it any more.

D Company had smoked about twenty tactical fags before they were given the order to move. It was time to get on with it. They sucked the last cough out of their fags then dragged their guts up from their boots and tabbed off up the track to put their lives on the line.

With a few shrugs, the reserve company was sent into battle early only to discover they'd already outflanked the enemy and gone past them. Although they'd tried to stay out of the firefight (a tactical bound) behind the point company, which was B Company, the two groups were now very close together on the right-hand side of the track running towards Goose Green, the northern flank of the attack.

★   ★   ★

As D Company moved up to look for H's enemy contact, the only sound that could be heard was some squelching as the Toms ditched their individual weapon sights into the bog. IWSs were pieces of optical kit designed for use with the SLR in Northern Ireland. They were shit. After a couple of days out on active service they fogged up with condensation and you could see fuck all through them, let alone take aim. They were just an extra bit of weight that got in the way.

There was a smaller sight, known as a FASUP, but guess what? – they were shit as well and wouldn't have got a dart onto a board after a couple of days out in the wind, rain and cold. What a fucking laugh. The Falklands are littered with bits of MoD optics that the lads had to 'lose' because they were so useless. Instead, the 2 Para Toms were going to rely on iron sights, bayonets and raw courage.

The order came for the platoons to shake out into their fighting sections with two up and one back. 10 Platoon under Shaun Webster and 12 Platoon under Jim Barry would take the point. 11 Platoon would be in reserve for the initial advance to contact, but that was to change very quickly.

Within minutes of moving forward, lighter by a couple of dozen or so crap rifle sights, 12 Platoon made contact with the Argies and came under effective enemy fire. EEF is the military under-statement for getting shot to fuck. They were taking casualties almost immediately.

Enemy machine guns erupted in the night, opening up from only forty metres away. Undaunted, two sections started crawling straight towards the enemy trenches, rounds constantly whining over their heads. One of the sections was led by Corporal Taff Staddon; the other was the headquarters section led by Lieutenant Webster.

That's when Lance Corporal Cork was hit. He was shot in the stomach as he was doing his job, courageously fighting forward to take on the enemy. At around the same time another Tom called Mort was hit in the arm. A third Tom – Fletcher – laid his own life on the line and lost it when he went to help his mate Cork.

That's what paras do. They go and help their mates. They don't listen to that bullshit about one wounded man taking four of his comrades out of the action to help him. So what? They drag their wounded into cover and carry on fighting. They reckon one para is worth four of everyone else's conventional troops in any event, so that makes it about right. What really matters is looking out for your mates. That's what makes paras strong; the knowledge that their mates will come and get them out of the line of fire. Fletch died in that tradition and his death strengthened the tradition. So it was that Cork and Fletcher became the first 2 Para soldiers to die in the battle.

Mortar bombs were now dropping all around D Company, but the soaking wet peat the men were crawling over was a lifesaver, absorbing a lot of their explosive force.

Still, it's fair to say that D Company were in the shit at that point, with 12 Platoon committed to heavy fighting and 10 Platoon pinned down under the weight of almost constant machine-gun fire and a fearsome barrage of mortars. There was no one but themselves to get them out of it. And that's what they set about doing.

As the men of D Company were giving their all, H was trumpeting down the radio nagging Neame to get on with it. He was pissed off because his timetable for the battle was being totally disrupted by the presence of an enemy who had the nerve to actually resist his advance. There were two and a half hours or so left to dawn and five klicks to go to Goose Green. Get a fucking move on! That was the clear message from the boss.

The lads in 11 Platoon were quickly in the thick of it led by nineteen-year-old Lieutenant Chris Waddington, but their fire was dangerously close to John Crosland's men further to the left and their tracer was making a dizzying pattern with the Argy tartan in the sky directly over B Company's heads.

Tom Harley of 11 Platoon was moving his section into dead ground when his second in command, Gaz Bingley, told him he was going to move the GPMG forward twenty metres and take up

(*Above*) We sent them home to think again! Argies embarking at Port Stanley for home. They were allowed to keep their weapons and equipment. However they left their mines behind – because they hadn't bothered to map them.

(*Above*) The end of the road. Proudly marching into Stanley well ahead of all the other Task Force units and flying my Goose Green flag on the barrel of my SLR.

(*Above*) The Para Memorial at
Goose Green. The grateful islanders
erected it within three days of the
battle. The Para whose face is
side-on is Bill Bentley, the Medic
who amputated Chopsey's leg
with a clasp knife under fire.
Bill got the Military Medal.

(*Right*) A picture taken in 2002
by Sleapy standing on B-
Company's start line. In the background is a herd of wild horses,
probably related to the ones that
nearly trampled us to death!

(*Above*) The view from an Argy Coastguard vessel approaching Goose Green from the sea.

(*Below*) The Argy flag flying over the Falkland Islands Company offices in Goose Green.

(*Above*) Argy helos deploying at Goose Green.

(*Below*) A party of Argy head-sheds arriving by Chinook for an inspection of the Goose Green garrison.

(*Above*) Hello mum! Some junior officers and Argy Special Forces types pose up for their souvenir picture.

(*Right*) A Harrier drops cluster bombs into the sea during the battle (background). The Argy troops didn't like that. The imprisoned islanders say they started screaming and running around when the Harriers swooped.

(*Above*) This is an Argy view of the schoolhouse attack. Look at the smoke plumes on the skyline.

(*Below*) A similar view. That looks like the dairy building in the foreground.

C (BRUNEVAL) COMPANY

NOMINAL ROLL AS AT 16 APRIL 1982

Company Headquarters

*	508073	CAPTAIN	JENNER	R D
*	507473	LT	KENNEDY	P
?	24135462	WO 2	GREENHALGH	B J
*	24171601	CSGT	TAYLOR	D A
*	24299883	CPL	CHURCH	P
	24533483	PTE	BROWN	D J

RECCE PLATOON

509087	LT	CONNOR	C S	
24053967	SGT	HIGGINSON	S	*
	CPL	EVANS		*
24299869	CPL	PEARSON	R M	*
24246397	CPL	RAYNOR	I T	*
24319855	LCPL	GRUNDY	P	*
24355312	LCPL	LINCOLN	A J	*
24366410	LCPL	PETTY	I J	*
24384212	LCPL	TURNER	B	*
24325003	LCPL	WOODS	S	*
24342730	PTE	ANDERTON	S A	*
24565418	PTE	BARNES	W	
24539292	PTE	BATES	M T	
24496155	PTE	BOLLAND	J	*
24600766	PTE	CHARTERS	R	
24431780	PTE	CROCKFORD	M J	
24600565	PTE	DAVIES	S	
24598561	PTE	DOCKERTY	L	
24596877	PTE	LOWTON	N A	
24603711	PTE	MOORE	D J	
24455553	PTE	MORRELL	R P G	*
24492095	PTE	RICHARDS	T	*
24472352	PTE	RUSSELL	S	
24464322	PTE	SMITH	D M	*
24599726	PTE	THEARLE	D J	*

PATROL PLATOON

*	497688	CAPTAIN	FARRAR	P R
*	24180546	SGT	SMITH	E D
*	24351010	CPL	BISHOP	E J
*	24339678	CPL	GRAHAM	J
*	24300786	CPL	McNALLY	R
*	24304581	LCPL	JACKSON	C L
*	24342317	LCPL	McHUGH	M J
	24440443	LCPL	SISSONS	K B
	24286592	LCPL	TIGHE	A
	24501128	LCPL	WALSHE	R D
*	24469859	PTE	COX	G S
	24493550	PTE	ELY	T D
	24554170	PTE	GRAY	D
	24472399	PTE	JONES	S
	24538567	PTE	MARTIN	M H
	24516624	PTE	MORGAN	T
	24491292	PTE	MORTIMER	K
	24554180	PTE	MYERS	P R
	24519328	PTE	SLEAP	M R
*	24469951	PTE	STOKES	E
	24527813	PTE	TENSON	R
	24472541	PTE	TRICK	D
	24557529	PTE	WARREN	P T
	24463368	PTE	WHEATLEY	J
	24441517	PTE	YOURSTON	

* Denotes married personnel

(*Above*) A Patrols Platoon roll listing the personnel who went to war.

SIGNAL JUST RECEIVED FROM THE BATTALION

2 PARA ARE EXPECTED TO BOARD MV NORLAND ON THURSDAY
24 JUNE 1982 AND HOPE TO SAIL HOME WITHIN THE NEXT
TEN DAYS. THE BN WILL NOT BE GARRISONING THE FALKLANDS
AT ALL. PSE PASS OUT ON FAMILIES NEWSLETTER. DATE TIME-
PORT OF ARRIVAL WILL BE NOTIFIED WHEN CONFIRMED.

(*Above*) A signal sent back to 2 Para families, telling them that their men are coming home.

ANNEX 'A' TO 2 PARA MFO/24
DATED   JUNE 1982

SYMPATHY AND CONGRATULATORY SIGNAL FROM CHIEF-GENERAL-STAFF

"FOR COLONEL OF THE REGIMENT AND PARACHUTE REGIMENT DEPOT FROM CHIEF
OF THE GENERAL STAFF. GREATLY GRIEVE THE LOSS OF COLONEL JONES,
HIS ADJUTANT AND THE OTHER 15 DEAD AND 30 WOUNDED OF THE GALLANT
2ND BATTALION: BUT WANTED YOU TO KNOW HOW IMMENSELY HIGHLY I AND MY
COLLEAGUES ON THE ARMY BOARD RATE THE PERFORMANCE OF THE BATTALION
AGAINST AN ENEMY OVER DOUBLE THEIR NUMBER, DETERMINED TO STAND AND
FIGHT. NOT ONLY WAS THE TASK GIVEN THE BATTALION OF VITAL AND
URGENT IMPORTANCE TO OUR COUNTRYS INTERESTS AND FUTURE AT THIS TIME
BUT ALSO IN ACHIEVING ALL ITS OBJECTIVES IN A TEN HOUR BATTLE AFTER
LOSING THE CO AND CAPTURING OVER 1400 PRISONERS THE BATTALION HAS
EXECUTED A FEAT OF ARMS AND GALLANTRY PROBABLY UNSURPASSED IN THE
GLORIOUS HISTORY OF THE BRITISH ARMY. IT WILL CERTAINLY RATE WITH
THE OTHER GREAT EXAMPLES OF COURAGE BY THE PARACHUTE REGIMENT SUCH AS
THE NORMANDY LANDINGS AND ARNHEM. I SEND YOU ON BEHALF OF THE ARMY
BOARD OUR WARMEST CONGRATULATIONS, WHICH IN DUE COURSE I HOPE CAN BE
PASSED TO THE BATTALION, WHILST AT THE SAME TIME OFFERING YOU OUR
DEEPEST SYMPATHY FOR THE LOSS OF SUCH FINE AND GALLANT OFFICERS AND
MEN".

(*Above*) Signal of sympathy and congratulations sent by Field Marshal Sir Dwin Bramall,
Chief of the Defence Staff.

position on a knoll that he could see ahead of them. This was a fucking bold move and as he crawled to the summit of the grass-covered hump with Baz Grayling, his number two, all hell broke loose.

Gaz and Baz had all but stumbled into an enemy gun trench and rounds were going everywhere at near point-blank range. But the lads were so close to the enemy that it was second nature to attack, so they just upped and assaulted the Argy position.

The firefight was a furious flourish of arms that lasted a matter seconds, killing some but not all the occupants of the trench. As they rushed the position, Baz took a hit in his water bottle, which exploded into shrapnel and fragged his hip. He collapsed to the ground but still kept firing to cover Gaz who was also continuing the assault, pumping bullets straight down the line of sight of the Argy machine gun which they eventually silenced.

Then, in awful twist of fate and at the moment of triumph, the Argy machine-gunner squeezed off one last burst in a reflex action as he died at his weapon and Gaz was down. It was a terrible wound through his eye and it was to prove fatal.

He was shouting 'my eye, my eye' over and over again. He went on shouting for about fifteen seconds. Tom Harley, fearful for his best mate Gaz, counted every one of those seconds.

Baz Grayling managed to half crawl and half drag himself to safety unaided. Safety? Actually there wasn't anywhere really safe to occupy as hundreds of machine-gun rounds whined over his head. Gaz's body wasn't retrieved until it was nearly sunrise and Padre Cooper, who seemed to be everywhere on the battlefield, found it. He brought Gaz to the RAP – or regimental aid post – with the help of a medic.

That left Tom Harley to avenge his friends and take the fight to the enemy again. In a typically unselfish act of courage, Tom, who knew full well the firepower he was taking on, rushed the trench and hurled a white phosphorous grenade into the enemy bunker to finish them.

The first medals of Goose Green had been won. All three got the Military Medal for their gallantry, though sadly Gaz's award was posthumous.

Chris Waddington, their platoon commander, had only been out of Sandhurst Military Academy and in the proper army for three months. He was a crow lieutenant known to the Toms as 'Boy Wonder' and he'd not even had time to get his mess tins bent in the field before he'd gone to the Falklands. Fuck, was he having a baptism of fire!

Waddington wasn't the only nineteen-year-old on the battlefield by any means. A lot of the Toms were young crows and the Argy ranks were also full of young guys in the last year of their teens. Chris took that incident when Gaz got hit badly. White-faced with fury at the death of one of his Toms, he started shouting and screaming at the smouldering shadows that lay still warm in the wasted position.

'You fuckers! You fuckers!' he kept yelling.

The lads stood and watched. Not their job to tell an officer what was what. Then Neame came along and put a steadying hand on Waddington's shoulder and muttered a few words in his ear.

No one could hear what was said between the two of them, but whatever the major said it quickly calmed Chris down and the lads in his platoon all looked the other way as he regained his composure. Lieutenant Waddington grew up very quickly that day and his emotive outburst over the loss of Gaz did him no harm at all in the eyes of the Toms in D Company.

While that was happening 12 Platoon were clearing out another six or seven bunkers. It was no picnic but the work done by Gaz, Baz and Tom Harley meant that the interlocking arcs of fire allowing the Argies to protect each other's positions had been broken. They were fucked.

At one point the lads spotted four shadowy silhouettes on a fence line. They didn't fire immediately, not wanting to risk a blue on blue with 11 Platoon, but instead they called for an illume which exposed the four shadows as Argies sneaking off the battlefield. Two of them were immediately shot up while the others dived over the fence into cover and managed to leg it.

Neame thought this spelt danger and ordered 11 Platoon to sweep through all the trenches on the ridge again. Just in case. It was a good job that he did because Tom Harley and his lads had to deal with more resistance.

The destruction of that Argy trench system led to a pause in D Company's battle and Harley went back to the RAP to check what had happened to his mate Gaz. That's when he learnt that an Argy round had entered his eye and had taken the back of his head off. Tom was told his mate would have been killed instantly.

But if that was the case then why had he been shouting those dreadful haunting words 'my eye, my eye' for fully fifteen seconds while he was supposed to have been dead?

Three of D Company's men had been killed and two were wounded in the space of an action that lasted no more than twenty minutes. It had been fast and furious and the lads of D Company had set the benchmark for bravery in the battle.

THIRTEEN

THE GORSE GULLY

IT WAS 7 A.M. Dawn and the Gorse Gully looked like an innocent enough feature cutting through the low ridge that straddled
the isthmus. To the left-hand side of it stood the higher mass of
Darwin Hill. The gully was the natural route through that ridge
to reach Darwin and Goose Green and the track ran through it.

It may have looked innocent but A Company were tabbing into
the funnel of a maelstrom. You couldn't blame them for thinking
that it was a walk-through; there'd been no sign of the enemy at
Coronation Point. True, there were reports of sixteen empty
trenches on the ridge behind the Gorse Gully and that would
have been enough to house a platoon full of trigger-happy gauchos.
But the bosses seemed to have fixed on the word 'empty' when
they looked at the map and considered those trenches. That was
a mistake, but it was a mistake born out of the fact that the
battalion had not been allowed to deploy its own eyes and ears:
the men of the Patrols and Recce Platoons of C Company.

I'm confident that if Patrols had been allowed to, we would
have been able to infiltrate around Burntside House without any
difficulty and then we could have sized up the scale of the problem
waiting for the battalion on Darwin Ridge. We could have done
that days earlier when we'd been limited to a few patrols for fear
of colliding with Special Forces. The decision to rein in H and
2 Para in the days after the landing while the battalion was

clinging to the side of Sussex Mountain was a major misjudgement on the part of the high command.

Without a proper CTR, A Company wasn't expecting to find any big Argy resistance, at least not until the outskirts of Darwin Settlement and maybe not until Goose Green itself.

As it was the battalion was halfway down the length of the isthmus, but our cloak of darkness was evaporating and on top of that we were out of kilter. We'd developed a bit of a speed wobble with two companies, B and D, slowed down by fierce actions on the right flank, while A Company, unopposed at Coronation Point, had bowled ahead. That had happened despite H delaying A Company until he'd checked their tickets like a bus inspector.

Major Chris Keeble, the second in command of the battalion, thought it could have gone either way at that point. He reckoned that the Battle of Goose Green might have been lost by 2 Para if anyone in the Argy command structure had had the guts to order a credible counter-attack on any one of our companies. We were on the back foot and we were about to come up against a heavily gunned, well-entrenched enemy in broad daylight across open countryside. The hours of full light became the Argies' best friend, giving them long, easy views of the approaching paras. Time to take aim and pour lead on the advancing gringos.

On went A Company regardless. They were determined and they had their own goal in mind. They wanted to be the first company to reach Goose Green. Word had got through on the signallers' rumour control that B and D Company had acquitted themselves well and fought good fights. A Company were eager to get a proper grip on the enemy's throat too. They weren't going to be outdone by those plonkers in B and D. No fucking chance.

Their route around the shore of Coronation Bay brought them bumping up against the flank of Darwin Ridge. 2 Platoon, under Lieutenant Coe, led the way with Corporal Tom Camp's section out on point. Behind him came Corporal Hardman's section to the rear and left and Corporal 'Monster' Adams's lads behind him to the right.

The orders from Dair Farrar-Hockley made complete sense. Use that the Gorse Gully to access your way onto the top of the ridge and from there you'll command high ground with views over Darwin and Goose Green. They'd occupy those empty Argy trenches on the ridge until C Company moved up behind them and took the keys to the high ground while A Company rolled forward to take Darwin then onwards again.

That was the general idea, but just as they entered the gully three figures silhouetted on a spur sticking out from the ridge above them cocked that one up. At first the lads thought they might be civilians because they appeared to be wearing duffel coats; in fact, they had the hoods of their military parkas up over their helmets.

Maybe they were shepherds, thought some of the lads. Perhaps some islanders were out dog-walking. Oh bollocks. Here we go again. More fucking scarecrows in the scenario. Why is it that in these situations you'd rather believe anything other than the obvious? It's the enemy. Who else would it be on an occupied island crawling with the bastards?

One of the blokes was closing in on them though, and he was no more than ten metres away in the diffused pre-dawn light when he noticed they were carrying weapons. Argies!

He shouted. In English.

One of them shouted back. In Spanish.

Both sides realised their error at the same moment, but Tom Camp's blokes were first on their triggers and they got the drop on the Argies immediately. Only one of them managed to escape.

But that invited a shit storm from the Argy bunkers that were finally revealed to the lads by arcing streams of tracer rounds as they poured machine-gun fire and heavy automatic rifle fire down onto them. EEF in spades!

When you come under EEF the best thing to do is move your

arse forward at the double into the nearest cover in front of you. Don't go back. However tempting that might be, just keep going forward. And that's what they all did. Tom Camp and Jock Hardman made it into the Gorse Gully with Farrar-Hockley and his Tac closely following. Not far behind them was 1 Platoon.

Most of them made it to cover because we're all taught in training that the first bursts of fire from a gun line, especially in poor light against a moving and often weaving target, are not usually accurate. There's a natural tendency for the gunners to shoot high and A Company took advantage of that built-in knowledge as they bowled into the Gorse Gully with very few casualties.

The company's main headquarters group and a couple of blokes from 1 Platoon were caught out in the open further behind the rest and came in for a harrowing downpour from the fire trenches above. They hit the ground and tried to fight back. Brave, but it was bound to be ineffective.

A party of five Royal Engineers attached to the Royal Marines then reattached to 2 Para were in that group. One of them, Corporal Melia, a mine-disposal and booby-trap expert, who was tagging along to make Darwin and Goose Green safe when they were retaken, was shot and killed. One of our medics was badly wounded but thankfully survived.

I didn't know Melia but I hear he was a cheerful and resourceful bloke, and let's be fair, anyone who volunteers to fuck around with mines and booby traps has to have a deep reservoir of courage.

Those that survived in that isolated section spent the next forty minutes on their bellies crawling down the line of gorse trying not to attract the attention of the Argy gunners until they made it to the shore of a creek on the edge of Coronation Bay.

Back in the Gorse Gully, Dair Farrar-Hockley had a ragtag mixture of about sixty or seventy blokes from various sections and platoons who'd all been scattered by the ferocity of that first Argy fusillade. If there'd been any Argies planted on the top of Darwin Hill itself, the commanding high ground of the entire isthmus, most of them would have been well and truly fucked. There weren't any. The Argy failure to take possession of that hill saved A Company from decimation and 2 Para from defeat.

I firmly believe we would have been in deep shit if the Argies had bothered to do that, but they hadn't and the truth is that they didn't occupy the highest ground in other positions too. Why? I think the answer is laughably simple. I think it was too fucking cold for them. They just dug lots of trenches out of the wind then sprinkled mines around in the gaps.

Thank fuck they were lazy soldiers, but at that moment it was no consolation to Monster and his boys. They were further over to the right when the first awesome machine-gun onslaught began and they put their heads down and loped towards the re-entrant just to the north of the Gorse Gully as fast as their legs would take them. It was just a notch in the contours, but it offered some sort of shelter from the lead. Or so they thought.

It was here that Monster made a bad discovery. The re-entrant was covered by fire trenches too! And they were on to Monster and his lads straight away, raking them with machine-gun fire. Four bullets slammed into Monster. One of them burst through his right shoulder. The others slammed into his back like blows from a jackhammer as he toppled forward, dropping like a rag doll into the bracken that clung to the side of the hill.

His mate Tuffen was shot twice in the head and with good reason Monster believed he was dead and wrote him off, but in fact he lay there for about three and a half hours, less than a hundred metres from the enemy positions, before the lads could retrieve him. He was a tough bastard though, and against all the odds he lived.

Monster is a tough bastard too. A West Country hard nut. You don't get a name like Monster unless you're one of the toughest. He crawled into dead ground, then picked himself up and worked his way back towards the others below the edge of the spur in the dead ground underneath the Argy positions.

His right arm hung like a pendulum from his shattered shoulder. His SLR bounced along the ground as he dragged it behind him with his left hand. A lesser man would have jacked in a dead faint but Monster kept going. It would take more than four Argy machine-gun bullets to keep him down.

Eventually he came across one of the dead Argies who'd been killed on the spur in those first moments of the action. The Argy looked like a warrant officer and he had a pistol in his hand. Despite his horrendous wounds Monster wanted that pistol as a souvenir but he wasn't entirely sure the bloke was dead, so he crept up on him and stamped on his helmet to make sure. He *was* dead. The pistol was Monster's.

Another fifty metres and he couldn't go any further. He could hear the voices of the other lads down in the Gorse Gully and he dropped to the ground and began to tend his wounds, clamping a couple of field dressings onto his back, then lying on them to put pressure on the wounds and slow the bleeding. He didn't know it but he was going to be there for a long time before he got proper medical help, and while he was there some of the lads tabbed past him as they tried time and again to break the Argy grip on A Company's throat.

One of the lads looked down at him and said 'You been hit, Monst?'

'Yeah.'

'Fucking poor skills that, mate.'

The next one to tab past asked Monster the same question.

'Yeah. In the back.'

'Shit field craft, Monst!'

A third Tom came along and asked the predictable question of his stricken mate.

'Yeah,' said Monster, resigned to the inevitable piss-take.

'Oh well, Monst, you won't need those gloves then, will you, mate?'

With that he relieved the wounded Monster of his black

Northern Ireland-issue leather gloves with knuckle padding on the fingers. That's paras for you. Always cheerful in the face of someone else's troubles!

But the truth is they did care and those seemingly unsympathetic comments and the nicking of his gloves were their way of seeing how much life there was left in Monster; how much of a reaction they could get out of him. When Monster told them to fuck off and threatened to kill them they knew he'd be all right.

However, as he left the re-entrant behind him, Monster wasn't to know that he'd discovered the position of the Argy command bunker, and the machine-gunner who'd plugged him four times was the one who was destined to kill Colonel H.

FOURTEEN

BOCA HOUSE

THERE'S AN ODD THING about the way time and space change when the chips are down. They slow to a time-frame exposure. Every sense is magnified and on the field of endeavour the best soldiers, like the best sportsmen, appear to make time and space their own. The difference is that while some sports imitate war, the usual way you get sent off on the battlefield is when you're killed or wounded. But there is another way, a better way: you march off the winner.

That's why all the senses of Little Bish and the boys from B Company were jangling and acute, and that's why many of them took time and space for their own as they crested a ridge on their way to the next objective on H's battle plan: Boca House.

The sun was rising. It was around the same time as Dair Farrar-Hockley and half of A Company were charging for their lives into the Gorse Gully.

B Company had regrouped after that first vicious action off the start line when they'd overrun a whole cluster of Argy fire trenches. That had taken a fair time, about an hour and a half, in the darkness just before dawn. But their blood was up. They'd tasted battle and there was more to be done.

Boca House was only 1,200 metres or so away, and though they didn't know it as they emerged onto the line of the ridge, it was going to be another six hours before the Argy trenches to the south of the house surrendered. It was going to be a gruelling, bullet-whipped day.

And when B Company eventually got to Boca House and looked around them for the home they'd liberated, a lot of the Toms were scratching their heads until they realised there was no fucking house at all. Their objective was the brick foundations of a building that had once stood on a fifty-foot circular contour on the ground above a beach on the Brenton Loch side of the isthmus.

Boca House commanded views over the local terrain. That's why the Argies dug in there and that why B Company had fought for a grid reference. They'd taken on the trenches that Taff Evans had recced across Camilla Creek from his OP in the gorse bank days back.

Only 1,200 metres to go, but at dawn as they left the smoking, body-filled trenches of the first Argy ramparts behind them and crested that one-hundred-foot-high forward slope overlooking Boca House, it may as well have been on the far side of the moon. It could only be approached across seemingly endless acres of open ground, and it was protected by two interlocking arcs of multiple machine-gun emplacements and flanked by minefields. It was a bed-wetting, fucking nightmare.

Crosland and his Tac unit were out in front as B Company headed down the gentle incline on the forward slope of the hill south towards Boca and into the mouth of a maelstrom of machine guns. Directly in front of them lay the line of gorse that went from one side of the isthmus to the other, cloaking the Gorse Gully on its way.

The slope offered a bit more cover than a slightly tilted bowling green but not much. There were undulations and lots of grassy hummocks standing proud in bare earth eroded by the sharp hooves of grazing sheep; there were a few boulders as well. To the left there were some small valleys, re-entrants notched into the side of the ridge that stretched across the Gorse Gully. It was no place for the faint-hearted.

Under Lieutenant Ernie Hocking, 4 Platoon were on John

Crosland's rear right, 6 Platoon tabbed to the rear left headed up by Lieutenant Clive Chapman and 5 Platoon, under Geoffrey Weighell, followed in reserve.

As they came down the slope, Bish in 5 Platoon could see some figures through the morning murk standing around with their hands in their pockets, kicking and stamping the ground as they tried to keep warm.

Some of the Toms opened up. No more fucking scarecrows, they'd learnt that much, but apparently one of their corporals hadn't.

'Cease fire! It's fucking A Company!'

It wasn't.

'Fuck off! They're Argies!' came the response.

'Right!' shouted the same wanker. 'The next bloke who opens up will be charged –'

He never ended his threat because that's when B Company were caught out in the open. The whole Argy gun line opened up on them, reaching a crescendo of heavy machine-gun fire that they kept up for hours.

Green and white tracer. Cobalt-blue tracer. Orange fucking tracer. Even in the swelling daylight the sizzling tracks of the tracer defined the area of the battlefield, reflecting off the sea in the near distance like a mesmerising laser show over Hong Kong harbour.

Fuck this, thought the lads, and they were nearly tripping over the heels of their leaders as the first three sections legged it towards some dead ground between them and the gorse line at the bottom of the hill. The first probing bursts saw the tracer go high and they knew they had seconds to make it before the Argy gunners readjusted.

Heavy-calibre bullets whined and strummed through the air, kicking up stones and mud from the eroded soil and splashing and hissing in the puddles around them. Machine-gun bursts whacked into the hummocks of grass with lethal force like lead machetes.

Moving back towards the ridge with 5 Platoon, Little Bish spotted two large enemy bunkers about five hundred metres directly forward and another about 150 metres on the opposite ridge leading back towards the Gorse Gully. In front of him, he could see Crosland's Tac group standing out like sore thumbs because of the hedgerow of radio antennae waving above them. The aerials wobbled ludicrously from side to side as the poor bloody signallers struggled to keep up with their heavy loads.

Panting and straining, their hearts fit to burst from the effort, they all sprinted over the fifty or sixty metres that took them into dead ground. Then they began working their way down into the thorn-covered haven of the gorse bushes another sixty metres or so ahead of them, using the field craft and combat skills that had been drummed into them over years of training and long tours in Northern Ireland's bandit country. They did well and got to the gorse line in one piece and then, barely pausing for a breath, moved on the enemy positions wherever they could.

The machine-gun nest to the left that Little Bish had spotted was the Argies' closest position. It was just in front of the gorse line and it was an urgent problem. The bastard was giving them gyp. Lance Corporal Dunbar of 4 Platoon had a bead on the bastards and lifted a 66mm rocket to his shoulder while his boss yelled at him not to fire.

'Watch out for A company!'

Good point. As it happened A Company was indeed in the line of fire and well within range about eight hundred metres away, but most of them were already out of sight on their bellies in the Gorse Gully.

Dunbar had work to do, though, and didn't heed the call. Those machine guns were going to kill some of his mates if he didn't sort it. He lined up the sight on top of the plastic disposable tube of the anti-tank rocket. The cool-headed bastard didn't rush the job. Steady. That's it. Breathe out. Press the plunger on top of the rocket. Fortune favours the brave. Then he just slotted the rocket right down the back of the Argies' throats. Whooph! A bunker shot!

One problem less, but there were plenty ahead of them. No one could put their heads up even to get a glimpse of the enemy without attracting a fury of machine-gun rounds.

The gorse line proved to be a better position than they'd realised, because hidden under the shelter of the blanket of gorse were some earthen banks that had probably been thrown up years back as sheep folds to gather in the flocks. They made decent cover, which was just as well because most of B Company was going to be sheltering there from the lead storm for a good while. They were well and truly pinned down and there was fuck all they could do about it without heavy fire support. Their obstacle was a set of thirteen trenches packed with machine guns.

One thing was for sure. The Argies had stiffened up with the arrival of daylight. They could clearly see 2 Para manoeuvring low and fast in front of them and there's something about a .50-cal machine gun in a prepared position and a bright clear view that turns a conscript frightened of the dark into a Johnny Rambo.

During their first engagements with the enemy, when they'd cleared their trenches, both D and B Companies had found that the Argy positions were stocked with huge quantities of ammo and rations. They'd insulated their trenches with ammo cases and they'd used them as duckboards at the bottom to keep their feet dry. In most trenches they were literally standing on more ammo than an entire 2 Para company could carry.

The addition of daylight and long clear views into the equation filled the Argies with confidence and made them brave as fuck.

Everyone from Crosland down to the most inexperienced crow in the company knew that going forward to attack those trenches in broad daylight would have been suicide.

Most of B Company were now hunkered down under that earthen bank in the middle of the gorse, which had been set on fire in places by the scorching tracer.

But that left the poor fuckers in 5 Platoon, who'd been giving them covering fire while they'd moved into the gorse, out in the open. In their position they were only about seventy-five metres from the bunker Dunbar had done in with the 66. They were ordered by Crosland to take out that bunker, so even though they believed it had been completely destroyed Little Bish and a half section moved to the right just out of view of the Argies to give supporting fire while Brummie and the other half rushed it.

It was empty, but then Little Bish saw his mate fall back screaming. Oh no! Not Brummie. The lads watched open-mouthed as Brum pulled his trousers down in the middle of the battlefield and started examining his wedding tackle. It looked like the poor bastard had had his balls shot off.

Brummie ignored the whining rounds whipping through the air around him while he got a field dressing onto his bollocks. It turned out that a stone had been chipped by a round, sending it flying like a meteorite to collide with his balls and cut his scrotum. And all Brum could think at the time was, 'Oh fuck, what will the wife say?'

As the platoon withdrew from the hill, the Argies got their range and bullets were cracking around their heads as they headed for the wiped-out bunker. Little Bish found a small depression and dived into it but it was no place to be and Brad, his platoon sergeant, had to scream at him twice to move.

He'd frozen for a moment but not for long, and he was quickly up and sprinting towards the safety of the bunker screaming with anger and fear. The last few feet saw him flying through the air like a hunted stag. He hit the mud and rolled over.

Thank fuck for that. He'd not been hit. He was safe but what had he done with his rifle? It must have spun out of his hand as he somersaulted into safety. As he looked up Little Bish could see it six feet away stuck in the ground by the bayonet. All he had to do now was run back under fire and get it! And that's what he did. With his heart in his mouth he leapt out and attracted a stream of machine-gun rounds as he grabbed the weapon and leapt back to safety.

Men were getting hit now and Scouse Margeruson was brought down off the hill wounded in the face, shoulder and stomach. The blokes watched him dragging on a fag with a huge dressing on his face wound, and every time he took a pull on his fag, smoke billowed out of the gaping hole in the side of his face and filtered through his dressing.

At that point a mortar man called 'Strasse' Street was hit on the slope after laying down smoke for the lads to get themselves into dead ground. One of the corporals, a stalwart guy called Les Standish, ran out with a Tom called Brookey, grabbed him, then manhand-led him up seventy metres of the slope to the summit and safety. Fuck knows how they weren't hit as the Argy machine guns ripped the ground around them into shreds.

Then more heroics as Private Hall was hit in the back. True to the unspoken bond between the lads, a couple of his mates skir-mished out to help him as 4 Platoon risked their necks to try and suppress the Argy fire.

Steve Illingsworth and Poole got to his side, quickly tore off his webbing to locate the wound, then dressed it before dragging him into dead ground. Again the Argies tried to cut them to ribbons but failed to get on target in time.

Steve was a man of redoubtable courage and without a selfish bone in his body. His mate safe in dead ground, he realised that the most precious metal in the battalion lay in the open in Hall's discarded webbing: the clips in his ammo pouches.

Without hesitating, he ran back out to retrieve the ammo and was shot dead in the attempt. That selfless courage won him the Distinguished Conduct Medal posthumously. 5 Platoon had one man dead and two wounded.

Then minutes later Captain John Young, Crosland's second in command, was hit by shrapnel from a mortar bomb and after his men had tended to him and done the best they could he had to lie out there on the bollock-freezing battlefield for twelve hours despite his grave wounds. He lived. A lesser man would have jacked up and died.

Now mortar and artillery fire from the Argy positions in Goose

Green were brought to bear on that ridge for the rest of the daylight hours. Huge eruptions of black peat momentarily obscured the view of the battlefield like ink blots on a manuscript.

Down in the gorse line one of the platoon radio operators who was sitting in a patch of burning furze radioed a request to be beamed up like Scottie. But there were no transporters at Goose Green apart from one ancient farm Land Rover and the Trekkie radio operator had to stay put!

Pinned down, B Company thought there was nothing for it but to make a brew and that's what they did. They got their hexi stoves out and turned the gorse line into the most dangerous picnic site on the planet.

Their mates in A Company were pinned down too and they, likewise, opted for a tea break while they sorted their ammo clips out. And as two companies of Red Berets gratefully slurped on their reviving mugs, most of them were wondering why the colonel didn't do the obvious. Because H had a solution to the horrendous machine-gun fire that was to keep them stalled for hours. The lads all knew what it was. So why the fuck hadn't he come up with it? Where were the bloody Milans?

FIFTEEN

HANGING ON

IT WAS FIGHT OR die over in the Gorse Gully. One of the signallers was even using a Tom's back to give a gimpy more elevation in the desperate struggle to try and suppress the endless stream of machine-gun fire from six or seven trenches on the spur between the gully and the re-entrant.

Corporal Tom Camp, one of four Camp brothers in the battalion, Captain Watson who was the FOO, together with a ragtag of different sections from 2 Platoon chiselled their way up the slope. Inch by inch they crept forward dragging gimpys and 66mm rocket launchers behind them.

This was dangerous stuff, but those guys were as bold as fuck and that's when Dey, the platoon's radio operator, stuck the gimpy on his mate's back to give the lads some suppressive fire as they took a tactical bound forward.

Sweat turned cold as it ran down their faces and the enemy machine guns dared them to move at all. But they kept going. Short scuttles. Crawls. Improvised ways of moving that would have got top marks in a drama class. It didn't fucking matter as long as they kept going forward. Bullets tore up the ground around them and whined in the air above as the Argies tried to rip them to shreds. No chance.

Their field craft was second to none and the boys kept moving up towards those bunkers because they knew that they weren't the only ones with an elevation problem. Maybe it is hard to shoot upwards on a steep hill with a gimpy but it's equally hard to shoot downwards with a machine gun housed in a bunker. The lads knew that the closer they got to the end of the Argies' barrels the more limited their arcs of fire would become and that created the narrowest sliver of dead ground right under their fucking noses.

They did get right under their fucking noses. Ten metres away. It was payback time.

Whoomph!

First, the 66 struck the right side of the fire trench with devastating effect. Blood and shredded kit were blended by the explosion.

Next, an L2 grenade and a white phosphorous exploded simultaneously, sending the occupants to oblivion.

The WP burnt as it clung to their combat gear, burnt as it clung to the cases of ammo lining the bunker. It stuck to everything and nothing could put it out until, hissing and spluttering, it guttered out. It even clung to the metal of the Argy guns, burning fiercely with the eye-stabbing, acetylene bright light of phosphorous. It was dripping off the machine-gun barrels so they looked like weird melting Halloween candles.

Screams of attack and screams of pain dominated the area. The whole ridge was alive with the brutal, vicious activity of war and shouts of command as A Company moved in, and they succeeded in clearing five or six of those misery-making bunkers on that spur and bought the battalion precious time to take stock.

They say necessity is the mother of invention so Sergeant Ted Barrett had organised some of the lads and a maul of six gimpys in one group and told the gunners to fire like fuck into the same trench at the same time. Forget the other fire trenches, he said, just pound hot lead into one while a pair of guys skirmish and crawl to within range to blast it with 66s or L2 grenades. Then when the lads who'd closed on the enemy position signalled that they were ready to rock, three of the gunners would switch their fire onto the next bunker that was about to be assaulted. The remaining three would hammer away on the first one.

Fire teams moved from one position to the next, whacking trenches from close range with 66s and grenades to finish it. The fuckers in the in-depth positions could plainly see what was coming their way. Not good for morale, that. And it destroyed the will of the Argies who were accessible on the lower part of the ridge.

On the other side of the gully Corporal Hardman's 2 Platoon section moved as well. They were going to attempt to push further up the gully to come around on the right side of the spur to outflank the positions on the high ground. No fucking chance. The whole area was a labyrinth of machine-guns nests and alive with tracer from the Argy positions further back to the right. It looked like the Argy guns had more layers than a fucking trifle.

They caused mayhem and Private Worrall, who'd been skirmishing his way up the incline with Lieutenant Coe, was shot in the stomach and had to lie in the open with rounds mercilessly hailing about him.

On the other side of the gully, a Tom called Kirkwood took a round in the leg and Ted Barrett was bowled over by the shock wave of a mortar blast while shouting for help to extricate Kirkwood from the shit. That's when Corporal Dave 'Pig' Abols and my best mate Steve Prior ran out under fire and dragged Kirkwood back into dead ground.

Worrall was still stuck out in the open and still at risk of being wasted by the enemy. What followed was an epic of military courage and comradeship and I'm not using that word 'epic' lightly.

Whenever I recall what happened I feel of wave of emotion at the loss of my friend, and I must confess I get a lump in my throat when I consider the raw courage and the modern chivalry displayed by Pig Abols and Steve Prior, backed up by a team of other paras. I'm glad to say Pig survived and was awarded the prestigious Distinguished Conduct Medal for his daring. Steve gave his life; he didn't live to tell the tale.

He was a mint guy, Steve. Quiet but no pushover and absolutely confident in his abilities as a soldier. Not only that but he was the first man in the battalion, officers included, to get a American Express card at a time when credit cards were so new they were still a status symbol. How could you top that one? In short, he was my hero back then and he's still my hero today.

Worrall was a mate too and he needed their help desperately. The boys responded with utterly selfless courage. Not just Pig and Steve, but Lieutenant Coe, Sergeant 'Sex' Hastings, four other NCOs and a few Toms as well. They risked their lives, either carrying the wounded and retrieving Steve when he died, or by exposing themselves to the Argies so that they could provide covering fire.

Paras don't leave wounded mates under fire. That is the bond that exists between airborne soldiers. The shared trust is that once fallen they will not be abandoned to die alone and to be left to the devices of the enemy; they won't be left under fire if it's humanly possible to retrieve them. To us that understanding is up there with Queen and country. Once out of the line of fire, the wounded are in the hands of fate as they wait for treatment while the rest of us get on with the fighting.

And that's just what happened. Pig and Steve had already burnt themselves as they skirmished forward through blazing gorse to back up the other lads who were attacking a fire trench. That's when they realised that Worrall had been hit and was lying on the other side of a low earth bank about thirty metres away in the killing ground of the enemy machine guns. They both ran forward to help him and Steve started giving his wounded mate first aid while incoming rounds screamed all around him. They could see it was bad and they were desperate to get Worrall over the other side of the bank and into some cover.

But thirty metres in that sort of hell is a very long way and it was snipers that they had to contend with next. They began crawling back on their bellies through the clumps of white moorland grass; Steve was dragging Worrall and Pig was at his shoulders helping to work their mate towards the earth bank. Every time a piece of their webbing or a glimpse of their heads was seen above the grass they could hear rounds from a single-shot Mauser sniper rifle whistling overhead.

It was a painstaking and tortuous process undertaken by both of them with absolutely no regard for their own safety, and it took them a mind-numbing half an hour to drag Worrall across twenty-five metres. At that point they couldn't go any further because they'd have had to drag him through the still smouldering and burning branches of the burning gorse.

Twice Pig went back and forth over the earth bank to organise covering fire, and on one of those times he discovered the guy who was supposed to be giving the fire had been hit himself by frag from an anti-tank weapon.

The plan was that the two of them would lob a smoke grenade as cover and as a signal for the fire to start in earnest, but when they'd done that and tried to leg it carrying Worrall they both tripped over because his webbing was getting tangled up in gorse roots. By the time they'd freed Worrall from the gorse, the smoke they'd laid had vanished, whipped away in the brisk wind, but they went for it anyway. They grabbed him and tried to leg it over the bank, but all the activity must have alerted a bastard of an Argy, who they'd already worked out was a sniper, and given him time to set himself up.

He was a predator waiting to take a chance, waiting to see what would be revealed when the smoke dissipated. He was in luck and as soon as Steve got up to make the run he was shot through the back of the head and fell stone dead onto the stricken and wounded Worrall.

Two more junior NCOs rushed to help Pig drag Steve over the bank when they realised he was dead. They then returned for Worrall. When it was over Pig dragged the guts out of a few fags, sorted out his ammo, then returned to the fight.

The prophecy Steve had made on the Norland had come to

pass. He had died so that someone else could live. Those words of his echo down the years and still raise the hairs on the back of my neck when I think of them.

There were fourteen untouched Argy fire trenches above the Gorse Gully and they were still dominating the battle. They'd brought the advance to a complete standstill.

And because those bunkers interlocked their arcs of fire with the group of machine guns eight hundred metres away at Boca House, they were also helping to keep B Company pinned down over on that side of the isthmus too. Same thing for the Boca House emplacements – they were helping to keep A Company on their faces. That's how interlocking arcs of fire work. It's a bastard to crack, and as daylight lit the whole scene Argy snipers joined in while it gave their mortars and artillery a field day.

Their artillery pieces, old but effective US-built howitzers, were back behind the front line of trenches in Goose Green and soon the battlefield was being painted with black blotches of exploding peat. Thank fuck for that peat; its cushioning effect saved many lives. On both sides.

As we watched events unfold, we quickly worked out that the Argy mortar and artillery fire was being very accurately directed onto our companies and sections as they deployed around the isthmus. It was plain that they were being orchestrated from behind our positions by observers tucked up in an OP on the high ground east of the area towards Cantera Mountain. They couldn't have been anywhere else to have seen so much of our deployment. Somewhere out there in a camouflaged position was a team equipped with high-powered bins and a couple of radio sets and they were literally calling the shots. We were spitting tacks about it as we lay on our bellies waiting for a move. If Patrols and Recce had been allowed to probe and penetrate the area while the battalion was stuck out on Sussex Mountain for six days we would have found those fuckers.

Fanning out across the country, stopping to observe the terrain closely, it's highly likely we could have tracked the bastards down to their lair. We had the skills and the knowledge, and we'd have bumped that OP, rolled the fuckers up and saved the battalion from a torrent of shit. We didn't because Brigadier Julian Thompson and the rest of the task force head shed had vetoed 2 Para forays out on the terrain in case we crashed into Special Forces. I reckon that was a crap decision.

While the Argy mortars and artillery were getting good coordinates from their OP at our backs and firing well-directed shots at multiple targets from well-embedded positions, our blokes were not faring so well. At least the artillery weren't.

They were set up back at Camilla Creek House and they lobbed about nine hundred rounds onto the set during the fourteen hours of the battle with little effect. Problem one was that they had the wrong strategy. They spent a lot of effort and shells trying to hit their rival team in the Argy battery. It didn't work because, unlike the Argies, we didn't have anyone who could eyeball their position and call in accurate fire. They were simply out of sight. Trying to shoot them up without a forward observer was like playing darts with a blindfold when the dartboard is in another room.

When they were tasked to give fire support to the rifle companies it didn't come off too well either because of various bullshit artillery technical problems. The wind factor, the trajectory, the depth of the peat the guns were on, the relaying of coordinates from the FOO, the price of fucking fish. Lots of problems with the artillery but very little effect. I know the gunners worked their bollocks off to keep their guns firing and they got themselves shot up by a Pucara for their troubles, but the truth is that they were pissing into the wind.

The mortar teams were another story. Low on bombs and knackered after carrying their heavy weapons to the battle, they still managed to keep banging bombs into the Argy positions.

However, without that old blue Land Rover stolen by the Argies, then nicked back again by 2 Para, the mortars would have been silent for much of the battle. There were no helicopters flying to resupply us with ammo and it was the light blue goddess that filled that vital role. One of the Toms stripped it of every seat except the driver's and even the radio to lighten it. Then it went back and forth between Camilla House five or six times during the night fetching bombs and ammo and returning with casualties.

As dawn rose, the Mortar Platoon had to move closer to the action, which meant humping everything to a new position 2,000 metres to the south of the original RV at the white bridge. And that meant the lads doing a shattering 4,000-metre round trip loaded with bombs to shift the stockpile they'd built up with the Land Rover earlier at the first position. They did the bomb-run marathon in a relay, taking it in turns, with every one of them doing it three or four times that night. Pure fucking endurance!

The lads were so desperate to hurt the enemy that they even stood on the base plates while they were firing to try to keep them stable. A couple of the Toms had their ankles snapped doing that and they were risking their lives with every shot. One slip could have found them leaning over the tube and they'd have earned themselves a flip-top head for their trouble.

But they soldiered on because the 81mm mortar can be a devastating weapon. I was with Mortar Platoon before I joined Patrols and one of the first lessons we learnt was that mortars were responsible for around a third of the British casualties in World War II; the second thing we learnt was that you have to move your hand quickly when you drop the bomb into the tube or you'll lose the fucker.

Operated by a good crew, an 81mm mortar can fire twelve rounds per minute. It's an interesting, though useless, bit of information but a good English bowman could loose the same number of arrows at the French during the Battle of Agincourt. That's some tradition passed down over the centuries. Coincidence? Heritage more like!

So there we all were, high and dry on Darwin in a shooting gallery with D Company out on a limb. A Company's swift dog-leg around the isthmus and the promising start to B Company's advance on Boca House had both hit brick walls. Not only that but the Argies had enough firepower in those combined positions to keep C Company pinned down well back from the stalemate, preventing them from rolling up behind A Company's own derailed advance.

Just to compound the growing chaos and dropping bollocks, the artillery support wasn't making a dent in the enemy, HMS *Arrow* had fucked off with her guns out of sorts and the Harriers couldn't fly because they were fog-bound on the carriers.

Most Toms believe that at this crucial point H's grip on the battle slipped a bit more. It's been said the battle could have gone either way. Wrong. It was rapidly sliding down the pan and it would only be the Herculean efforts of the ordinary paras that would stop it being completely flushed away.

The truth is that H's timetable was being torn to shreds by the Argy .50-cal rounds and he was rushing forward to move it on.

SIXTEEN

STAYING ALIVE!

THE AIR WAS SO thick with enemy rounds that Scouse McVeay thought he was going to get lead poisoning.

He was lying against a slight drop on the face of the spur leading out of the Gorse Gully, formed by the side of the track leading to Goose Green. His face was pressed against the wet grass and the enemy rounds were passing about three inches over his head. All the time.

The rounds whined in the air, then whacked into the ground a few feet behind him. His eyes were watering, his radio aerial had been snapped off by a round and he felt like he was naked in a hornet's nest.

Scouse was a larger than life character and his job was to be up front with the Toms to select targets for the mortars and call in their fire, but the only decent view he had that day was of the rim of his helmet. Alongside him were a party of bombardiers from the artillery battery. They had a similar job and a similar sodding view.

They knew exactly what their situation was because they'd fought and manoeuvred their way into it with the rest of A Company. They were pinned down and all that was between them and a coffin was that four-foot bank of peaty earth.

Marksmanship, courage, discipline, endurance and stoicism are all signs of a good soldier. But the skill that regulates all the rest, the one that keeps him alive, is his feel for the ground.

It starts off with training, where the basics are laid down. 'Stay low, move fast' is the one the airborne lives by but there are others. That feel for the terrain is developed on exercise and finely honed on active service; in our case on operations in the hostile IRA territory of South Armagh.

You can only explain so much of it in training; it's experience that counts and it suddenly clicks so that a good soldier adds an eye for contours to his collection of skills. It's a three-dimensional understanding of the ground around and in front of you in relation to your position and of course to the enemy's as well.

Experienced soldiers can tell at a glance if they should move to a point ahead or to one on either side, and factor their judgement of the elevation of the enemy guns into the instant equation. If it all adds up they will have found dead ground to evade the enemy's fire. Get it wrong and they'll be malleted.

That art of finding dead ground in the midst of mayhem and making use of it is crucial. And it's a fine art, where the best soldiers develop an intuition that will find cover with only inches of difference between life and death.

When they get to the dead ground soldiers know that the shape they make can define them as a target to enemy guns; they know that a silhouette against the skyline can be fatal and they understand how camo can help maintain their security. In the military it's called field craft, but at its most developed I'd class it as a sixth sense and there can be no doubt that a lot of good soldiers are born with it.

When a man breaks out of that invisible cone of safety he's established, it is usually a calculated and well-weighed risk and it's done for two reasons: to kill the enemy or to save a friend.

I believe that field craft together with courage were the two most important elements in 2 Para's success at Goose Green. Field craft saved scores of lives on that day and Scouse was one of its best exponents; he knew that the bullet-free bubble he was surviving in was small and could burst at any time but he knew exactly where it began and ended.

Because of their forward-spotting role, his group was bristling with radio antennae. Most of the signallers had snapped their aerials in half – the radios still worked but there was far less chance of them being pinpointed by the enemy.

One of the bombardiers shouted over to him: 'Can you see anything?'

He's joking, isn't he? thought Scouse.

'Someone had better have a look.'

'OK!'

Fuck it, thought Scouse. He was fed up. They'd been there for ages – he didn't know how long exactly but it was too long. They were sitting there like a tableful of blokes in a pub waiting for someone to call for a round. That's what he should have been doing, calling for a mortar round, so he slowly raised his head above the parapet.

'Whack!'

Scouse felt as though an invisible hand with a giant cricket bat had slammed the front of his helmet. He was thrown back across the track and for a few seconds he couldn't see anything and he didn't feel much either. He'd been hit. Fuck. Was he still alive? It seemed so, as the reality of the battle came swimming back into his consciousness. He looked for blood. There was none. He'd definitely been hit but he'd been lucky, and as rounds were slamming into the ground around him, he bundled himself back into the dead ground.

There was nothing he could do there any more. Scouse needed to be somewhere where he could see what was going on. He decided to move back a bound. A calculated decision. It was going to be dangerous.

Right! And Scouse was off like a bolting hare, weaving his way back under fire down to the big bank at the bottom of the incline on the shore of Coronation Bay. That's where Tac 1 were holed up.

As he sprinted the last few yards towards the narrow beach,

Scouse watched a group of paras walking the other way towards the most intense machine-gun fire imaginable. He couldn't make out who they were at first, he was too busy running, but then as he came up level with them he could see the colonel was striding out front.

'Calling in mortars, McVeay?' asked H, who knew everyone's name.

'No, sir,' answered Scouse. 'Just staying alive!'

With that, Scouse bundled over the earth and stone bank of the shore, then turned to watch H's party still moving up the incline towards the Gorse Gully with H ramrod-straight as his party skirmished around him.

Scouse managed to work his way back up to a spot where he could get a proper view of the enemy and then he was able to direct the mortars successfully. I know that because it was Scouse who saved my patrol when he called in fire to knock out that Argy tracking us with his mortar across the open ground.

Scouse thought that H's advance to the battle was one of the bravest and certainly one of the maddest things he'd ever seen. It was a bit of a Charge of the Light Brigade moment and Scouse reckoned that anyone who doubts H's determined courage should try walking with a straight back down the butts of a rifle range while live rounds from a gimpy are spinning around them.

Scouse removed his helmet to feel the bump on his head when he got into the beach cover and as he lifted it off it fell into two pieces. The Argy 7.62mm machine-gun round that had batted him off his feet had also split his helmet like a conker.

It was around 8.20 a.m. H and his Tac 1 group had already crossed an exposed piece of ground on the shoreline using a smoke grenade tossed by H to cloak their movement. That got them into a patch of gorse which would give them a bit of cover as they worked through it, then H came out of the gorse and strode on in no mood to be fucked about by anyone.

When he arrived at Dair Farrar-Hockley's side, those Argy trenches on the lower slopes had already been dealt with, but all efforts to sort out the line of trenches on the top of the ridge hadn't paid off. Going forward out of the gully was generally reckoned to be suicidal.

But H wasn't ready to accept that, he wanted to be certain. So he ordered Lieutenant Coe to get up to the gorse line in the neck of the gully to call down mortar fire on the trenches. Coe thought it was fucking hairy but he was game to try and he was going to go with the Tac 1 mortar officer, Mal Worsley-Tonks. They set off into the teeth of a gale of enemy fire tacking from side to side, but even as they were moving up the gully Dair was arguing fiercely that H was sending two officers to their deaths.

At first, H disagreed but Dair was absolutely certain they were taking their lives in their hands, so H took his word for it and he himself shouted after them and called them back. Just as well because the Toms who were watching, fascinated by the unfolding suicide mission, were also convinced the two officers were heading for a mortuary slab.

Another attempt by Coe to take a section to the right foundered in the face of a torrent of fire coming from the ridge. Bollocks.

With the stalemate showing no signs of lifting, the A Company Toms settled into a routine of firing between brews of tea so hot that they had to put masking tape on the rims of their tin mugs so they didn't burn their lips.

Some of the lads in the more exposed positions were constantly reminded of the fragile perimeter of their cones of safety by machine-gun fire whipping and whining above them. They were lying nearly horizontal as they slurped their brews or spooned porridge into their mouths.

Others with a bit more space were huddled in two or threes. They'd had no sleep for over thirty hours, and they weren't going to get any either, but they were able to warm themselves with a hot drink and rations, sort out their ammo and check their weapons.

One of the lads was even heard asking if anyone had a paper he could have a look at and some were dragging hard on cigarettes. A lot of Toms took up smoking during the war, then gave it up on the way home after puffing their way through their free issue of a thousand tactical fags.

But while some of the guys were refuelling, others were stagging them in the fight, and their platoon and section leaders were constantly chiselling away at the hill, looking for an opportunity to muster a unit together and then try to take it to the enemy. As a Tom from up North put it, the Gorse Gully was really a place for miners not pit managers. This was work for Toms and their corporals and they were already testing the ground. They didn't need the colonel to do it for them or even to tell them how to do it! They needed the colonel to arrange air strikes and bunker-busting fire support to bear down on the Argy trenches to help give them some leverage on the enemy.

As the deadlock continued, H was becoming more and more agitated and told one officer over the net who'd offered support, 'A Company got themselves into this and they'll bloody well get themselves out of it.'

I don't think A Company had got themselves into anything. Like the rest of the battalion, they'd been poorly served with intelligence about the enemy, and from day one they'd been denied every conceivable form of military support, from vehicles and tanks, through ammunition resupply to air strikes.

Now, to top it all, they had the worst possible nightmare to contend with: a boss who wanted to get down and dirty and re-invent the military wheel.

SEVENTEEN

MY BALL!

'DON'T TRY TO TELL me how to run my bloody battle!'

Not even the crackling interference on the radio net could disguise the cold indignation in H's clipped public-school accent.

It was about 9 a.m. and A and B Companies' stalemate along Darwin Ridge was in real danger of becoming a checkmate for the Argies when D Company's boss Phil Neame called on the net to offer a helping hand.

Neame and the lads were about three hundred metres from the narrow, shingle beach on the west coast, the other side of the isthmus, and he believed he could hook round on the Argy positions from the right, flank them and turn them over. He suggested to H that it was at least worth going round to have a look at the situation, but H was having none of it. His mind now seemed to be soldered onto A Company's problems and he snapped at Neame, giving him short shrift.

It wasn't the first time that H had been offered a leg-up and Neame wasn't the only officer to have suggestions and possible solutions to the continuing hold-up across the isthmus rejected with a snarl across the battalion net.

Because of our specialist role, C Company patrols could listen in to all the battalion frequencies and we heard a couple of H's comments flying over the net among the tracer rounds.

The first time he'd fucked off Neame's flanking suggestion was shortly after dawn when it would have been clear to a blind man that we'd just washed up against the main Argy line of defence. Fair enough. Early days, you may think. Let the boss see how things pan out before he calls on any other assets.

D Company was in a fold on the north-west side and spotted a trickle of about twenty Argies using the shoreline to their right as a rat run to get back to their mates. It was pretty obvious they were men who'd been caught out by the fighting with B Company. It was also pretty obvious that the fuckers wouldn't trolley along the beach if it had been seeded with mines – and if they could use it so could D Company.

Neame had been ordered to hold fast in that position as a reserve and await further orders, but seeing a good opportunity handed on a plate he radioed H and put the idea to him.

'Stop clogging the net; I'm trying to conduct a battle here,' was H's response.

Sitting out there in full view, D Company soon attracted the attention of the Argy artillery spotter in his OP behind our lines and shells started screaming in closer and closer until Neame decided to up sticks and fuck off into a fold where the lads couldn't be DF'd.

Even that simple and sensible use of his noggin, by a major no less, incurred the wrath of H who, when he was told that D Company were manoeuvring, obviously thought Neame was trying to pull a flanker. Literally! He seemed to think that a flanker pulled on the Argies was a flanker pulled on him, and H wasn't having any of it!

'Where the hell do you think you're going?' he shouted down the net to his company commander.

H wasn't happy but Neame promised him he wasn't going to interfere in the game plan and was only moving so that a third of H's troops weren't taken out by the howitzers. This was not good. Aggro with the Argies was the idea, not aggro between the bosses.

We were being held back in reserve in C Company too, although that had never been our role when we'd trained hard over the years. We were trained to infiltrate, recce, hold start lines, patrol and recce. We were the eyes and ears of the battalion.

When the action began we'd be used as a pretty flexible supply of battlefield replacements for the other companies as they began to take casualties, or else we'd be put into action immediately alongside one of them. I can't remember us ever being used as a reserve because we were considered too small a number.

That day though, the big day, we were being held back by Argy fire that had us pinned down and by H's seeming lack of the will to use us. We just lay out in the terrain, impotent to help A Company. Yet from our position well back behind the Gorse Gully we were staring at one target in particular which we would have loved to take. Darwin Hill seemed to be crying out for investigation.

'I wonder if there's a pub up there?' said one of the lads.

'Shouldn't think so,' I said. 'But I bet you there's a fucking good view down on those Argy bunkers.'

The reason we were so interested in Darwin Hill was that as the battle progressed it became obvious that there were no Argies up there on the highest feature in the battlefield. If there had been they'd have already shot the shit out of half or more of A Company and entered the history books as the winners. They certainly wouldn't have allowed A Company to take out those first few trenches on the lower slopes of the Gorse Gully before they'd finally hit a lead wall from the ones above. But there'd been no firing from Darwin Hill. We were certain there was no one up there.

There was a reason they hadn't taken that top spot and I think it was down to the weather. As the battle progressed most of us had worked out that a lot of the Argy positions weren't necessarily in the most strategic spots but they were definitely in the warmest ones. The fuckers didn't like that constant bone-chilling wind cooling down their thin tropical blood and it showed in the layout of their trench system.

That's why there was no fucker on Darwin Hill. Mines? Yeah, maybe they'd sown a minefield on it. That's what they'd done elsewhere on the battlefield. Their system on the Falklands seemed to be dig a trench in a warm spot and leave a wind-chilled minefield on the cold high ground.

So what? If we didn't have the knowledge, the training and the will to get through a minefield on Darwin Hill then we shouldn't have been on the battlefield in the first place. We had some kit that would make a path through a minefield called a Bangalore torpedo. It was an old Second World War weapon that was basically a long pole with charges attached down its length. You laid it on the mine-infested ground in front of you and blew the charges and in turn they set off the mines in the area and cleared a path.

The lads were all chomping at the bit to tab round with a few Bangalores, climb up onto Darwin Hill and get some LMG fire down onto their bunkers. We reckoned that all being well it would take us about an hour, an hour and a half to tab it and then we'd be in a commanding position above the whole trench system.

I still don't know why we didn't do that but I believe the order to scrub the idea came down the chain of command from H, though I'm not absolutely sure of that. I am sure that we missed a good opportunity to help end the bollocks in the Gorse Gully and give the enemy a severe slapping because it turned out we were right. There were no Argies on that hill and A Company were pinned down a lot longer that it would have taken us to do the tab to the top.

As it was we'd gone to ground in an extended line to the rear of the action, where we were in the money seats if all you wanted to do is watch the battle. We didn't want to watch, we wanted to fight, and our second in command, Lieutenant Kennedy, came up with another useful idea. It wasn't a battle breaker but it would have lent powerful support to the gimpys of A Company.

In our unit there were a dozen light machine guns and that amounted to a kick-arse collection of firepower which had fuck all to do because we were well back and our gunners, including my patrol's gunner Kev, couldn't make out who was friend and who was foe because of the distance.

Why not? thought Kennedy. Better than sitting on our arses doing nothing. So he got onto the net to A Company and asked for some help to direct our LMG fire. All he wanted was someone up front with A Company to tell our gunners who was who and get them on target. Our guns had the range but it was just a bit too far for the gunner's eyeballs.

Same sketch as with Neame.

'Get off the bloody net,' said the agitated H. 'I'm trying to fight a battle.'

Kennedy was well pissed off. We could see that. I doubt he was annoyed at any snub. That's not the army way. Short, sharp statements are a way of life for us and we get a lot worse verbal bollocks than that. No. I think Kennedy was just plain fucking frustrated. He'd come up with a valid use for our guns and been fucked off for no really good reason that I can think of.

An LMG is a pinpoint accurate weapon. Kev, who was a shit-hot shot, would often say that it was too accurate to be a real machine gun because they usually have a much wider beating zone. But from that range twelve of them smashing into one position after another with dartboard precision would have given A Company a real bunk-up.

One more officer was going to have a go at suggesting a way of breaking the deadlock in the battle. That was Major Hugh Jenner of Support Company. He'd been told by his Milan man, Captain Peter Ketley, that his crews were spotting quite a bit of movement on top of Darwin Ridge.

It was a fair bet that they were seeing Argies dashing here and there between trench positions. That meant Support Company had a bead on the actual trenches too, and in their armoury they had several Milan anti-tank missiles which, in the hands of a skilled operator, could be used as a devastating bunker-buster.

Good news you'd have thought. We had no effective artillery. The Royal Navy had fucked off with their 4.5-inch guns and there didn't seem to be any chance of a neat load of cluster bombs being delivered onto Darwin Ridge by a Harrier because they were all fog-bound on the aircraft carriers.

But at least we had one ace up our sleeves. The Milan crews could see the enemy trenches! Brilliant. Ketley was desperate to come forward and have a better look at the ridge to identify the targets and bring his missiles to bear on the Argy bunkers.

'No,' said H and he meant it. 'I don't want anyone coming forward until we sort this thing out. We've got enough trouble as it is; it's a difficult situation.'

It wasn't as brutal a rejection as 'Don't tell me how to run my bloody battle!' but it must have been fucking frustrating for Support Company.

The point was that Neame, Kennedy and Ketley all wanted to fight a battle too. They were professional officers, not time-wasters and not yes men, and they could see the way it was going. From their positions all three of them were able to offer suggestions that could have brought their units into play with devastating effect and could have tipped the battle our way. They were all back from the main clash of arms and had a clear picture of the action across much of the battlefield and they all had workable ideas.

And guess what? That's where H should have been. Not out of the line of fire altogether but far enough back to get an overall view of what was happening to his battle plan.

H wasn't bothered about their remedies for the Argy fire line. He was far too busy micromanaging A Company.

Nodding towards the top of the spur above the Gorse Gully he told A Company's OC, 'Dair, you've got to take that ledge.'

Ten minutes later Farrar-Hockley had gathered a force of about fifteen soldiers from various sections, among them Captain Dent, still lugging round the radio H had ordered him to carry, and the battalion adjutant Wood who was to his utter credit straining to have a go at the enemy.

The mortars laid smoke and off they went in a bit of an disorganised charge up the slope, with most of the blokes doing their own thing, weaving here and there under fire on the slope.

Dent got it first. Shot in the chest. He fell back on that bloody radio and was shot again. Wood was next. He was urging the lads on, saying, 'That's it. Airborne all the way. Remember Arnhem!' Then he died.

Jock Hardman was the third to die, shot up by the deadly interlocking and overlapping machine guns above in the ill-fated assault. Another one of the lads was forced to use Hardman's body as cover and a rest for his LMG and he could feel more rounds making his friend's body twitch as even in death Jock defended him.

My mate Gerry Toole called out to Dair, 'For fuck's sake, boss, if you don't get back now, you've had it; you're never coming back.'

The rest of the assault group worked their way back under intense fire, cursing the day as they did.

It had been a desperate waste of life, but H was still stubbornly refusing to budge from the Gorse Gully and take a look around himself, get his bearings, assess the situation properly. He seemed to be mesmerised by that smoke-filled hole of a gully.

God knows what he was thinking at that moment, because H had just sent his best mate Wood to his death.

EIGHTEEN

PIG'S LAW!

'COME ON, A COMPANY, get your skirts off!'

What a cry to battle! H was fired up and he was calling on his troops to follow him into the attack. At the same time he was calling into question their manhood as he tried to galvanise A Company and rally them to his side with a taunt.

'Follow me!' he yelled.

Guess what? They didn't.

A Company were in no mood for public-school gestures or bullshit rallying cries from the pages of *Commando* comic. They had the situation weighed up already. They'd watched the futile loss of three men's lives and they were in no mood either to get their skirts off or to follow him. They knew what was waiting for them up there in the Gorse Gully and they were going to sort it out in their own way and that didn't include charging into machine guns First World War style.

If H had bothered to ask them, they'd have told him that the route he was intending to use around the back of the spur led into the re-entrant where Monster and Tuffen had been shot up. There was no way through there. They'd tried that one.

If he'd stopped for just a moment and asked the Toms, they'd have also told him that A Company weren't out of the action. The gimpys were still stoically working away on eroding the will of the Argy trenches with their six-to-a-bunker attacks. A few of the blokes, notably NCOs, including Sergeant Major Price, Pig Abols and Gerry Toole, were still chiselling up the hill and about to start the fight again.

But H didn't stop to ask anything; he didn't even stop to brief his team or outline his intentions.

The only people who followed H were his 'personal' soldiers; his driver, the battery commander Sergeant Blackburn and his personal bodyguard Sergeant Barry Norman, together with a couple of his radio operators. They were brave professionals obliged by their duty to follow him come what may and they acquitted it with honour.

H was a fit guy and he was so quick off the starting blocks that when his team reacted he was already thirty metres ahead of them, rounding the spur of the re-entrant and preparing to take out a bunker to his left.

Then there was a warning shout: 'Look out, there's a trench to the right!'

Barry Norman instinctively hit cover while H turned to attack his bunker, going down on one knee to check the mag on his Sterling sub-machine gun before rushing on. Norman emptied a magazine into the trench H was attacking in a bid to give his boss some supporting fire. It was a terrible dilemma because he knew that the guns in the other trench were bound to open up. Of the two, the nearest was the better choice but really there was no best thing to do in those circumstances.

So he kept firing in support and screamed a warning to the colonel over the racket of machine-gun fire: 'Watch your fucking back!'

It was too late. The next burst of fire dropped the colonel, hitting him in the back. One of the Argies in the trench that H was rushing to attack leant out to try to finish him off. The colonel was lying directly in front of the trench but Norman kept the bastard back with a stream of accurate fire.

At that point H's radio operator, Blackburn, flashed out the message over the battalion net using the boss's call sign.

'Sunray is down!'

That signal was to become one of the iconic sound bites of the Falklands War, but as the word spread there was no panic in 2 Para, just steely resolve. We just added H's name to the list of mates we were going to avenge.

Norman couldn't do anything at all with such devastating firepower in front of him, but just lay there in cover unable to help his wounded colonel for over quarter of an hour.

Then suddenly the battle was turned by a quite independent attack and Pig did the biz in breaking the deadlock. He'd chipped away up that slope until he'd got into an outflanking position on the ridge, which had a view from one spur across the re-entrant to the other. Now he could see the machine gun that had killed H still knocking out bursts at anything that moved.

Pig bided his time. He hadn't got this far to waste the opportunity. He lay there with less cover than a stripper and waited for his moment. Lying on the ground next to him in the tussocks of grass and wilted bracken was the green plastic tube of a 66 rocket.

Slowly Pig prepped his weapon. Every movement was calculated not to alert the enemy to his presence as he prepared himself for a literally explosive burst of action. He slipped the front and back covers off the end of the disposable tube of the US-designed rocket, designated the 66 light anti-armour weapon. The LAW. He depressed the detent clip on the 66, releasing the telescopic tube to its full length, and as he did so the front and rear sights flicked up simultaneously and the weapon was primed. Still lying there in the midst of a bedlam of machine-gun fire, he slipped off the safety catch.

Then, in an inspiring act of courage, Pig jumped to his feet in the middle of a howling gale of machine-gun fire, lifted the rocket to his shoulder, lined it up on the bunker opposite, breathed out and squeezed down the rubber trigger on the top of the tube.

Whoomph!

The blistering white ball of an explosion enveloped the Argies in the trench. It turned out that the position he'd aimed at was the command bunker for the chain of trenches on the ridge. With that one act, Pig had broken the lynchpin in the Argy arcs of fire and shattered their resolve.

What he didn't know then was that he'd also avenged H's death. The last thing the bastard who shot the colonel saw was a para rising up from the ground to be his nemesis. Cool as fuck, Pig had delivered his verdict and carried out the sentence. It was Pig's LAW.

Scouse McVeay watched that action and told me Pig had stood in the lead storm as if he was fucking bulletproof. Pig puts it down to a calculated risk and he's right. He made his calculations in a soldierly way, then put in his attack at the moment of best opportunity. But it was a spectacularly brave act and white flags started appearing all along the Argy line.

In the space of twenty minutes two of our comrades, H and Pig, had carried out attacks that were so brave they would put the fear of God into any enemy. But they were very different in their nature. I believe H's death-or-glory dash into action was motivated by anger, passion and regret at the loss of his friend Wood. It was lion-hearted but ill-conceived and futile. It didn't make a difference to the battle.

Pig, on the other hand, had looked over the ground and seen the slimmest of opportunities. He had an idea and he was going to try it. It took half an hour for him to work his way into a place where he could show the Argies who was boss on that battlefield.

And it was that action, the culmination of a lot of nerve, balls and superb field craft, which broke the Argies, not H's emotional charge into the Valley of Death.

Only when Pig had bust the fire line could Barry Norman get to H's side to treat his wounds. He clamped field dressings onto them and then got a line into the boss and poured two bags of Haemacel drip into him as he slipped away into shock.

Scouse knew that something was seriously fucking wrong when

he heard someone calling for help. He thought it might have been Dair.

'Straight stretcher! Straight stretcher!'

Fuck. Must be serious. Someone needed a proper stretcher with poles down the sides on a day when most of the wounded had been dragged around on ponchos.

Up in the re-entrant someone ripped a piece of corrugated steel off the trench H had been assaulting to use that to carry him off the hill to a spot where a casevac airlift could be called in.

Dair had already been calling headquarters for a casevac for over an hour to attend to the other lads who'd been wounded and obviously he called again for H, but the colonel bled out waiting for a helo to arrive. He'd been hit in the groin and it was a femoral injury. No one thought he was going to make it. He died at 10 a.m.

'Boss! Sunray is down!'

When Crosland got the message from his signaller he did a double take and said, 'Are you certain?'

'Roger that, boss. The CO's down.'

Crosland's reaction is now legend among B Company's Toms and within 2 Para as well. He didn't waver or panic. His company was still pinned down by the Argy positions at Boca House. There were two or three bunkers where the bastards just wouldn't budge and they were dictating what moved over the ground.

He thought for a second then turned to his Tac team and shouted, 'Break out the Milans!'

At last, a solution to the deadlock. Things began to move quickly from that moment on.

Chris Keeble, the battalion second in command, was going to take over H's role but he was well back with Headquarters Company, so he put Crosland in charge for the hour or two that it would take him to get onto the battlefield.

Neame couldn't raise Crosland on the net – he was too busy

organising the Milan attack. But Keeble sanctioned a move along the beach by D Company.

Crosland and Neame were in the thick of it now, no longer held back by H, they were getting on with organising their renewed crack at the Argies. I'm not going to speak for the two of them, they're Ruperts and they live by the Ruperts' code, but the belief in the ranks is that H's death, tragic as it was, lifted a dead hand off their role in the battle.

The units galvanised themselves. Neame pushed his blokes along the beach and they set up a fire line of gimpy's facing the Argies in a flanking move.

B Company geared up for a push forward after being told by their OC that a Milan anti-tank team had been moved up with 5 Platoon about seven hundred metres to the rear. They were chuffed. They'd been waiting for a bit of support. But it wasn't going to come easy, as a mortar landed near the Milan team and some of them got fragged.

That didn't put the fuckers off though. In fact, nothing was going to stop those leery fuckers in the Milan team firing their missile, because if they managed to fire one and hit the Argies on the nose it would be the first claimed hit from a Milan fired in anger by British forces.

History beckoned, but it was nearly history for some of B Company when the guys from Support Company unwrapped their Milan, taking the protective 'feet' from either end and tearing off its plastic covering. Once set up on its firing post, they sighted it on the most dangerous of the bunkers.

'Fire!'

The first missile dribbled off the firing position, fizzing like a wet firework, then started wandering around B Company's position like a jump-started spaceship trying to work up some speed. Little Bish ducked as it zipped around between him and Headquarters Company, then breathed a sigh of relief as the rogue spluttered and dropped out of the sky.

Two more were fired and B Company watched as the fireball of the rocket slammed into the bunker. A survivor leapt out and began dancing around in pain and terror. He ran to the next bunker and dived into it. There was nowhere to hide, though, as the next Milan slammed into his new refuge. Game over. And it was for the rest of them too.

Outflanked by Milans and D Company's gimpys, the Argies had witnessed a fatal firepower display that they didn't want to see again. The white flags began appearing over bunker after bunker.

NINETEEN

SUNRAY IS DOWN

THE FIRING HAD STOPPED and an eerie silence had fallen over the battlefield when we entered the Gorse Gully, where A Company had fought their hearts out during the night. Here and there tracer rounds and white phosphorous grenades had set the gorse ablaze and the peculiar acrid smoke of a heath fire blew over us, but it failed to fumigate the stench of battle.

That's where I found Gerry Toole exhausted, spent by the ferocity of the battle and the loss of our mates, but alive. That's where I found Steve and Jock Hardman too, laid out on the cold ground, their bodies shrouded by ponchos.

I walked over and took one last look at them. Their hands had been put in their pockets. It was strange. They were paras; you never saw them with their hands in their pockets. But Scouse McVeay said that way it would be easier to get them into the body bags later on.

We saw Dair there too, sitting on a bank, smoke from the burning gorse lifting and billowing over him, making his eyes water, as tears cut streams through the camo cream on his face.

Sleepy had been in his company before he'd joined Patrols and Dair called him over.

'Mark.'

'Boss.'

'It was terrible. Bloody awful. The colonel's gone, you know.'

Scouse was scooping food out of his tin mug into his mouth. Dent was dead, hit by three rounds, so Scouse hadn't had to share his last packet of porridge with the captain. He was glad at the time. Not that the captain was dead but that he didn't have to share his food with him. That's the way it was. The need to survive came before anything else. That promise they'd made to share his last sachet of porridge didn't have to be kept and Scouse felt guilty that he was glad.

Then we went up into the waxworks to sweep through the Argy bunkers and mop up any of the enemy left behind and I found that young Argy officer and took his surrender as he died.

'If you're ever in the Shot, I'll buy you a beer.'

Nearby, Sleapy found another Argy clinging on to life, his guts hanging out from a wound. The area was littered with the dead and dying, blood-soaked shell dressings, bits of used medical kit, thousands of empty cases and lots of shit. The guy he'd found was older than the rest and he was sporting a big gaucho moustache. He was obviously a warrant officer, one of the professionals in the Argy army. Lying near him was a discarded, scoped Mauser bolt-action rifle. He was a sniper.

He was sitting up, and called out '*Médico*' to Sleapy, probably because he had a small red cross painted on an old 44 pattern water-bottle pouch that held his med kit. Sleapy was ex-A Company. His mates were dead so he didn't like the look of that fucker.

He couldn't see the sniper's right hand so he stuck his boot square on his chest and pushed him over just to make sure he didn't have a hidden weapon. It was rough handling but justified by the need to keep alive.

Sleapy admits to feeling a deep hatred well up inside him when he saw that sniper rifle and thought of his dead mates. He considered using an Argy .45 Colt pistol he'd picked up to finish the wounded man off, but he fought back the urge and like the rest of us kept discipline. Even so, we'd become desensitised.

I'd had those same feelings of hatred and a burning urge to

blow away the young officer I dealt with, even though I could see the man was on the point of death. The loss of our friends robbed us of compassion. They were the enemy. They'd killed our mates. They were just dummies in the waxworks to us.

Sleepy doesn't know whether that sniper survived. His injuries were severe and he probably didn't make it, but all the wounded Argies were casevaced and given good treatment once the fires of battle had cooled.

As we stood around at the top of the ridge, there was a lot going through our minds. Why had H done that? Why had he charged up that the Gorse Gully? It seemed like madness to us.

Much has been said and written about H's death, but my opinion is not one made with the benefit of hindsight. It was formed there on the top of that ridge in the half-hour or so after the colonel's death. It is an opinion that is held by most of the Toms who were there in the battle too.

The first thing I have to say is that H Jones was the best boss I ever had in the army. He was a cracking bloke and when he joined the battalion he made an immediate impact. The hard-core Toms loved the way he would call a battalion meeting in the drill hall and then announce, 'Right, now that you're all here we're going on a ten-mile run.'

All the fat HQ wallahs, drivers and officers, who would normally be able to skive off a battalion run, were trapped and H would run the fuck out of them. He worked us hard and he'd given us a touch of the old-time airborne-assault identity that tended to come and go depending on who the CO was.

It was as if he had some premonition that we would be doing something extraordinary, outside the normal run of the British Army's duties; something even more dangerous than our anti-terrorist role in Northern Ireland.

To that end he worked us on battalion-scale exercises and that training was to serve us well on the Falklands. Without his audacious attack on the generals we wouldn't even have been in the Falklands. It was H who persuaded them to bin the Anglians and send us as the spearhead battalion instead.

Not only that, he made one vital decision without which we would probably have been creamed by the Argy gun lines at Goose Green. H insisted that we should double up the number of GPMGs we took to the Falklands and we actually nicked most of the poor bloody Anglians' gimpys to take with us. Talk about adding insult to injury.

Having said all that, I do not believe it's right to shirk away from the fact that he unravelled at Goose Green. I'm a soldier and I don't criticise him for it in any angry sense because I understand the pressure he was under. I blame the task force command for much of it. When we went into battle at Goose Green it was the spearhead attack of the war, the first clash of arms on the ground. H and 2 Para were carrying the pride of the nation on our shoulders. Fuck knows, people get lathered up enough when England plays Argentina in the World Cup, and there was a lot more at stake at Goose Green than a trophy.

I don't know what was going on with the head shed but all I can tell you as a guy on the ground is that we didn't have air, sea, tank support, proper intelligence or even basic supplies of ammo. I'll never believe that 'gun out' bollocks unless one of the ordinary jack gunners tells me it's true. Then again, the day after the battle the sky was alive with helicopters flying missions. Volvo Snowcat cross-country vehicles appeared as if by magic the day after we'd so desperately needed transport for kit and ammo.

The pressure was on H but he put pressure on himself too. His tendency to micromanage came bursting to the fore and got worse when the battle began. One moment he was urging Dair and A Company to get on with it; the next, after they'd swept through Coronation Point, he held them up for an hour while he came to check the situation personally.

This refusal to give his officers their head and trust their judgement on that day was a real problem. D Company could have made that left-flanking move early in the battle but he just gave Neame an ear-bashing over the suggestion.

To be honest, a lot of D Company guys don't have much of a good word to say about H. They believe that he saw Neame as some sort of competition. Neame was pure para, not a blow-in from a crap-hat regiment; he was popular and he was a laid-back winner.

At any rate, there were moments in the battle when Neame, Crosland and Kennedy of my Company, C Company, all offered credible suggestions to rip into the enemy and had them kicked into the long grass.

But the decision that most Toms found unbelievable was H's rejection of Ketley's offer to mallet the Argy positions on the ridge with Milans. The battle was in the balance. Men were losing their lives. Why not break the gun line with rockets and then let the Toms sweep through without running the gauntlet of the withering fire that was putting their lives at risk?

What made it worse is that we knew that H was conserving his supply of Milans because intelligence reckoned that the Argies had Panhard armoured vehicles on the islands. H was keeping the rockets in case they showed up somewhere along the line. But the French-built Panhards were light armour and they weren't even tracked vehicles. They certainly wouldn't be able to operate off the tracks, criss-crossing the camp, and anyway our immediate problem was the need to bust the bunkers holding us back. Break out the Milans! That was the right order.

Neither did any of us rate the fact that H was so close to the action. He was not doing the Toms in his battalion any favours. We needed him to be near but not underfoot. He should have been conducting the battle, not fighting it. H was doing Toms' work but he could never do it as well as we could. He was the colonel; we were the fucking cannon fodder.

I believe that he simply became mesmerised by the battle in the Gorse Gully and his judgement became unbalanced. When his friend Wood died I reckon he then decided to do what he believed was the honourable thing and try to sort it out himself. It's been suggested that he may not have known that Wood was dead. Rubbish. News like that spreads fast by shouts across the battle.

'Wood's down! Dent's down!'

That's the way the news would have travelled the eighty metres or so from the ridge to the dead ground where H was lying up. Dair himself came running back to that position after seeing them die and I know the guys all around him were aware of the three deaths on the ridge.

I think that news tipped H into an ill-conceived action, and he rushed off without a plan and without too much concern for the danger he was putting his personal team into either.

His 'get your skirts off' call to arms was not inspiring and his action was all risk and no calculation, and contrary to the citation for his Victoria Cross he never fired a shot. It didn't break the battle and it didn't inspire his troops. They were just getting on with it and quite honestly wishing the boss would bugger off and bother some other company.

No surprise then that the award of the VC to H was controversial. The citation in the *London Gazette* on 11 November 1982 reads:

On 28th May 1982 Lieutenant Colonel Jones was commanding 2nd Battalion The Parachute Regiment on operations on the Falkland Islands. The Battalion was ordered to attack enemy positions in and around the settlements of Darwin and Goose Green.

During the attack against an enemy who was well dug in with mutually supporting positions sited in depth, the Battalion was held up just South of Darwin by a particularly well-prepared and resilient enemy position of at least eleven trenches on an important ridge. A number of casualties were received. In order to read the battle fully and to ensure that the momentum of his attack was not lost, Colonel Jones took forward his reconnaissance party to the foot of a re-entrant which a section of his Battalion had just secured. Despite persistent, heavy and accurate fire the reconnaissance party gained the top of the re-entrant, at approximately the same height as the enemy positions. From here Colonel Jones encouraged the direction of his Battalion mortar fire, in an effort to neutralise the enemy positions. However, these had been well prepared and continued to pour effective fire onto the Battalion advance, which, by now held up for over an hour and under increasingly heavy artillery fire, was in danger of faltering.

In his effort to gain a good viewpoint, Colonel Jones was now at the very front of his Battalion. It was clear to him that desperate measures were needed in order to overcome the enemy position and rekindle the attack, and that unless these measures were taken promptly the Battalion would sustain increasing casualties and the attack perhaps even fail. It was time for personal leadership and action. Colonel Jones immediately seized a sub-machine gun, and, calling on those around him and with total disregard for his own safety, charged the nearest enemy position. This action exposed him to fire from a number of trenches. As he charged up a short slope at the enemy position he was seen to fall and roll backward downhill. He immediately picked himself up, and again charged the enemy trench, firing his sub-machine gun and seemingly oblivious to the intense fire directed at him. He was hit by fire from another trench which he outflanked, and fell dying only a few feet from the enemy he had assaulted. A short time later a company of the Battalion attacked the enemy who quickly surrendered. The devastating display of courage by Colonel Jones had completely undermined their will to fight further.

Thereafter the momentum of the attack was rapidly regained, Darwin and Goose Green were liberated, and the Battalion released the local inhabitants unharmed and forced the surrender of some 1,200 of the enemy.

The achievements of 2nd Battalion The Parachute Regiment at Darwin and Goose Green set the tone for the subsequent land victory on the Falklands. They achieved such a moral superiority over the enemy in this first battle that, despite the advantages of numbers and selection of battle-ground, they never thereafter doubted either the superior fighting qualities of the British troops, or their own inevitable defeat.

This was an action of the utmost gallantry by a Commanding Officer whose dashing leadership and courage throughout the battle were an inspiration to all about him.

That's why H got the VC, but the opinion of his bodyguard Barry Norman was a bit more stark. He reckoned that as a strategy H's action wouldn't have passed Junior Brecon – that's a basic battle course run on the wilds of the Brecon Beacons for junior NCOs.

Should H have got the VC? Well, certainly the battalion deserved a VC and in that sense the award to its colonel may have some justice in it.

But the Toms' award for Man of the Match goes to Pig Abols, not just for that cracking piece of work with his LAW up on the ridge but for the two rescues of wounded comrades he'd carried out under fire earlier in the battle. The hard-arsed rescue he carried out with my mate Steve was VC stuff all on its own.

It would have been quite something if Pig had got the VC. His father was a Latvian, who like many of his countrymen and the entire nation of Finland decided to fight for Hitler against the Russian Communists. Not much of a choice really, Hitler or

Stalin. They were as bad as each other. But if Pig had got the VC he could have stuck it on the mantelpiece with the German Iron Cross his father won on the Eastern Front!

Pig didn't get the VC of course, H did, but nothing that I say is a criticism of H in that sense, even if it does sound harsh. Toms don't think that way. We just say it like it is because to do otherwise would be disloyal to our mates who died that day. Christ knows how I would have performed if I'd had to lead a whole fucking battalion. H did what he did; it's just that some of it wasn't great on the day. I just know that H shouldn't have been where he was when he died. And I wish he'd survived. I wish they'd all survived.

There's no hindsight in any of this. A lot of these thoughts were going through my mind after speaking to my mate Gerry Toole, who gave me a quick sit-rep on what had happened in the Gorse Gully. Most of my opinions were formed on the day up there on the ridge surrounded by the blasted and shot-up Argy positions. They haven't changed over the years. They were formed while me and the guys in the patrol spoke over a brew on that freezing wind-buffeted ridge. We had muted, clipped conversations about the mates we'd lost and of course about that most extraordinary happening for any soldier: the loss of our leader.

It was a weird one. The colonel's not supposed to die. He's the chief, we're his tribal warriors. We're the ones who are supposed to get it if anyone does. But in this battle 2 Para had lost two captains and their colonel in the space of half an hour in the same godforsaken gully. It was a moment to pause, time for a double take, but it wasn't a morale-busting blow. We were just more determined to steam into those Argy bastards.

Not much time to crack our jaws about it all then, though; there was more work to be done. But as we picked up our kit Steve said, 'What the fuck was H doing there? He shouldn't have been anywhere near that shit.'

'Yeah,' I agreed. 'Remember? He did the same thing in Kenya. He was always rushing to the fucking front of the queue for bullets. I tell you, there's nothing more dangerous than a Rupert without a fucking plan.'

That's when our captain, Paul Farrar, came along and I asked him, 'Boss, when the fuck are we gonna get some in?'

We could see Goose Green about two klicks away in the distance, the sea shining lead grey where a shaft of sunlight had managed to squeeze itself through a layer of cloud so thick it looked like it was going to fall on us.

'Nah,' said the boss, 'don't think so, Geddes. They'll be surrendering soon, a walk-through talk-through. It's going to be pretty academic from now on.'

TWENTY

THE SCHOOL HOUSE

'COME ON! COME ON! Move! Move! Move!!'

Here we go again! We were playing Russian roulette with a dozen .50 cals and a bewildering array of Argy support fire. Same sketch as the run in to the Gorse Gully, but this was worse. Much worse.

It was the second time in the space of an hour that we'd advanced into battle in broad daylight across open ground in full view of the enemy, and I was shaking like a shitting dog.

The random chattering of machine guns was joined by the deafening explosions of Oerlikon anti-aircraft rounds fired directly at us. They were soon joined by artillery, Pucara 20mm cannon, napalm and even Viper mine-clearing explosive charges catapulted into the air like some deadly giant serpent from a fairy tale.

And there were more snipers at work than before too. Single-shot Mauser rifle bullets ranged in and smacked the ground too close to call. Nothing random about them. Individual rounds telescoped for an individual's death.

'Move! Move! Move!'

I gritted my teeth and went for it. Fire and manoeuvre! Fire and manoeuvre! The patrol fanned out around me and we went for it. Young Pete Myers wasn't pretending he was out for a jog any more. Steve Jones had a steely look as he went all Men of Harlech on us and Greg Cox had his Geronimo grin pasted onto his face. The redoubtable Kev, weighed down by the LMG, brought up the rear as usual.

As we ran, crouched, fired then ran again, men were going down wounded all around. I saw half of one guy's arm draped over a tussock of grass like a glove lost on a walk. Then our company Tac was hit and two signallers went down to sniper rounds, marked out for deadly attention by their radio aerials.

'We're going to pop over to the airfield and see who's over there,' Farrar had told us when we'd set off from Darwin Ridge five minutes earlier. 'Shouldn't take long. We'll probably mop up a few air force personnel and that'll be that.'

He believed the Argy defences had been dealt with and the rest of the battle would be a walkover, so we gathered up our weapons and headed down the long forward slope.

The ground fell away towards a small, saltwater creek before it rose again more sharply to flatten off into a small plateau above the sea. We could see the simple grass airstrip to our right, almost straight ahead of us was the schoolhouse and between the two lay a dairy building. The houses of Goose Green itself were clearly visible behind those first three features.

Down in the narrow valley between us and the airfield, I could see D Company coming in from the right-hand side having hooked around the back of the completely subdued Argy main lines on the ridge.

They looked like a crowd of soccer hooligans as they marched along exhausted, spread out but not in any recognisable skirmish formation at all. I could see the bandoliers of ammo around their necks glinting in the sun. Soccer yobs? Maybe not. More like Viking raiders looking for a church to sack.

As we advanced towards Goose Green, it must have occurred to our second in command that we looked a bit like the opening scene from *Dad's Army*. He began whistling the theme tune to the series.

Pop over to the airfield? A walk-through, talk-through? I don't fucking think so. We hadn't gone more than fifty metres when the shit hit the fan. Suddenly Kennedy's whistling of the *Dad's Army* theme tune stopped and the Argy mortars started whistling *Evita*. Havoc followed in spades.

Over to my left, somewhere among Dick Walsh's patrol, Sleapy heard a high-velocity round thud into the ground a few feet to his right. That's not effective enemy fire, he thought; no need to take cover.

Twenty seconds later, another round came in, still slightly right. It was obviously long-range. A fucking sniper! But he didn't forget his field craft. Sleapy went through a mental inventory. Why had the fucker picked on him? Did he think he was a Rupert? Maybe a radio operator? He checked to make sure his map wasn't showing, making him stand out from the others. It wasn't. Another round thudded in, still wide. Sleapy took the hint and began to skirmish his way down the ridge.

All along the line of the ridge, from the schoolhouse to the airfield, machine-gun bunkers revealed themselves with stabbing points of muzzle flashes and streamers of tracer rounds. The landscape erupted again with the hellish pyrotechnics of war and confusion of battle.

Crackling machine guns and whistling mortars began their terrible music and then the Argy artillery sited somewhere in Goose Green opened up. Twenty-five-pounders and 105mm US howitzers. Their crews must have been frantically spinning the wheels that angled the barrels to get our range. Their shells screamed in as they joined the mayhem.

But the Argies had saved some surprises for us too. More weapons joined in the symphony.

Boom! Boom! Boom! Boom!

The base line was provided by Oerlikon anti-aircraft guns stationed around the airstrip as the crews reset them in their ground role. They sounded like slave masters beating out a rhythm for the rowers on an ancient galley. With four barrels each, firing two at a time, they'd also been spun down to fire straight over the slope and airburst shrapnel above and around us. Just what we fucking needed.

There was more though. The bastards has stripped the anti-tank rocket pods off a disabled Pucara and strapped them onto the school playground slide then rigged the electronic firing trigger with a car battery. Very inventive. We heard the rockets leave the pods and watched their smoke trails as they streaked out into our lines before exploding with sharp cracks.

'Fucking hell, Steve! They're giving it fucking everything. They must have known Patrols were coming for them!' I shouted to my second in command.

'It's no fucking joke, Johnny,' he screamed over the racket of the armaments trying to cream us.

We were flat on the ground now, trying to work out what was what in the midst of the bedlam. I reckoned the notch of a valley leading to the salt creek beneath the schoolhouse was the only option.

'Move! Move! Move!' I shouted to the lads.

Forward. No going back. No one even thought of going back. Fire and manoeuvre. Stay low, move fast. Eyes like a bulldog's bollocks, constantly seeking cover or the slightest depression that might offer dead ground. Return fire. Manoeuvre.

Keep moving forward. We were running across open ground again under effective enemy fire. We were pushing our luck to the limit; we had no more cards to play.

The incoming was unbelievably intense. The anti-aircraft bursts made strange explosive patterns ten feet above the ground and they were coming over us at a huge rate from the four-barrelled monstrosities pumping them out. Mortars kicked up plumes of black peat that spurted into the air like small oil strikes around the battlefield. The rockets kept piling in from the school slide.

There were so many munitions going off that cordite smoke billowed across the face of the long slope in thick clouds. We took it as a gift from the enemy – in some places that smoke from expended munitions was the only cover we had.

We'd set up the gunners with their LMGs on our right flank to give supporting fire to the advance should we need it. Should we fucking need it! The enemy were throwing everything at us and the LMGs were going to be lifesavers with their deadly accuracy at long range.

Kev was firing away at the Argy trenches with Bob McNally alongside him using a pair of bins to direct his fire as they tried to suppress the Argy fusillade. Then Bob saw a peach of a target.

'Kev!'

'Yeah.'

'There's a fucking Pucara taxiing on the runway!'

Kev looked up from his sights and saw the plane too. It was a gift. Kev had a grim smile on his face as he angled the LMG and pumped out a burst at the aircraft.

'Left five.' Bob corrected his fire as he watched the tracer in Kev's rounds splashing in towards the plane.

Another burst. This time Kev was bang on. Bob watched tracer rounds hit the fuselage and burst off it like showers of welder's sparks while the other rounds tore holes in the side of the aircraft. The cockpit windows burst inwards as the bullets struck.

'Got him! Same again!' Bob's voice was the urgent voice of a hunter not wanting to lose his quarry.

Kev squeezed another burst out and tore more strips off the fucking aircraft. Maybe it was the one that had shot down and killed the Scout pilot Dick Nunn. Kev gave it his all, but the Pucara had already stopped moving. Bob reckoned no one got out of it, and the pilot was dead.

Nice shooting, Kev. What a star! He'd banged up an Argy Pucara on the runway. That's one hell of a notch to have on your holster.

But Kev's triumph was in stark contrast to the bollocks raining in on us, and within five minutes C Company had as many wounded. There were bits of blokes everywhere.

Tony Tye went down to my left, shot in the upper arm, and I heard Big Bish calling on Chopsey to go and patch him up while he kept firing furiously at the enemy. Chopsey worked his way over to Tony and was dressing his wounds when an Oerlikon anti-aircraft shell ripped his leg off.

'Fuck! Chopsey's down too!'

I could hear myself thinking, 'Poor fucker – he's only just got over his sunburn!'

Then halfway down the slope our OC, Major Jenner, and his Tac group were hit by a shell, howitzer or Oerlikon, I'm not sure. But it was a direct hit on their group and it knocked his gunner over with a chest wound. Jenner was hit too and so was one of his radio operators. Charlie Holman-Smith, another of Jenner's signallers, dashed forward to retrieve the wounded gunner's gimpy. It was desperately needed.

Charlie had the weapon in his hand and he was on his set giving a sit-rep to Tac 1 because the boss was wounded.

Dick Walsh heard Charlie call it on the net: 'We've got three down.'

'Whack!' A round struck him. Maybe it was a piece of mortar frag.

'Make that four! I've been hit too!'

Charlie died almost as the words left his lips. What a man. He kept doing his job right up to the end.

The only thing we could do was to keep moving. Dick and Sleapy were working their way through this fucking turkey shoot when Sleapy heard a big thud ahead of him. Time seemed to slow down, as he found himself staring at the fins of a big Argy mortar round about ten feet away. As he ran for his life he swears it felt as though his feet were going nowhere.

A hundred metres from the valley and rounds marked by our own red and white tracer started whining over our heads much too close for comfort. The machine-gunners in Support Company were up on Darwin Hill at last, giving the trenches around the school a hammering. A couple of them fired so much that the flash suppressors on the ends of their barrels melted and dropped off. And still they kept firing!

But the machine-gun platoon's fire was so close that they were about to hammer us too, so a couple of the guys in Jacko Jackson's patrol took their red berets out of their patch pockets, stuck them on the end of their bayonets and waved them around. It did the trick: they switched their fire.

By then we understood the confusion. A few dead Argies, who came from an Argy rangers unit, were wearing black or green woollen combat hats. So a lot of the guys put their red berets on – to keep the friendly fire away.

By this time Big Bish had all but taken over as platoon sergeant and screamed out a fire control order: 'Three hundred. Top floor. Schoolhouse. Rapid fire!'

This focused most of the lads and brought many weapons to bear on the Argies in sandbagged positions up there. The whole platoon opened up simultaneously and ripped into the top floor of the building, turning window frames into matchwood.

'Fix bayonets!' Fuck, this was getting really serious.

We fixed the steel on our rifles, peeled right and headed down into the maelstrom. About forty metres left to the small valley leading up from the small saltwater estuary at the foot of the schoolhouse slope and I was sprinting for my life again. The firing had become more and more intense the closer we got to their positions, but ahead of me I could see the sanctuary of the dead ground.

It was weird but the area sheltered from the Argy fire had an almost tangible sense of tranquillity. The air around was alive with gunfire and danger as I was conscious of the mounting casualties. I was aware of the rounds in the air. You're not supposed to be able to see supersonic bullets in flight but perhaps there's another level of awareness when there is so much fucking danger about. Running like hell, I headed for tranquillity.

'Come on! Come on!'

As we dived into the haven of the gully we bumped into a load of lads from Recce Platoon looking shocked and chin-strapped.

The patrols were now spread to the four winds. I think the platoon commander and his team were on the far left as we fought forward.

Baz, the sergeant major, had joined up with us after the Tac HQ had been wasted on the forward slope. He was the only one of us with a helmet on. I remember feeling really jealous of his helmet.

We all took a breather in the dead ground. And what a place! The tide was out and the creek we were hiding in was a mesh of thick-skinned saltwater plants resting on a slimy bed of mud, and all around were the carcasses of dead sheep in various stages of decomposition. My stomach churned from the stink. It really was dead ground.

Head count! Are the boys all right? A quick look around and a patrol roll-call reassured me. All present but not a lot was fucking correct.

I spotted Tom Harley from D Company up on the ridge above us. He was point man in the point section again. Right up the front of the fucking bus as usual. Tom quickly organised anyone who had a gimpy or an LMG into a fire support platoon tucked away in a little cleft to the right of the schoolhouse.

What was left of the Patrols Platoon amounted to ten or twelve guys; a mixture of several patrols. Taking cover in a ditch, the dirty dozen huddled in a snake with me and Baz at the head. Quick battle orders were being briefly formed as the two of us weighed up the approach to the schoolhouse. Tom barked orders from the high ground. Then Pete Adams, captain and second in command of D Company, joined us. He was a former commander of Patrols and I could see the pride on his face as he waved in acknowledgement. We were still his boys and we both knew that soon there would be a free-for-all scrap and it was going to be fast and furious. Very furious.

News of a white-flag shooting had reached us with the arrival of the lads from D. In snatched breathless bits of conversation they told how they'd fought some Argy trenches to the point of surrender at some bunkers near a flag pole at the furthest end of the airstrip.

A young Rupert, Lieutenant Barry, had gone forward under an Argy white flag of truce to arrange the surrender with Corporal Sullivan and Lance Corporal Smith. There was some fire from their in-depth positions and from our own machine-gun platoon flying around. The Argies must have known there was confusion about but as the three paras approached they opened fire. It was a heinous crime according to the Geneva Convention and according to the laws of war. It was a fucking bushwhack!

Colour Sergeant Taff Meredith, a fearless fighting man, couldn't believe his eyes and instantly took action. Single-handedly, Taff assaulted the bunker and the forward sections also joined in and devastated the position with gunfire as Taff took a terrible revenge. There were no survivors.

What the cowardly bastards had done was to shoot all three of our men where they stood out in the open. I've heard excuses for what they did, but they'd shot our mates from behind the cover of a white flag and we had no excuses for them.

Above us was the schoolhouse which the Argies had sandbagged and fortified. All around it were machine-gun trenches. They'd dug in there because the school overlooked a bridge carrying the track over the estuary creek into Goose Green.

I was seething. We were all seething. I looked up at the school-house where Argies were pouring fire out of the windows and from trenches in the playground. Killing under a flag of truce! Trenches in a playground! Automatic rifle fire from a school! Bastards. What the hell were they doing in a place where kids should have been learning and playing?

Suddenly I felt an ice-cold anger sweep over me. I'd been furious at Warren Point in Ireland when the IRA bombed the lads. But this was different. It was a cold clinical anger because there at Goose Green I could see exactly where the enemy were and knew exactly what I could do about it. Those shits in the schoolhouse were going to get some. And I could feel that very same anger pulsing almost tangibly from the men kneeling around me.

Sleapy had a horrible fixed smile on his face. Jonesy had a faraway killing look on his face and Dick Walsh, ever the professional, looked like a dentist about to pull a tooth. I know I had some bastard's death in my eyes. This was going to be an NCOs' and Toms' action from start to finish.

Baz Greenhalgh, our company sergeant major, was the senior rank in our group and he uttered two simple words that had inspired men all day on that battlefield.

'Follow me!'

As we moved off to attack the building, we passed Tom Harley and told him we were going to storm the schoolhouse from the left flank and then dropped all our heavy kit off with him. I stuffed a fresh matchstick into the sears of my SLR. I remember slapping Kev on the shoulder and saying, 'Remember the Alamo!' What was all that about? Perhaps I'd slipped into my film-star fantasy.

Oh shit! Here we go! As we manoeuvred into our FUP, our forming-up position, I heard the roar of aircraft engines. First one in was an Aeromacci and cannon fire started hitting the ground over to the right near D Company. The next thing I heard was an explosion and a cheer from D as the jet hit the ground whacked by a Blowpipe missile.

The whine of another aircraft over to my right. A Pucara! It was swooping low over D Company.

I called out to Steve, 'Funny their planes can fly but our fuckers can't.'

'Yeah,' he agreed, 'very funny!'

Something silver flashed out from under its belly and began to drop slowly almost like a dream towards the ground. It was a canister. Then a blinding, searing flash followed by the warmest moment I had outdoors on the Falklands. It was like sitting in front of a nice coal fire back home, even though I was over a hundred metres away from the blast. Napalm! It was close and a big patch of the slope was turned to ash. But the bomb had fallen behind D Company – if it had fallen among them they'd have been barbecued.

Then the bastard came over us and the whole battalion opened up on it, piling rounds into the Pucara until the pilot lost his bottle and ejected. I watched him parachute safely down to the ground where he was grabbed by some D Company Toms. I was going to meet him myself soon.

Had to get on though. There was work to be done.

Tom Harley knew exactly what to do with the gimpys and LMGs he'd organised. He laid down a torrent of fire on the schoolhouse as we moved out. We made it to the FUP and went firm for a few minutes, shooting anything that moved and blasting anything that didn't with 66s.

All we had to do now was make our last dash to some dead ground on the reverse slope of the L-shaped building that was going to be our final assault position. With a desperate sprint we made it. A massive amount of firepower was smashing into the school as Tom and the boys blasted away with everything they had while I crouched down in the FAP prepping WP and L2 grenades. Dick Walsh and Dave Trick were doing the same.

Let's go!

We dashed forward, firing as we ran, and a massive fist of lead followed us from Tom's position to punch into the schoolhouse too.

The Argies opened up and we discovered that we were caught in a crossfire, so all three of us slammed into the foundations at the apex of the building and lay down in the cover of six courses of bricks. It was the only hard cover. The rest of the building was made of wood.

My heart was pounding. But I felt no fear at that moment.

Breathe in! Breathe in! Right, what next?

I looked around me and saw Dick near one of the windows

starting to post grenades through a window. Me and Dave Trick joined him.

An L2 followed by WP. The L2 had a five-second fuse time and that's an eternity when you're in a tight corner. I'd heard of a D Company Tom fragging himself when he'd grenaded a tent.

'Keep down by the bricks!' I shouted. I wasn't taking any chances. I didn't want a splintered school wall turning me to mince.

Six deafening explosions went off almost simultaneously, turning the school into a charnel house. Flames started flickering inside as the WP took hold.

Dick heard the sound of feet pounding around in the classrooms and desperate voices shouting in Spanish. Shadows moved past the windows. Men were screaming inside. I left Dick and Tricky behind in cover and ran to the front door of the school. Flames began leaping out of the windows.

I swung my boot round and kicked the door in. I remember thinking, 'Where the fuck's my helmet?'

I felt vulnerable all of a sudden. I still had that stupid black woollen hat on. Good protection from cold. Shit for lead. My right side was exposed to Argy bunkers and I had my back to the fearsome fire from D Company and by that time from fifty metres in the fog of battle I must have looked like an Argy! What the fuck was I doing there?!

Almost immediately air rushed past me into the hall, fuelling the blaze with a surge of fresh oxygen. A firestorm roared up inside and I swung my rifle into the open doorway and fired two bursts from the SLR.

For some reason I couldn't hear screams any more. Perhaps I didn't want to hear them. Volcanic heat was erupting inside the building, and I could see hideous stumbling shadows and crumpled figures that had once been men. It looked like a scene at Pompeii.

At the far end I saw the school stage, a little platform for the kids to perform on. I don't know why but I just had a flashback to my days in the Birmingham Drama School. Men were dying and all I could think was that I was never meant to be an actor. I was born to be a soldier. It's weird where your mind wanders in extremes.

It was time to move. Dave Trick was covering me as I leapt ten feet into my next position. As I moved the retreating Argies fired a missile from the pod strapped to the slide on the other side of the building. It screamed through the building, cutting a vicious vapour trail right between me and Sleapy, who dived down under the bricks again!

By now the school had turned into a hell house. Some of the Argies had got out of the far end and were squirming into the trenches that flanked it, but they were sent to oblivion.

At the same time the Argy artillery came into play on the building. The Argy commanders must have known that we'd overrun the position and the game was up for their men in the school. As they'd DF'd the place earlier, they quickly began laying accurate fire down on the building as they tried to kill us. They didn't seem bothered that they might kill their own wounded at the same time.

It was kicking off all over the place. Two Harriers screamed over us too late to take out the Argy planes, but on the west side of the airfield they had a run at the Oerlikons that had been smashing rounds into the schoolhouse. Two misses and the cluster bombs they'd been carrying killed fish as they exploded in the sea just off the settlement. A fuel tank was ablaze near the school and somewhere in the distance near the airfield an Argy ammo dump went up.

Still more to be done. The guys were swarming round the sides of the burning building to occupy the Argy positions. We kept up a withering fire from those positions.

Bursts of fire from my matchstick automatic echoed out to the Argy in-depth bunkers. We took no prisoners at the schoolhouse. We didn't shoot anyone with their hands up or under white flags. They just didn't have time to get their hands up.

Tom Harley and his guys were suppressing the fire from other

Argy trenches, but as we poured through the schoolhouse position we discovered there was yet another defensive line nearer the town itself. Another firestorm, and we took cover wherever we could.

I jumped into one of their shell scrapes with some other guys. We pulled Argy bodies out of the bottom of the bunker and piled them up onto the rampart to give us some extra cover. Argy rounds whacked into Argy bodies as we crouched and waited to make our next move.

A few yards away Dick Walsh and a dozen Toms had found some dead ground. They were lying in the hollow created under the swings by the children's feet. Dead ground dug out by kids! Jonesy, the Falklands horse expert, was in that scrape with Dick and Pete Myers and they were chatting about shit; passing time in the hour that followed, until we could move on.

We'd become isolated now and we were drawing more and more incoming fire. Pinned down we were going nowhere. Time for a some tea and a few happy snaps. My mate JY had jumped into the scrape next door and he passed me a brew, then, cool as cucumber, he started taking a few pics.

The boss, Paul Farrar, turned up and filled what was left of my shell scrape. He went on about something but I didn't take any notice, then he leant out and took a long slow snipe at an Argy in depth. It was like a poking a stick into a hornet's nest and all hell broke loose for another five minutes.

'Great, boss, but let's not attract any more attention for a while, eh?'

The seats of the swings had been taken down, leaving just the tubular steel frames, and an incoming round clipped a frame, ricocheted and smacked Jonesy in the chest. His hands went up to his chest. Dick and Pete looked on in shocked silence. He'd been hit. Then he lifted his hands away and found that a 7.62 round had been stopped by empty magazines he'd thrown into the chest pocket of his smock in the last engagement. Nice souvenir, but time to leg it.

The trench I sat it out in was in the direct view of the next layer of Argy machine guns. I may as well have painted a bloody bullseye around the trench so much shit was coming in. They were also bringing yet another weapon to bear on the schoolhouse. Vipers! The Viper is a US anti-mine weapon which is a long cable with explosives along its length. You fire a rocket and the Viper snakes out behind it off a reel, banging off charges as the line hits the ground. We had Bangalore torpedoes; they had state-of-the-art Vipers! And they'd begun firing them towards us.

Baz Greenhalgh was in there with us. We were in a really dodgy position, pinned down and about to be pinned up as soon as the Argy mortars gave us any attention. We should have been falling back to reorganise, but Baz, an old-time para, wouldn't have any of it. His blood was up. He'd decided that no Argy was going to push him back. Ever.

I said, 'Baz, It's time to fuck off!'

'I'm not going back. OK?'

I could see there was no arguing with him, but we couldn't stay where we were. We were in deep trouble. There was a shitload of incoming, it was getting closer and more accurate, and D Company had lifted their fire.

So I said, 'We're not going back, but we'll go sideways.'

He thought for a moment. 'OK. We'll go sideways. But I'm not going back.'

The volume of fire was massive and I took my webbing off and threw it behind me, so that I could get my belly closer to the ground as I crawled backwards but definitely to the side of the position into dead ground. It took me a lifetime to do it. All of ten minutes. But it nearly was my lifetime as rounds hammered into the ground all around me until I made it into cover.

The sun was about to set and draw a curtain down on the battle. Something strange happened then. There was no formal ceasefire but both sides stopped fighting as dusk fell and we were ordered to withdraw to the gorse line. It was a strange anticlimax after an action that was so intense it left us all drained. We walked like half-living androids back down the steep slope into the estuary then up the gully to join A Company.

We'd lost men and had some wounded, but the next day Dick Walsh and I stopped counting the number of Argy bodies that were recovered from that position when we reached eighty-five. We'd got some in!

TWENTY-ONE

THE WOUNDED

IN THE GREY LIGHT of dusk, as we left the gully at the school-house behind us, we heard someone moaning. It had to be a wounded soldier and it was more than likely one of D Company's blokes. We rooted around behind a low embankment and found a Tom called Shevill.

He was a gunner who'd been wounded at the white-flag incident and retrieved by his mates, who were giving him an infusion of drip through his backside when the Pucaras had struck with the napalm. Even though he was badly wounded he'd jumped up with his trousers round his ankles and dived over that low wall. In the confusion that followed his mates couldn't find him again, but luckily we had and he had more holes in him than a cabbage strainer.

We pressed field dressings on about eight wounds before we carted him back to the Gorse Gully on a poncho. I thought he'd be crippled for life, but Shevill was a wild Geordie lad and I saw him just six months later in Newcastle, pissed and stripped to the waist showing off his scars as he danced on a pub table.

He was lucky. There were many men who waited a lot longer for treatment than him – yet another failure of our illustrious commanders who'd sent us into battle with First World War medical backup. One officer was laid out on the battlefield in pain for twelve hours; a couple of Toms, Cork and Fletcher of

D Company, spent more than twenty hours out there before they were found.

We had no bandsmen to take on the stretcher-bearers' job, although some of Headquarters Company were organised into that role and so were the Assault Pioneer Platoon. It wouldn't have been so bad if we'd just left the bandsmen but we left their bloody stretchers with them too.

That's why H had to be carted out of the re-entrant on a piece of corrugated tin and badly wounded men were being lugged around on ponchos. Casevac airlifts? Forget it. Despite constant requests none materialised until the very end of the day, but when they did they were magnificent. The first to fly was in response to the 'Sunray is down' signal.

The flight ended in tragedy near the Gorse Gully when the Royal Marine helicopter pilot Dick Nunn flew in his Scout to airlift the 'wounded' H to the field surgeons back at San Carlos. There were two Scouts flying in formation and they stopped first at Camilla Creek House to drop off ammo for the guns. Then they flew up to the battlefront and that's when two Pucaras swooped down on them.

Nunn's mate managed to weave his way out of trouble but Nunn's helo was blasted by a Pucara flying head on towards him. He was shot in the head and died instantly as his Scout dropped to the ground and bounced. His gunner, Royal Marine Sergeant Bill Belcher, was thrown out of the chopper on impact and against all odds survived but needed to have one leg amputated. They were brave men and 2 Para hasn't forgotten them.

Another pilot who's entered our folklore is Captain John Greenhalgh (no relation to Baz) of 656 Squadron RAF. The squadron often did training missions with 2 Para before the war, so the two units were working buddies and Greenhalgh went the extra mile to carry out a dodgy casevac under the nose of the enemy.

He took a medic, Lance Corporal Bill Bentley, right up to the forward slope of the schoolhouse approach to fill his helo with wounded. He knew he'd arrived at the right spot when he saw flashes of gunfire from the Argy bunkers. They were aimed at him!

He filled the chopper with the injured Toms then left Bill to walk back. Greenhalgh flew the last mission of the day in darkness to B Company's regimental aid post, guided in on the green light of a right-angled signal torch. One of the blokes he brought out was Captain Young – fourteen hours after he'd been hit. Young and Greenhalgh had become friends over the years in the officers' mess. Nice one.

Throughout it all our 2 Para medics performed superbly and there was a piece of real heroism and cool skill on the forward slope to the schoolhouse when our company Tac got it and Chopsey's leg was blown off. Bill Bentley was coming down the slope behind us and he ran straight to Chopsey's aide. The poor bastard's leg was hanging on by flesh and skin, so Bill took out his clasp knife and cut it clean off before sorting out Chopsey's stump. He was operating under withering enemy fire; he set a brilliant example and won the Military Medal for his fantastic work under the worst possible conditions with few resources.

During one of the night dust-offs made by John Greenhalgh on the forward slope, we had one of our wounded mates, Smudge Smith, ready to put on the helo. Smudge had a gut wound and he was being a real sport about it, lifting his shell dressing up so that curious Toms could take a peek at his intestines. Smudge needed a surgeon badly, but he was a stretcher case and there was no more room on the skids of the helo.

'Sorry, lads, room for one sitting wounded only,' we were told.

A whingeing fucker with a twisted knee said, 'That'll be me then.'

I fucked him off and encouraged Smudge, 'Come on, mate. If you can sit up a bit we'll get you the fuck out.'

The helo was drowning our voices and flattening the tussocks behind us, but Smudge was a proper bloke and he went for it.

He put his hands behind his neck as if he was doing a sit-up in the gym and gently pulled himself up with us helping. Eventually he got himself into a sitting position and we quickly bound his knees up to his chest by binding masking tape around his body then we put him on the last seat in the chopper.

Monster was taken off for treatment to his back wounds and made a full recovery, but he had a serious health scare seven years later when a lump appeared under his left armpit. He was still in the army and the docs got him in quickly for exploratory surgery. They tried to syringe the swelling but nothing came out, so they cut it and held a Petri dish underneath to catch the growth. Out tinkled an Argy 7.62 machine-gun bullet!

Some of the wounded just didn't want to be evacuated. Our boss, Roc Roger Jenner, was hit on the forward slope with his Tac and was ordered onto the next casevac. He didn't want to leave his blokes and went out into the gorse for the night to hide from the head shed. When Keeble spotted him the next day Jenner was given a Rupert-style bollocking and his marching orders, but he was quickly back with us before our next battle, Wireless Ridge.

One miraculous injury was suffered by a D Company Tom called Parr, who called out saying he'd been hit in the stomach. His mates looked with the help of a torch, but they couldn't find a wound until they noticed the spent head of a 7.62mm machine-gun round right in his belly button. It hadn't even broken the skin, though he was badly bruised when it struck him. A couple of days and he was right as rain and back in the thick of it. But Parr's fantastic luck ran out on Wireless Ridge, where he was killed in a tragic blue on blue.

Once they'd been evacuated, the wounded, from both sides in the conflict, received the attention of some top-notch surgeons, who were operating in a special theatre appropriately set up in an old meat refrigeration plant at Ajax Bay. Four surgeons and their staff carried out 202 operations during the war and more than a third of them were on Argentine prisoners. After one air raid two unexploded hundred-pound bombs hit the roof and were sandbagged. The surgeons just kept on cutting.

All the medics are agreed that the freezing conditions closed down blood vessels and stopped people bleeding out. So it was that the doctor who saved most lives on the Falklands was Jack bloody Frost.

TWENTY-TWO

THE AFTERMATH

HELMETED MEN MOVED QUIETLY around the makeshift camp on the ridge above the Gorse Gully. Night was falling and the temperature dropped like a stone while the wind fanned up the dying embers of the gorse fires.

Miserable groups of prisoners, fearful of what we might do to them, their souls tormented by defeat and the loss of their mates, huddled together and dreamt of home and their loved ones.

It was a desolate scene, one that I'm certain soldiers from down the centuries would have recognised. It was after the battle. A time of low voices and few words. They'd certainly have recognised the battlefield raven from our own ranks picking over the corpses of the Argy dead. It was a Tom called Dennis Wheatley and I spotted him with a pair of battlefield secateurs in his hand. We used them for cutting foliage for camo on OPs and for snapping barbed wire. But Wheatley was leaning over an Argy corpse and for a horrified second I could see that he was about to take a finger off it to steal a gold ring from the corpse.

'What the fuck are you doing?' I said.

'Spoils of war,' he muttered.

I stuck my SLR in his face and told him to fuck off or I'll waste ya. I would have too. Later I discovered one of the other guys had taken a pistol to the ghoulish bastard earlier on when he caught him doing the same thing. Wheatley's dead now. Let's hope he was buried with all his fingers.

As we walked through the smoking holes of the Gully I noticed that half the Argy dead weren't wearing boots. It was obvious that the A Company boys had helped themselves to better quality boots just to survive, and binned their crappy, cardboard DMS.

It was a bleak, depressing place. We had very little food and we knew that we'd have to sleep out in the open again. It was going to be a miserable, energy-sapping night and we didn't know what fighting the morning would witness.

The truth was that we had just half a clip of ammo each, and although we'd given the enemy a hell of a beating and seemed to have them cornered, it was us who were really under siege. They had us outnumbered and outgunned and if they came out of their corner fighting we'd be in big trouble. Our edge was the terror we'd instilled in those of the enemy who'd witnessed first hand the formidable way we fought. Terror is infectious and while we waited we hoped it would be spreading through the Argy ranks in Goose Green.

We had our immediate survival to think about as well and ravenous men started sharing meagre rations and getting ready to bed down on the cold wet ground. A lot of us spooned each other to keep warm as we slept. Scouse McVeay took a poncho covering a body to help keep himself warm during the night. He knew his mate wouldn't have minded. He put it back over him at first light.

Dick Walsh and I had work to do though. The boss had told us to make a white flag. That's not the sort of item a para is in the habit of carrying around in his webbing – we weren't surrender specialists.

'You two are going to deliver the CO's terms to the Argies in the morning, unarmed, so you'll need a white flag,' Farrar told us.

Nice one boss. Memories of the three guys shot in the white-flag incident were more than fresh. Still, if that's what we had to do that's what we had to do.

So Dick and I had to hunt around and find a piece of white cloth from somewhere, tear a piece off and tie it onto a radio aerial. We discussed our strategy and decided we'd go down fighting like one of my heroes from fiction, Corporal Steiner, did in *Cross of Iron*.

'I'm going to stuff a pistol in my belt in the small of my back,' I said. 'If the bastards open up on us I'm going to take at least one of them with me. Hopefully an officer.'

'Good plan, Johnny. I'll do the same.'

'Yeah, if any shooting starts I'm going to go down like Steiner,' I said.

Dick knew what I meant and grinned. 'This could be our first suicide mission, Johnny.'

'And our last,' I answered. We both laughed, even though there was nothing much to laugh at; after all, we had no scoff so we had to scrounge some garibaldis to dunk in our tea.

The night was bone-chillingly cold and events were taking on a sort of kaleidoscope effect as fatigue and a low blood sugar level started to make me space out a bit. I needed proper food and a good kip, we all did, but we weren't going to get it yet. Out in the open again, I remember us all spooning each other on the ground as we desperately tried to keep warm.

Never play poker with Chris Keeble. 2 Para were outnumbered, outgunned and low on ammo. OK, we were tougher by far but all those .50 cals were waiting for us and Vipers, Oerlikons and shit knows what.

Keeble didn't care. He was a Rupert with attitude and he penned his ultimatum to be handed to the garrison commander, but in the end Dick and I didn't have to do a Steiner.

I suggested to the boss, 'Why don't you send a couple of Argy prisoners in to do the delivery?'

There was a quick confab with the head shed and Keeble thought it was a good idea, so they sent the English-speaking

Argy pilot who'd dropped the napalm and an NCO to walk in and deliver the ultimatum to their commander.

Keeble spoke to the POWs when he handed them the note and gave them the nice guy/nasty guy routine. Basically in Rupert-speak it went along the lines of 'You're Catholics, I'm a Catholic. We're all God's children and I don't want to see more Christians die, but this lot are Red Berets – they're hard and mad and they don't give a shit.'

With some D Company guys, we walked the POWs up to the edge of the schoolhouse area and then they followed the track into the town. They were expected; a short-wave radio message had been sent to the Argy commander.

Keeble didn't mince his words in his terms of surrender and its clipped British directness is stirring. It went like this:

To the Commander, Argentine Forces, Goose Green
From the Commander, British Forces, Goose Green Area

MILITARY OPTIONS

We have sent a POW to you under a white flag of truce to convey the following military options:

1. That you surrender your force to us by leaving the township, forming up in a military manner, removing your helmets and laying down your weapons. You will give prior notice of this intention by returning the POW under the white flag, with him briefed as to the formalities, no later than 0830 hours local time.

2. You refuse in the first case to surrender and take the inevitable consequences. You will give prior notice of this intention by returning the POW without his white flag although his neutrality will be respected, no later than 0830 hours local time.

3. In any event, and in accordance with the terms of the

Geneva Convention and the laws of war, you shall be held responsible for the fate of any civilians in Goose Green, and we, in accordance with the laws, do give you prior notice of our intention to bombard Goose Green.

It was signed by C. Keeble and dated 29/5/82, and I reckon it scared the Argy commanders shitless, because well before the deadline the POWs appeared under a white flag to say their commanders would meet ours on the airfield for a parley.

Piaggi, the Argy commander, believed that he was completely surrounded by a superior force in numbers and firepower simply because of the hammering his men had taken. Keeble had guessed that would be the case when he played his hand and laid down his card in the ultimatum. He was right. The Argies folded their hand.

They met in the tin hut on the edge of the airstrip and there was some knockabout over terms, the way the prisoners would be treated, repatriation, and from our side the location of minefields.

The Argies strode off and then within half an hour about 250 air force personnel were paraded near the church and ordered to sing their national anthem, which was a bit of a tuneless effort by the demoralised men. Then their boss, some form of air commodore, handed his pistol over to Keeble.

Next in order of rank was the army boss, Colonel Piaggi, who marched his garrison out. You could have knocked us down with a feather. They just kept coming from between the houses of the settlement. I reckon there were about eight hundred of them and they took off their helmets, placed down their weapons and were then allowed to go back to collect their belongings from the settlement.

While we were gaping after them, wondering why so many of them hadn't managed to mallet us, the bastards were vandalising, looting and generally shitting all over their former billets in the islanders' homes.

★   ★   ★

We found 114 civilians banged up in the community centre, where they'd been forced to stay for a month while the Argies seconded their homes, the cheeky bastards.

They were overjoyed to be liberated. They were island folk and not given to big displays of emotion, but there was a real feeling of jubilation in the town and we joined in with a low-key, no-booze celebration. They had a real party when the Argies were booted off the island completely.

Victory was tempered with a sense of mourning for our mates, and we were genuinely touched when the Goose Greeners went out onto the battlefield and built a memorial to the lads within a couple of days of the battle. I think that was the true expression of the gratitude they felt for what we'd done.

And we were all put up in various lodgings out of the incessant Falklands wind, which was a real relief.

That night of the surrender, Goose Green was filled with screams of torture. Don't worry, it wasn't the Argy prisoners, we didn't touch them; we just left them glowering at their officers who'd requested and been allowed to keep their side arms to protect themselves from their men. What an army!

No, the screams came from the guys who were having rationed baths. Two inches of water per bath and they were trying to soak the masking tape off their thighs. A lot of the guys taped their thighs to stop their ammo pouches from rubbing them raw as they tabbed. I never seemed to get any chafing so I never bothered with the tape. Normally you can soak it off in a good bath but there just wasn't enough water, so they were ripping it off each other. I remember Dick Walsh howling in pain when one of the lads sneaked up on him and gave it one big fucking yank.

We spent a lot of time cleaning our weapons and kit and getting ourselves back into some sort of soldierly shape and order for whatever else the Falklands and the Argentines had to throw at us.

There were some laughs like when an L2 grenade rolled off

a shelf, hit Pete Myers on the head and bounced onto the floor of the sheep shed we were kipping in. He moved like a cat on a hot tin roof!

That night the islanders put on an old 8mm film in the community centre for the lads; *Soldier Blue* went down like a lead fart!

But for most of us it was a quiet, inward-looking time. Paras like to think that gallows humour and a cynical shrugging-off of adversity is the currency they deal in and that's true – up to a point. But the loss of our mates who'd been killed and the injuries that a lot of our other mates were having to bear left us feeling a little bit more hollow than we'd been before the battle.

And there was one terrible incident during the days after the battle that was indelibly printed on the memories of those who witnessed it.

We had the POWs housed in sheep-shearing sheds. They were comfortable enough, but a few of them were tasked to do different jobs, such as clearing the mess they'd made in the town and collecting up the considerable quantity of munitions they'd left all over the place.

I think it was the second day we were there at Goose Green. My patrol was on POW stag inside a huge sheep shed when I heard the familiar double throb of the twin rotors of a Chinook inbound. Thought nothing of it. Then suddenly there was an almighty explosion.

'Fuck. We're under attack!'

Rifles were raised at the POWs. Just in case. The rest of us piled out to see what the hell was going on.

An ammo pile had gone off just outside the door of the shed and there was a huge boiling flame that had engulfed three of the POWs tasked to do the clearance. I watched as one of them came running out of the flames. He was turning into an obscene charcoal caricature of a man in front of our eyes. It was a pitiful sight as he ran towards us then blindly ran back into the flames again, and a spark of compassion made me reckless. I moved to double over to him and drag him out of the flames. Greg Cox saw it coming and grabbed me as I moved and said, 'Don't you fucking dare.'

He could see the man would be better off dead than alive. The prisoner's legs crumpled underneath him.

A medic was in tears screaming, 'Fucking do something.' Someone took Steve's rifle and put two rounds into the prisoner. But if he'd looked hard enough, he'd have realised that the corpse was already burnt out.

That was a terrible death, not only because of the manner of it but because that young man had surrendered and was entitled to look forward to returning home to see his homeland and his loved ones. It was no one's fault. He wasn't destined to see home again. His fate had been a small charge of static.

TWENTY-THREE

MEDALS IN THE SNOW

THE BATTLE HAD BEEN won. 2 Para triumphed against all odds and in the couple of weeks that followed, Britain prevailed over Argentina and sent the invaders packing.

So who were the winners and losers? Let's take losers first. Of course they must include the hundreds of servicemen killed or injured on both sides in a war generated by the fascist regime of the Argentine junta.

To this day, twenty-five years on, the war is still being fought by men suffering from post traumatic stress disorder. Many get treatment but a shocking number take their own lives. In fact, the total number of PTSD suicides since the war is nearly three hundred; larger than the number of British servicemen who died during the conflict.

Quite a few 2 Para blokes have succumbed to the syndrome and Les Standish, who won the MM at Goose Green, has worked unstintingly with the South Atlantic Medal Association (the Falklands War veterans group) to help wherever possible. I have no idea how much help or even sympathy the Falklands veterans in the Argentine receive.

Militarily, the Toms in 2 Para reckon Phil Neame, the admirable OC of D Company, was a loser in the medal stakes. Both the other rifle company commanders, Dair Farrar-Hockley and John Crosland, were awarded the Military Cross. Neame, whose D

Company were point company through most of the war, wasn't. We think he was a victim of army politics because of his frictional relationship with H.

Chris Keeble, another fine Rupert, was given command of the battalion for the final stages of Goose Green, played a blinder and was then replaced by another officer. The Toms think he richly deserved a battlefield promotion and should have led us onwards.

The junta were losers of course. Galtieri got the boot immediately and a caretaker colonel took over for a few months while a democratic election was organised in Argentina.

But there were political losers in Britain as well. Lord Carrington, the Foreign Secretary, fell on his sword and resigned immediately, which is as it should have been after the FO bollocks in the run-up to the war. The Defence Secretary, John Nott, offered to resign but he was needed; there was a war to be fought and so he stayed on. After the war he did the honourable thing and slipped out of politics.

The McVeay brothers were losers of a sort too. There were three of them – Scouse and his brother in 2 Para, and the twin of Scouse's brother, was with the SAS, where all three eventually ended up. They met at Port Stanley and posed for a historic family photo together. Guess what? It didn't come out.

The winners? 2 Para won the Battle of Goose Green and Britain won the war. The Falkland Islanders were obviously winners because they had their freedom restored. The Argies had already ordered them to drive on the right-hand side of the road and told them that a Spanish curriculum would be introduced into the islands' schools. Cheeky bastards!

But in the years since the spring of 1982 history has been rewritten by the liberal left and BBC types, so now the Falklands War seems to have been all about Maggie Thatcher. It's said that Maggie was the only winner and she's been painted as a prime minister who cynically went to war to help her win an election.

What a load of bollocks! Clever people who know a lot more

about politics than me reckon she'd have won the election anyway without a victory in the Falklands.

Those who accuse her of that cynicism should remember something else. We weren't guaranteed to win. Her victory wasn't a given and the plain fact is that we could easily have lost and she would have gambled away her political future on the turn of a card.

It amazes me, too, that the accusations should come from the left of British politics, because what Maggie was doing was taking on a fascist military dictatorship that she knew full well was abducting, torturing and executing thousands of their own people. She knew that she was taking on a regime of baby snatchers. Maggie may not have been everyone's cup of tea but she was a principled woman. She could no more have left the British population of the Falklands Islands in the hands of such a regime than she could have done the taxpayers of the Isle of Wight.

Her critics are informed people and I'm sure they know what was going on in the Argentine as well as she did and that's why I believe they are guilty of rank hypocrisy.

The plain truth is that the real winners of the Falklands War were the 30 million people of the Argentine, because the Falklands War, which began decisively at Goose Green, led to the downfall of the oppressive junta dictatorship. Afterwards, the people of the Argentine got a vote, they got a popular government and they got rid of the shits in the secret police; abductions ended, torture ended, summary executions stopped and no more babies were snatched.

It didn't end there. They regained control of their economy and got rid of the hyperinflation that had crippled them financially for years; they could hold their heads up in the international community again. They were no longer a puppet people with soldiers pulling their strings.

We did that. The lads in 2 Para started the ball rolling at Goose Green when the junta's policy of a patriotic war to divert attention from their own evil doing blew up in their faces. I believe that the Toms of our battalion were the original ALF; not the

Animal Liberation Front, but the Argentine Liberation Front. Our fight freed those people.

But a quarter of a century on, after all those years the Argies still hanker after the Malvinas. They still believe they have a claim over the islands and Britain is painted by them as an imperialist power in the region.

It's balls of course. The fact is that the Argentine establishment and government is itself the rump of the old Spanish colonial one. Their claim on the Malvinas goes back to the days when there were clashes between land-grabbing colonial powers all around the globe.

France, Spain the US and Britain all contested the islands at one time or another, in those days wanting the place as a whaling station. Britain won out and ended up with it. We actually populated the place because no bugger had lived there permanently before. Then when Argentina became independent from Spain they decided on a whim to take on the old Spanish colonial claim for the Falklands. Trust me, Mexico has a better claim for Texas than the Argentine has over the Falkland Islands.

There's another sinister twist to the fallout from the Battle of Goose Green and the Falklands War. Recently, there has been a series of trials in the Argentine of police and military chiefs who operated the regime under the junta. Those brutes had been hiding for twenty years under an amnesty hastily arranged by the military in the months after the Falklands War to protect themselves when they got the boot. That Amnesty was rightly lifted in 2004 so that justice could at last be done.

In September 2006, a seventy-seven-year-old retired bricklayer called Julio Lopez vanished from his home in Buenos Aires. He had been due to give evidence at the trial of a former police chief who'd been one of the torturing baby snatchers. Lopez hasn't been seen since and other witnesses have had twenty-five-year-old tape recordings of torture sessions dropped through their letter boxes to intimidate them.

And so, on the twenty-fifth anniversary of the Falklands War and the Battle of Goose Green, I've got a message for the Argentine people and it's this:

The military adventurers, the torturers and the secret policemen are alive and well in your country and they're waiting in the shadows. So why don't you forget about the Falkland Islands and look after your fragile democracy. We'll look after our own. And by the way, there's no need to thank us for toppling the junta.

Over those twenty-five years a lot of water has ebbed and flowed on the tide at San Carlos Bay, but the day after the Argy surrender my patrol had one honourable task to perform and the memory of it is still fresh for me.

It was the morning of 30 May 1982 and C Company were relaxing in the warmth of a sheep shearers' dormitory on the edge of Goose Green. We were eating our heads off, drinking lots of brews and sleeping away the battle fatigue that had left us hollow inside.

The Argies had trashed the dormitory when they were being evicted but one treasure had survived and that was an old-fashioned, bright red record player with a lid top and a needle on an arm. Amid the smashed vinyl of broken LPs which covered the floor, one record was still intact. It was a single. 'Down in the West Texas Town of El Paso' sung by Marty Robbins.

We played that record to death and sang along so that the words became etched on the minds of every man in Patrols Platoon. It became our anthem and when we got back to the Shot we insisted it was on every pub jukebox.

It was playing again when the padre, David Cooper, came into the room and asked for volunteers for a sensitive job. At the start of the battle I'd told my guys we were all going to get through it and we had; I believe we were the only patrol or section in the battalion that hadn't taken a casualty. I'd also told them we weren't going to volunteer for anything, but with the padre standing there and us the only ones with full roll call, I stepped up.

'What d'y want done, boss?' I asked.

'I've commandeered a Snowcat and I'd like you guys to go out in it and bring our dead off the battlefield. They've been there long enough.'

I nodded. Nothing to be said. We wouldn't come back without them and we headed out of the settlement in the Snowcat. It's an Arctic warfare vehicle with a tractor unit that tows a heated trailer, also on tracks, behind it. You can get three blokes max up front and half a dozen in the trailer. Kev and Pete went in the back, Eddie Stokes came along with us.

Snow had fallen overnight. It was the first snow of the winter and we could see right across to Sussex Mountain. The whole scene was lit up by the luminous covering and it lay like a crisp, newly pressed white shroud over the battlefield, hiding the paraphernalia of war. It made innocent hummocks out of discarded helmets and weapons.

We stopped to search around the flag pole at the far end of the airstrip, quite close to Goose Green. Hard as we looked we couldn't find Lieutenant Barry who'd been shot in the white-flag incident, but then as if from nowhere another young officer appeared. He didn't say anything, he just walked straight to the spot where his friend had died as if he was locked onto it by radar. We put the body in the trailer and the officer just walked silently back to the settlement.

As we drove on, feeling sleepy in the heat of the cab, mesmerised by the throbbing of the big Volvo engine, the battlefield became a unified landscape again. During the fighting it had been chopped up into unnatural military segments where different engagements were being fought. Boca House. Gorse Line. The Gorse Gully. With the battle over it had been returned to the sheep and the wild horses, and we could wander freely over it too as we looked for our mates. Most of them were shrouded with a sheet of snow. We only found them when we saw the crimson medals of the blood on their para smocks that had stained the snow.

Captain Wood and Captain Dent, who'd died probing the Gorse

Gully. Gaz Bingley, Steve Prior, Jock Hardman, Steve Illingsworth, Tony Cork, Paddy Sullivan, Charlie Holman-Smith. We gathered them all in.

Kev found Tam Mechan frozen to his LMG. His finger was still on the trigger and he was still smiling in death. Kev gently prised him from his weapon and tears froze on my eyelashes as I helped put brave Tam with the others.

The Snowcat trailer was full and there was nowhere for Kev and Pete to sit, so I suggested what we were all thinking.

'You'll have to go on top of the guys,' I said.

Kev paused for a moment, then resigned himself to it and said, 'Yeah. OK.'

Young Pete looked horrified. 'I can't do that!'

'It'll be all right,' I said. 'We'll cover them with ponchos and make a nest on top with sleeping bags.'

'No, John, I can't do it. They're my mates! I'll hang on to the back!'

'No you won't! Get in the back or you'll freeze to death before we get back to Goose Green. Because they're your mates they won't mind.'

Pete and Kev climbed carefully on top of the pile of heroes' bodies and we drove back across the battlefield to the church at Goose Green where the padre was waiting for us.

There, when I lifted up the canvas on the back of the trailer, I found Kev and Pete. They'd fallen fast asleep with their friends.